Egypt's Long Revolution

The millions of Egyptians who returned to the heart of Cairo and Egypt's other major cities for 18 days until the eventual toppling of the Mubarak regime were orderly without an organisation, inspired without a leader, and single-minded without one guiding political ideology. This book examines the decade long of protest movements which created the context for the January 2011 mass uprising. It tells the story of Egypt's long revolutionary process by exploring its genealogy in the decade before 25 January 2011and tracing its development in the three years that have followed.

The book analyses new forms of political mobilisation that arose in response to ever-increasing grievances against authoritarian politics, deteriorating living conditions for the majority of Egyptians as a consequence of neo-liberal policies and the machinery of crony capitalism, and an almost total aban-doning by the state of its responsibilities to society at large. It argues that the increasing societal pressures from different quarters such as labour groups, pro-democracy movements and ordinary citizens during this period culminated in an intensifying culture of protest and activism that was vital in the lead up to the dramatic overthrow of Mubarak. It, also, argues that the features of these new forms of activism and political mobilisation have contributed to shaping the political process since the downfall of Mubarak.

Based on research undertaken since 2002, *Egypt's Long Revolution* is an essential resource for scholars and researchers with an interest in social movements, comparative politics and Middle East Politics in general.

Maha Abdelrahman is a Lecturer at the Centre of Development Studies and the Department of Politics and International Studies, University of Cambridge. Among her publications are *Civil Society Exposed: The Politics of NGOs in Egypt,* (2004), 'The Transnational and the Local: Egyptian Activists and Transnational Protest Networks', *British Journal of Middle East Studies* (2011). 'NGOs and the Dynamics of the Egyptian Labour Market' *Development in Practice* (2007), 'The Nationalization of the Human Rights Debate in Egypt' *Nations and Nationalism* (2007).

Routledge Studies in Middle Eastern Democratization and Government

Edited by Larbi Sadiki
University of Exeter

This series examines new ways of understanding democratization and government in the Middle East. The varied and uneven processes of change, occurring in the Middle Eastern region, can no longer be read and interpreted solely through the prism of Euro-American transitology. Seeking to frame critical parameters in light of these new horizons, this series instigates reinterpretations of democracy and propagates formerly 'subaltern' narratives of democratization. Reinvigorating discussion on how Arab and Middle Eastern peoples and societies seek good government, *Routledge Studies in Middle Eastern Democratization and Government* provides tests and contests of old and new assumptions.

Egypt's Long Revolution

Protest Movements and Uprisings

Maha Abdelrahman

Routledge
Taylor & Francis Group

LONDON AND NEW YORK

First published 2015
by Routledge
2 Park Square, Milton Park, Abingdon, Oxon OX14 4RN

and by Routledge
711 Third Avenue, New York, NY 10017

Routledge is an imprint of the Taylor & Francis Group, an informa business

British Library Cataloguing in Publication Data
A catalogue record for this book is available from the British Library

Library of Congress Cataloging in Publication Data
A catalog record for this title has been requested

ISBN: 978-0-415-63304-8 (hbk)
ISBN: 978-1-315-76226-5 (ebk)

Typeset in Times New Roman
by Taylor & Francis Books

Contents

Acknowledgements

This book examines Egypt's revolutionary process. Like this process, it has been long in the making. The idea for the book project started in the second part of the 2000s with the aim of analysing the protests and movements that were gaining momentum in the streets, factories, offices, universities and rural areas of Egypt. In the course of realising this project, momentous events overtook Egypt and the book's range was extended to keep up not only with the breath-taking uprising of 2011, but the three turbulent years that followed. For several years, the writing of this book went through different stages not dissimilar to those of its subject matter: moments of soaring elation, periods of uncertainty and self-doubt, instances of retreat and dark days of potential defeat but always the knowledge that its completion relies on the sustenance of a great many people.

I am hugely indebted to the generosity and time of many friends and activists who shared their direct experiences, knowledge and enthusiasm for change with me over many hours of interviews over the years. They are too many to mention by name but I particularly want to thank Wael Khalil and Rabab El-Mahdi.

Some friends have read earlier draft chapters of this book and their feedback and support was invaluable. I want to thank Gilbert Achcar and Ray Bush for their useful comments and their unfailing support. Needless to say, the book would have been a great deal better had I listened more to their and other friends' comments.

I want to thank Kat Rylance and the rest of the editorial team at Routledge for overseeing the whole production process.

The Centre of Development Studies at the University of Cambridge was my intellectual home during the writing of this book. I am grateful to many there for their support and collegiality especially Ha-Joon Chang, Shailaja Fennell, Diana Kazemi and Peter Nolan. I am eternally indebted to my colleague Glen Rangwala from POLIS for walking into my office one day in January 2011, when he offered to teach my lectures while I headed off to Tahrir.

The intellectual and emotional support of so many friends in the Netherlands, UK and Egypt kept me going through the difficult task of writing this book that took place mostly away from Egypt which added to the emotional strain of the exercise. They are too many to name but I want to thank my Cairo friends Lamia Bulbul, Iman Hamdy, Malak Rouchdy, Reem Saad and Hanan Sabea for a wide range of support from 'book project discussions' to actually not asking how the book was going and everything in between.

Finally, I want to acknowledge Gary Debus; only he knows how much I owe him for this book and for a great deal more.

Introduction

Arab countries and their peoples have always posed a challenge to commentators and analysts of the region as they have systematically failed to act in ways expected of them. For example, Arab countries were at 'the bottom of the class' after the third wave of democratization had come and gone. The inability of the region to join other countries in ridding themselves of dictatorial regimes gave rise to a robust industry devoted to deciphering the enigma of this anomaly, looking for signs everywhere but mostly in the dark recesses of the region's cultural and religious systems or, occasionally, in a reductionist version of the 'rentier' thesis. No sooner had the mainstream orthodoxy become comfortable in its assured pronouncements on 'durable authoritarianism' and that reform (not revolution) would only be possible in the region as an outcome of international pressure and elite pacts, than a wave of mass uprisings gripped successive countries from the end of 2010. The uprisings successfully overthrew the heads of three regimes and created shock waves in almost every other country. The ripple effect, in fact, went well beyond the region, inspiring groups of people across the globe. Having quickly adjusted to these new developments and celebrated the rise of the Arab masses from their deep slumber, analysts were again let down by the blatant resistance of the same countries, Egypt in particular, to follow a graceful route of democratic transition. Promptly, the obituary of the 'Arab Spring' was articulated in unambiguous terms. Declarations of 'failed revolutions', 'aborted transitions', 'Arab Spring turning into winter' and a whole gamut of such clichés started to appear only months after the uprisings. Such quick pronouncements are not only characteristic of mainstream analysis of the region, but also go hand in glove with readings of revolutions that regard them as events rather than continuous processes of transformation.

The events of the 25 January 2011 uprising have by now been documented and their details preserved for posterity. If indeed any revolutionary moment were ever 'televised', then it was the momentous 18 day uprising. Millions of people pouring out onto the streets, the occupation of major squares across the country, the birth of the 'republic of Tahrir', the carnival-like atmosphere it engendered and the brutal violence the regime used against the protestors were not only televised but tweeted, blogged, Facebooked, instagrammed,

You Tubed and a lot more. The debate on whether the January uprising, the downfall of Mubarak, and the fast-moving events which have since ensued constitute a revolution, a transition to democracy, a 'refo-lution'[1] or a military coup or two, will continue to occupy analysts for a long time to come.

While the outcome of the ongoing events is likely to take years if not decades to become apparent, it is without doubt that the uprising marked a juncture when new and old actors became locked in a power contest which held, for a while, the potential for redrawing the political map of the country. The 25 January uprising will remain a unique moment in Egypt's recent history, irrespective of the course of events that has since followed or will ensue in the future. For one thing, it marked the bursting of the masses onto the political stage with a single-mindedness to bring down a regime that they recognized as their enemy. The resoluteness of the masses emanated from grievances against the Mubarak regime which united a *melange* of factory workers, middle-class professionals, pensioners, students, the unemployed, small artisans, football ultras and street vendors. The uprising also marked a rare moment when the same masses appeared to hold the power, albeit fleetingly, to threaten the stability of the existing order. As the days progressed and the millions continued to throng the streets, the well-established political actors of the military, the state–capital nexus, regional actors and international powers were preparing their next move and their contingency plans. In the early days of the uprising, however, the die had not yet been cast and the balance of power seemed relatively open to contestation between old and new actors. A rare glimpse into a world where the promise of 'bread, freedom and social justice' could be attainable flickered for a moment for millions, not only in Egypt and the Arab region but across the world. In an age when almost the whole world lives under the hegemony of a global order antithetical to these hopes, such moments need to be valued and not underestimated.

However, the dramatic 18 day uprising was only one episode in a far longer struggle against the same order; a struggle which spanned more than a decade before the uprising and one which has not abated since the downfall of Mubarak. While the marches on 25 January 2011 ended in a most unexpected turn of events, the occasion itself was one of numerous series of protests, marches, occupations, sit-ins, rallies and other forms of contentious action which had dominated opposition politics and gripped the country since the outbreak of the second Palestinian Intifada in 2000. Widespread support for the Palestinian cause had ignited street protests and demonstrations, transforming opposition politics into a vibrant, multifaceted activism that ushered in a new era in Egyptian politics. The intensification of protests and the flourishing of activist groups mobilized large swathes of Egyptians across different socio-economic groups, crossing rural–urban divides, creating cross-ideological coalitions and using new forms of loose organizational structures outside decayed traditional, political organizations. Likewise, the 25 January uprising, crucial as it was, did not mark the end of this long revolutionary struggle. Neither the symbolic downfall of Mubarak, nor the work of the counter-revolution since has been able to subdue the desire of millions for more radical change. Contentious action has not only continued; it has, if anything, intensified.

This book tells the story of Egypt's long revolutionary process by exploring its genealogy in the decade before 25 January 2011 and tracing its development in the three years that have followed. This task is undertaken by investigating the historical lineage and the political economy of the uprising as well as the dynamics of the regional and international context in which it took place and the actors who shaped it. Understanding the lineage and the course of the uprising within this framework not only helps us grasp how such a momentous event came about but, more importantly, guides us in making sense of the revolutionary process as it unfolds.

The book gives centre stage to the groups and individuals who have carried the weight of this long revolutionary process. The millions of activists, workers, farmers and individuals from other social groups who have fought across the country against the order established by the Mubarak regime before, during and after the uprising are my concern. They and they alone provide the momentum for Egypt's long revolution. Only days into the uprising, those who until then were protestors, activists, strikers and members of the disgruntled masses, quickly acquired the status of 'revolutionaries'. The book shows how, since the downfall of Mubarak, these 'unintentional' revolutionaries have been marginalized from the ensuing political process: at times co-opted, at others vilified, but usually outmanoeuvred by a well-entrenched political class experienced in playing the game. This has led political and academic analysts, who had 'discovered' and briefly celebrated the power of the masses, to turn their gaze from them. After the initial euphoria and laudatory comments, the supposedly victorious masses were soon relegated to a back seat while the focus returned to traditional political actors: the military, the Muslim Brothers and regional powers. The millions and their continuing struggle receive cursory attention and only in so far as they are seen to have been subdued and defeated by counter-revolutionary forces.

In bringing the focus back to them, this book is neither a eulogy for the heroism of these millions nor a lamentation of their 'failure' to resist the forces of the counter-revolution. The goal of the book is to provide a sober analysis of the experience of mobilization, activism and protest movements that has shaped the revolutionary subjects and of their ability to take the struggle to another level within a new phase of a long revolutionary process. Attention is focused on the inability of the millions who had challenged Mubarak's order to give rise to a counter-hegemonic project with a more radical, revolutionary agenda. Revolutionary alternatives, it should be emphasized, are born of long struggles and the ongoing revolutionary process is where such alternatives could still be born. As Marx argues in the *Civil War in France*, the 'working class did not expect miracles from the Commune ... . They know that in order to work out their own emancipation ... they will have to pass through long struggles, through a series of historic processes, transforming circumstances and men [sic]' (Tucker, 1978: 558–59).

Between waves of advances and ebbing tides of retreat, a learning process is continuing and new possibilities can still be born.

Increasing poverty, high unemployment rates and a youth bulge combined with the absence of political freedom under an authoritarian regime are by now the staple ingredients of the mainstream narrative of the causes of the Egyptian uprising. However, increasing poverty and deteriorating living conditions as well as the erosion of political freedom, from which the majority of Egyptians suffered under Mubarak, were but symptoms of a much more complex story. It is the story of a definitive and violent end to an old order and its replacement with another. On 25 January, millions of Egyptians were revolting against the incrementally implemented but ultimately brutal end to the post-independence, developmentalist state and the birth of a neoliberal order. In the making for decades, the hegemony of the neoliberal order during the last years of Mubarak's rule had become complete. Building a modernizing, developmentalist state in Egypt from the 1950s was, first and foremost, a political project, backed by a global capitalist system and reliant on the rise of a new political class, new institutions and a new social base. Neoliberalism is similarly a political project that requires the dismantling of old foundations and the construction of a new basis. For Harvey, the building of the neoliberal project is necessarily based on strategies of accumulation by dispossession. Essentially a state-led project, under neoliberalism the state carries out a dual function. On one hand, it serves to 'roll back' regulatory frameworks that protect labour, the environment and any group hoping to defend common property rights won through long struggle (Harvey, 2003). On the other, it 'rolls out' institutions and alternative regulatory frameworks that support its strategies of dispossession, mainly privatization and liberalization of markets and of the commons. For the majority of those dispossessed, a neoliberal order requires the 'destruction of any sense of entitlement built up through the period of the broad welfare state' (Gordon, 2005: 60).

Chapter 1 examines the construction of this new order in Egypt since the 1990s, focusing on the rise of a growing political class, its strategies of dispossession, the institutions it relies on for its dominance and the methods it employs to extend and protect its hegemony. The chapter goes on to describe the context in which millions of Egyptians have risen to engage in a wide range of struggles against the ascendancy of this new order and the regime that represents it.

Structural factors grounded in political and economic institutions are key to understanding the proliferation of waves of protest that swept the streets of Egypt for almost a decade. Nonetheless, as Gramsci (1971) points out, objective structural conditions do not necessarily by themselves create successful mobilization on such a large scale. The process of small- and large-scale mobilization, its dynamics, the forms it takes and the actors involved, therefore, need to be examined. This is particularly necessary given another element of the mainstream narrative of the January uprising that is embraced by Western media, the Egyptian political elite, global institutions and even some Egyptian activists. In this self-serving version of reality, the events of the 18 days of Tahrir were quickly portrayed as a peaceful protest led by middle-class, technology-savvy, urban youth demanding greater political freedom. Given this representation, the only logical path to follow after Mubarak's ousting would be a transition based on the market economy and 'democratic' elections. Absent from this narrative is the role of large sections of the Egyptian population, such as workers, farmers and the urban poor, who have equally shaped events before and after 25 January 2011, with their overriding motivation of achieving social justice conveniently ignored. Chapters 2 and 3 interrogate the history of mobilization in the ten years before the uprising by showing that, apart from the pro-democracy movement, *workers, farmers and,* (indeed), *almost everybody else* was at the heart of this process. Efforts to classify the mobilization and protests during this decade have tended to categorize them either by the content of their demands, usually economic or political (Joya, 2011), or mobilization structures such as workplace, neighbourhood or association (El-Ghobashy, 2011). In this book, the classification is based on the processes of dispossession that provoked a burning sense of injustice, which in turn engendered the original protests, and on the level of interconnectedness between these multiple protests.

The ease with which the forces of counter-revolution – the military establishment, the state–capital nexus, the leadership of the Muslim Brothers (MB), conservative regional powers and global financial institutions – have been able to undermine a potential revolutionary project is analysed by examining the mobilization process. Each of the following three chapters, therefore, identifies one of the characteristics of the process of mobilization and the features of the revolutionary subject and analyses the challenges they pose to post-uprising 'revolutionaries'. Chapter 4 begins with the question of organization and its relevance to the development of a revolutionary project. As Gramsci reminds us, no social or political activity is ever completely spontaneous. They are always under the *de facto* influence, even if implicit, of a set of ideas, a leader or an organization (Sasson, 1982: 16). Conceptions of organization and the praxis of creating organizations are central to the discussion of Egypt's revolutionary process. Chapter 5 moves on to focus on the subject of tactics and the challenge of building broadly-based coalitions during and after the Mubarak era. Chapter 6 focuses on the rift which has to date split the struggle along 'economic' and 'political' lines.

The book is a detailed case study of Egypt. However, the story told here, despite its specificities, is not unique to one particular context. The dismantling of the old order and the imposition of a new one, the struggles that such a watershed has engendered, the ways global capital, the global political elite and their national agents are working to crush these struggles and undermine their revolutionary potential are all facets of a single global reality. Egypt's revolutionary forces are not alone in facing daunting questions about their potential for creating and realizing a transformative project which could replace the country's powerful ruling class and the order it protects. Activists everywhere, not only in countries of the 'Arab Spring' or the global South, are more than ever confronted with the pressing question of how to make another world possible – a question to which the conclusion of this book returns.

Note

1 Asef Bayat used the term in 2011 to explain the potential of uprisings in the Arab world within the context of existing models of revolutions and political transformations.

1 Mubarak's brave new world

From the mid-2000s, Mubarak's Egypt was a poster child for a new neo-liberal order in the region. For several years, it had been hailed by the World Bank for its 'reforms' as one of the world's top-ten most improved economies. In 2010, the year before the 25 January uprising, Egypt topped the list (World Bank, 2010). Successive Mubarak governments had indeed made many strides to earn such a celebrated position. From the 1990s, they had acceler-ated privatization of public assets, introduced drastic cuts in social expendi-ture, launched legal reform to guarantee 'flexible' employment, privatized agriculture, removed trade barriers and generally put the interests of capital above all else.

The impressive success of Mubarak's regime in dismantling the remaining heritage of the old order of public investment and import substitution strate-gies, which had been introduced in the 1950s and 1960s, would not have been possible without the restructuring of important institutions and the introduc-tion of new ones. At the heart of this institutional restructuring was the rebranding of the ruling National Democratic Party (NDP) and the govern-ments it put in place. Gamal Mubarak, widely tipped to succeed his father as president, was invested with the task of reorganizing the NDP as the strong-hold from which to launch a new local version of the neoliberal order. Under the banner of 'New Thinking', the young Mubarak quickly rose through the ranks of the party to head its newly created policy committee in 2002. He surrounded himself with a group of 'reformers' who shared his fervour for scrapping the remaining elements of the developmentalist state. While this state built by Nasser had already started to show cracks under its own weight as early as the 1960s, the task of reducing it commenced in earnest in the 1970s under Sadat as part of his open door economic policies. Unlike Sadat and the early Mubarak governments, the new NDP reformers embarked on their task with a singular commitment and an unwavering disregard for any possible social cost of their project. Steeped in private capital and hailing from top positions within international financial institutions (IFIs) such as the World Bank and the IMF, the pedigree of the new reformers was indisputable. The infamous Ahmed Ezz, for example, was a business tycoon who made his way up the NDP hierarchy and the government, culminating in his heading of the powerful Economic Committee of the Parliament in 2005. Mohamed Mohieldin, a World Bank economist, Taher Helmy, president of the American Chamber of Commerce in Egypt and Hossam Badrawi were among the most loyal supporters of the new project.[1] In 2003, the NDP launched a document prepared by the policy committee that outlined a blueprint for its project of transformation: a greater role for the private sector, the removal of trade barriers, a bigger role for IFIs in overseeing domestic market dynamics, attracting foreign investment, reducing tax on capital and creating a public opinion supportive of these policies.[2]

The advances that Egypt had already made in privatization, reduction of subsidies and trade liberalization in the late 1990s were deemed acceptable by its neoliberal taskmasters but with the observation that there was still considerable room for improvement. According to a USAID evaluation report in 2004, Egypt was not doing enough to attract investment. Among the many 'controllable' impediments to investment in the country were 'issues of contract enforcement, excessive bureaucracy, foreign investors' unsatisfactory past experience, and excessively discretionary customs and taxation practices' (USAID, 2004: 17). More work needed to be done. Only too eager to deliver, the NDP reformers pushed for the appointment of a new government with the commitment necessary to carry out the remaining steps.

The appointment in 2004 of the Nazif government, dubbed the 'businessmen cabinet', was a watershed in sealing a new order in Egypt. Nazif's government included a large number of business tycoons who controlled some vital portfolios. For example, Rachid Mohamed Rachid, appointed as minister of foreign trade and industry, was a senior executive of the Unilever group and the owner of Egypt's main food company (Fine Foods). Ahmed El-Maghraby, owner of Mansour and Maghrabi investment and real estate companies, was chosen as minister of housing. They were joined by Mohamed Mansour, owner of the Mansour Group conglomerate, which is the distributor of General Motors and Chevrolet, as minister of transportation. The minister of finance, Youssef Boutrus Ghali, was chosen for his experience as a former senior economist in the IMF. With Ahmed Ezz at the apex of the economic decision-making structure in the country and his fellow business tycoons dominating the government, policies and laws to promote the interests of domestic and global capital were now guaranteed.

Under the new Nazif government, a new ministry of investment was created, bringing together the public enterprise ministry, the general authority for investment and free zones, and the capital market authority. The principal task of the new ministry was to facilitate the privatization process. The new minister, Gamal Mubarak's close ally, Mohamed Mohieldin, and the government which appointed him, embarked on this mission with gusto. Compared to a mere nine public companies with a total value of $17.5 million sold in 2003, the new government privatized an impressive 59 companies worth $2.6 billion in 2005–6 alone. The privatization project was a clear ideological commitment to a new order. While neoliberal logic justifies the need to privatize public firms on the grounds of inefficient management and the supposed inability of state-run businesses to make a profit, among the companies listed for privatization in the same year were some of the most profitable public sector companies in the country, including Sidi Krir Petrochemicals and the Alexandria Mineral Oils Company (Rutherford, 2008: 222).

While a new political project requires a new and committed political class, it also needs new ideologues to advocate and justify its founding principles. Harvey (2003) reminds us how neoliberalism, as a new political economic doctrine in the 1940s, developed into a coherent project through founding exclusive think tanks which produced a steady stream of analysis and polemics in its favour. The Egyptian Centre for Economic Studies (ECES), a think tank established in the 1990s with the support of USAID and a group of powerful businessmen, provided the space for Egypt's new ideologues. The first director of the Centre was Ahmed Galal, a former World Bank economist, a close friend of Gamal Mubarak and later minister of finance in the military-appointed interim government in 2013. Among its board members were Gamal Mubarak himself, the all-powerful Ahmed Ezz, future cabinet ministers such as Ahmad El Maghraby and Mounir Abdel Nour as well as other business tycoons such as Mohamed Farid Khamis, chairman of Oriental Weavers, one of the largest machine carpet factories in the Middle East, and Ahmad Bahgat, owner of the giant Bahgat Group. The Centre was an invaluable institution that produced prolific research emphasizing the necessity and inevitability of the reform being carried out by the regime. Among the research produced were recommendations for accelerating privatization and extending it to new economic sectors such as the airline industry (Ragab, 2005). Government subsidies were the subject of a great deal of research that offered a critique of the subsidy system as costly, burdening the treasury and causing price distortions and commodity arbitrage (Helmy, 2005). Forecasts were provided for phasing out subsidies on strategic commodities such as petroleum energy products (Abouleinein, El-Laithy and Kheir-El-Din, 2009). To promote the liberalization of trade and a commitment to international free trade agreements, research was published on the inevitability of trade liberalization and on the success of the highly controversial Qualifying Industrial Zone (QIZ) protocol on the textile and garment industry (Refaat, 2003; 2006).[3] Very quickly, as Rutherford (2008: 211) commented, 'The ECES became the primary institution for translating the broad principles of neoliberal reform into specific policy proposals ... Through ... [its] efforts, the private sector's aspirations for change were converted into a coherent policy agenda'.

Heavily invested in the building of a neoliberal order, Egypt's new political class was set on a seemingly unstoppable course. Having successfully dominated political institutions, the leviathan of domestic capital was by now enjoying parliamentary immunity, preferential access to public resources and contracts, unlimited credit and, above all, the ability to fashion legal tools necessary for the smooth functioning of its project. Exploiting public office in the service of private interests is not unique to the late Mubarak era. Already in the 1970s Osman Ahmad Osman, a close friend of Sadat and the father-in-law of one of his daughters, was a minister of construction as well as the long-serving chairman of the Arab Contractors Group, a sprawling network of private and public-sector companies. Osman, who secured multi-billion dollar government contracts during Sadat's rule, was known to subcontract many of these contracts to his own private companies. While Osman was certainly the most obvious example, he was by no means the only one. Over the next two decades, a 'network of privilege', a term coined by Sfakianakis (2004), was steadily being woven between capital – or the ranks of the 32 – state bureaucracy and a new political class.[4]

The 2000s saw the rise of a new political class that dominated the policy process allowing the building of new forms of oligopoly unique to this era. Monopolies and oligopolies are central features of neoliberalism (Harvey, 2005) and should not, therefore, be explained in over-simplistic terms of corruption or crony capitalism. In Egypt, as elsewhere, monopolies were both an outcome and a servant of new strategies of dispossession. Whether it was steel, cement, telecommunications, food and beverages or agribusiness, almost all sectors of the economy became dominated by monopolistic and oligopolistic practices. In the strategic market of iron and steel, for example, by the end of the Mubarak era all production was in the hands of 22 companies. A mere three of these companies controlled over 90 per cent of total production with over 50 per cent of this share taken by Ahmed Ezz's Ezz Al-Dehkeila.[5] Similarly, by the end of 2010, almost 90 per cent of total cement production was dominated by only four multinational companies: Lafarge, Italcementi, Cemex and Seymour. This was the culmination of a long process that commenced in the late 1990s when the Arab Swiss Engineering Company, chaired by Mohamed Abdel Wahab, a former minister of industry in the early 1990s, facilitated the majority share sale (51 per cent) of the highly profitable, state-owned Ameiryah Cement Company to Lafarge in 1997. In 1999, the state sold large majority shares in its profitable top cement companies: Alexandria (74 per cent), Assiout (90 per cent) and Beni Sueif (95 per cent) to multi-national groups. The ensuing oligopoly has not only had negative effects on prices but also grave ramifications for national production plants.[6]

Favouring global capital by offering a large share of domestic markets to multinationals was part and parcel of the new neoliberal order. Following its accession to the WTO in 1995, the Egyptian government had to swiftly take measures to comply with the basic principle of the organization: the euphemistically named 'non-discrimination' rule.[7] By 2000, Egypt's government had removed most of the measures protecting key local industries against competition from imports. The textile industry is a case in point. The sector, which employed over 100,000 workers and generated about $1.25 billion in export revenue in 2000, enjoyed government protection in the form of high tariffs on low-cost imports from Asia. The original 40 per cent tariffs were gradually reduced to no more than 12.5 per cent in 2005, with a view to eliminate them completely by 2015 (Rutherford, 2008: 200). As a result, domestic producers lost a dramatic share of the market to cheaper imports from China. In a mere four years between 2001 and 2004, domestic production sales halved from $6 billion to $3 billion as cheap exports drove local companies out of the market (Al-Haddad, 2013).

Blatant crony capitalism became the trademark of Mubarak's regime and a foundation stone of the variant of neoliberalism it fostered. Of course, neoliberalism works hand-in-hand with crony capitalism everywhere. However, by the end of his rule, crony capitalism in Egypt had reached a highly developed state. Three-quarters of all subsidies on hydrocarbons and energy, for example, were consumed by industries owned by Egypt's new political elite (Springborg, 2011). Innumerable examples illustrate how crony capitalism had become a well entrenched system essential for the capital accumulation of the new ruling class. Changes in the global capitalist economy were at the heart of the functioning of this system. The financialization of the economy, starting in the 1990s under directives from IFIs, for example, had led to the increased value of particular assets such as land, which was crucial to the booming real estate market. Cases like the 'Palm Hills' and 'Madenati' gated communities, which received huge media attention both before and after Mubarak's downfall, are notorious examples of how the Mubarak family, the NDP, the cabinet and the state–capital nexus in general colluded to exploit public assets for personal profit and enshrine the new rules of the game in the legal system. In the first case, as one researcher puts it: 'the Mubaraks and their associates and relatives together with two ministers could unlawfully allocate large plots of public land, at low prices, to a company in which they hold shares'.[8] The details of the complex deal involved flagrant under-pricing of public land, a favourable bidding process and exploitation of the emergency law to put a seal on the operation. The example of the business tycoon Ahmad Zayat's capturing of the market for alcoholic beverages is another case in point. Through his strong ties with the state bureaucracy and his business partnership with the military complex in its Safi mineral water venture, Zayat was able to manipulate the privatization process of Al-Ahram Beverage Company, another public sector company that was consistently profitable. By means of a long, convoluted process, Zayat bought the company for EGP 231 million after the government had rejected an earlier bid of EGP 400 million from another company on the grounds that it was too low. For a while, he was able to monopolize the whole market.[9]

The price of 'success'

While the World Bank and other IFIs were hailing Egypt for its impressive seven per cent growth rate, mostly derived from labour remittances, Suez Canal fees and high energy prices, especially of natural gas, the UNDP pronounced 44 per cent of the population to be living at or below the poverty line (UNDP, 2008). The accuracy of this figure, indeed any attempt to measure poverty in any context, is fraught with methodological and political problems. In any case, poverty and even the fact of increasing poverty, cannot in itself be seen as the major explanatory factor for the 25 January uprising and the preceding decade of protest.[10] The new neoliberal order, more than just impoverishing the majority of Egyptians, was signing the death certificate of an old order which, while long waning, had continued to provide a sense of security and entitlement for many social groups. However, by the 1990s, many Egyptians had begun to realize that the state was no longer keeping its part of the 'social contract' in which it had committed itself, decades ago, to providing social security to a wide range of social groups. Moreover, Egyptians were becoming increasingly aware by the 2000s that this gradual but persistent chipping away of entitlements was not a temporary anomaly. Nor was it contingent on the policies of one particular government or a transient phase that would eventually be reversed. There was a growing realization that state–society relations were being permanently restructured to their disadvantage. The evidence was everywhere. The dismantling of the old system was systematic and universal. It left no area untouched; labour rights, rural livelihoods, progressive taxation, social security and pension schemes were all targets.

Labour and employment rights

The modernization project of the 1950s and 1960s gave a huge role to state bureaucracy across post-colonial societies. Devotees of the project in the words of one author saw the state bureaucracy as the 'midwife for Western development by creating stable and orderly change' (Dwivedi, 1999). The provision of universal education and health care systems as well as the introduction of land reform and the nationalization of private assets translated on the ground to rapidly increasing public service employment in many developing countries. Egypt was no exception and during the 1960s the growth rate of the bureaucracy substantially exceeded that of population, employment and production, with the number of employees in the public bureaucracy increasing by 70 per cent and salaries by 123 per cent. At the end of this period, the public sector employed at least one-third of Egypt's non-agricultural labour force, with some estimates putting the figure as high as one half (Ayubi, 1988; Owen, 1992). Furthermore, state employment under the populist regime of Nasser was characterized by the immense sense of entitlement it provided. All graduates of tertiary education institutions were not only guaranteed automatic employment but permanent jobs with concomitant social benefits. As a result, large numbers of the educated middle classes became not only reliant on the state but based their lives on its promises of life-long security.

Similarly, Nasser's populist regime extended major privileges to workers, guaranteeing them legendary levels of job security that won Nasser the support of the overwhelming majority of trade unionists and workers. One of his earliest decisions was to pass Decree 165 of 1953, which guaranteed workers' job security by making it financially and bureaucratically almost impossible for an employer to dismiss a worker without a very strong reason. Nasser's 'social compact' with workers, as well as with large sections of the middle classes, not only granted them job security but further instituted a generous regime of subsidies which supplemented the often low nominal wages, thus preventing any significant drop in real wages (Goldberg, 1992; Hansen and Radwan, 1982).

However, these privileges, which would have been impossible to sustain over the long term in any case, were gradually eroded by Nasser's successors. Over the decades, the share of public employment of total employment decreased steadily. In the period 1981–2008, it fell from 40 per cent in 1981–82, to 30 per cent in 1990–91, then to 29 per cent in 2007–8 (El-Wassal, 2013: 4). Privatization of public sector companies and slimming down of the civil service meant the loss of large numbers of jobs. In the first decade of the twenty-first century, while public sector employment remained more or less stable, the burgeoning of the labour force from 17 to 27 million meant a severe reduction in available jobs (Springborg, 2011). Needless to say, the private sector had no capacity to absorb laid-off workers, let alone the millions of new entrants in the labour market. The lucky ones among the hundreds of thousands of redundant workers managed to join the ranks of the informal sector. Like most countries of the global south, the informal sector in Egypt remains a major source of employment. Accounting for almost one third of total GDP in 2004, it provided employment for 8.2 million workers, considerably higher than the 6.8 million hired by the formal private sector (Galal, 2004). The informal sector remains outside the purview of labour laws and its workers are hence excluded from any form of protection, social security, unionization, access to credit or health insurance.

Perhaps even more relevant to the loss of a sense of job security was the dramatic rise in precarious or vulnerable employment. Among major achievements on the road to reform, Egypt was lauded by IFIs for having removed a great deal of labour market 'rigidities'. The private sector was especially lauded for not having minimum wages, while both the private and public sectors were commended for cutting down on non-wage costs and for fostering weak unionized activity (Hassan and Sassanpour, 2008). In 2004, a World Bank recommendation for slimming down the public sector was to rely on 'lowering remuneration for new entrants, adjusting the pay scale to strengthen the link between compensation and productivity, and focusing on non-wage benefits that distort labour decisions, such as generous pension systems and family allowances that add to the allure of employment in the public sector' (World Bank, 2004: 133). The infamous Law 12/2003 was enacted with the aim of providing more freedom for employers to dismiss workers summarily as well as the power to modify contracts at will. Under Mubarak, new employees, both in the private and public sectors, were increasingly hired on short-term contracts in order to avoid providing any social security. More alarming were reports of newly hired employees being required to sign resignation letters at the moment of hiring which their employers could use to dismiss them at any time. Even those with more secure contracts could not rely on any social security benefits as part of their employment. The overwhelming majority of firms across the economy (91 per cent) employ fewer than five workers, which means they are not required by Egyptian labour laws to provide workers with social security (Abdel-Fadil, 2011: 22). On the eve of Mubarak's downfall, even by the World Bank's conservative definition of vulnerable employment, 21 per cent of all male and 44 per cent of all female workers in Egypt were considered vulnerable (Springborg, 2011).

Rural dispossession

Integral to Sadat's policies of de-Nasserization in the 1970s, were the commercialization of land and agricultural production and the dismantling of state institutions that had been designed to provide support to small farmers. Nasser's land reforms[11] were criticized for not going far enough in creating a more equitable distribution or in reducing the old landowners' positions of economic power in rural areas (Richards, 1993; El-Ghonemy, 1998). However, the reforms were, undeniably, the most extensive in the whole of the Middle East (Bush, 2009). As was the case with labour and public sector laws, Nasser's land reforms afforded small farmers a huge sense of security, backed by laws protecting their rights, especially tenancy rights. In order to liberalize the economy and attract FDI, successive Mubarak governments followed in the footsteps of Sadat by whittling away benefits that had accrued to small farmers under Nasser. The tenancy law, in particular, was regarded by neoliberal policy-makers as the last obstacle on the road to 'freeing' Egyptian agriculture from the 'distorting' control of the state. Therefore, Law 96 of 1992, which came into effect in 1997, revoked the previously state-determined rents of small farmers, allowing landowners to charge any rent they saw fit. In some cases, landowners charged market-based rents, permitting some farmers to continue with their tenancy. But in other cases, landowners charged rents that immediately skyrocketed by up to 400 per cent in some areas, allowing them to terminate the contracts of those unable to pay the exorbitant rents and not issue new contracts to poor farmers, especially in the case of female-headed households (ibid.: 59). Millions of tenants were put at the complete mercy of landowners without any state protection, resulting in many peasant families, especially female-headed households, being dispossessed of their rights (ibid.: 58).[12]

Although agriculture was the slowest growing sector in the period 1990 to 2008, rural poverty had been declining until the introduction of Law 96. However, in the period after the mass eviction of tenants, it increased rapidly from 22.1 per cent in 2000 to 28.9 per cent in 2009, representing an increase of almost a third in only nine years (see Table 1.1). The plight of Egypt's small farmers and landless peasants was further exacerbated by the intensifying pressure of other neoliberal policies. For example, the country's much

Table 1.1 Poverty headcount ratio using national poverty line, 1990–2009

Region	1990	1995	2000	2005	2009
Urban	20.3	22.5	9.3	10.1	11.0
Rural	28.6	23.3	22.1	26.8	28.9
Total	25.0	22.9	16.9	19.6	21.6

Source: Bargawi and McKinley (2011) (based on CAPMAS and WB)

criticized food subsidy programme had a distinctively urban bias. In 2008–2009 rural areas benefited ten per cent less than urban areas from food and other subsidies (World Bank and Ministry of Economic Development, Arab Republic of Egypt, 2010).

The poor pay taxes and service the debt

Mubarak instituted a truly regressive tax regime, thereby even further increasing the inequality engendered by the neoliberal order. In 2001, the pro-rich fiscal system drew only 4.4 per cent of all revenue from taxes on industrial and commercial profits. Nonetheless, only a few months after its appointment in 2004, the Nazif government abolished progressive income taxation and introduced a flat rate of 20 per cent, with an exemption only for those with an annual income less than EGP 5000 (approximately equivalent to US$700 in early 2014). More importantly, corporate tax was slashed from 42 to 20 per cent. By 2009/2010, salaried workers paid EGP 13 billion in tax while the contribution of multi-billion dollar corporations was only EGP 22.9 billion (Gamal, 2010).

Not only did the burden of filling the coffers fall on the shoulders of the poor and their meagre incomes, they also had to service the country's huge debts. On the eve of the 25 January uprising, Mubarak's Egypt was servicing a domestic debt of EGP 962.2 billion, which had more than doubled from EGP 434.0 billion in 2004. This rapid rise meant that in 2009 domestic debt reached 67.4 per cent of GDP (Soliman, 2011). At the beginning of 2011, the country's external debt was $34.9 billion. The cost of servicing the total debt equalled 23 times a taxpayer's share of government spending on education and 3000 times that on housing (Abdel Wahab, 2011). Domestically, the major creditor of the government as well as domestic capital was the National Investment Bank, an institution described by Hazem El-Beblawi as suffering from complex problems and financial entanglement connected to the entire financial situation of the country.[13] In a study of the fiscal crisis under Mubarak, Soliman (2011: 106) shows that the National Investment Bank not only had financial problems but was financing a wealth of private enterprises. Of course, this is in complete disregard of the main purpose for which all national investment banks are created: to finance national infrastructure and other public projects with funds that are drawn heavily from the savings of millions of tax-payers in the form of social security and pension fund contributions.

One of the precepts of global neoliberal orthodoxy, which has been propagated since the late 1970s, is the need to 'roll back' the overly powerful and pervasive state. Ironically, neoliberal restructuring has led to the opposite in the state's more coercive functions: security and policing. With increasing dispossession, marginalization and disentitlement, neoliberal regimes everywhere have had to resort to new systems of governance in order to manage and control popular mobilization against the consequences of their policies. New modes of regulation have included the growing centrality of security and policing and the criminalization of groups which have been hardest hit by neoliberal policies. In Egypt, the restructuring of the security system has been an integral part of institutional support for the new order.

Policing neoliberalism: a state of terror

> The ministry will not tolerate any breach of the dignity of an honourable citizen ... [However] I have reservations [about calling] terrorists, thieves, drug dealers and such others as humans with rights[14]

In Marxist analysis, the police is not simply a state institution set up to fight crime and guarantee law and order but an agent in the service of capital. It is responsible for the reproduction of power relations and for crushing the expectations of labour in regard to wages and job security (Neocleous 2000; Gordon, 2005). The rise of industrial capitalism necessitated setting up institutions that would not only 'organize' new labour relations, but more importantly, quash new industrial workers' hopes of transferring a system of entitlement based on feudal tradition in the countryside to the industrial workplace. In the new industrial context, these workers' expectations could include appropriating part of the product of their labour (Coleman, 2003). In this reading, state coercion and police power are not seen as a coincidental outcome of authoritarianism but as an integral part of the capitalist state irrespective of the prevailing political system. With the rise of neoliberal capitalism and the consequent increase in large numbers of the working classes that have been dispossessed of their rights and entitlements, the state has invested heavily in enlarging the scope and power of the police to keep them quiescent.

Mubarak's Egypt was an excellent exemplar of this analysis. Immediately after Sadat's assassination in 1981, the country braced itself for yet another long stretch of rule by the infamous emergency law.[15] No other piece of legislation has endowed the police and security forces with more unchecked powers than this law. Under the pretext of fighting Islamist militants, the law gave the police a wide-ranging mandate to ban public gatherings and any form of demonstration, to inspect personal correspondence and search individuals and places without the need to follow the provisions of the Criminal Procedure Code, to censor publications, to detain suspects indefinitely without charge and to try civilians under military courts where no judges preside and where there is no prospect of appeal.

The emergency law notwithstanding, the ministry of the interior (MOI) also enjoys a monopoly over a wide range of aspects of the life of individuals. Managing prisons, providing security during elections and supervising the medical care of prisoners are the least controversial of the MOI's mandate. More controversially, the MOI controls the issuing of passports and birth certificates, grants nationality and provides permission to work abroad for millions of Egyptian migrant workers. To ensure the regime's control over the provinces, the MOI is further entrusted with the responsibility of appointing *umda*s (mayors) of villages too small to have local councils. Repeated calls to appoint civilians to these functions and a politician rather than a member of the police force as minister of the interior have gone unheeded.[16]

As the regime became increasingly reliant on the MOI to fight its war against Islamist militants, the police were gradually accorded more resources and liberties. Like the military, the MOI can count on a huge reservoir of free labour: conscripts, particularly those from poor and rural backgrounds, who provide the manpower for the Central Security Force (*amn markazy*).[17] Created in the aftermath of the 1968 student demonstrations, the *amn markazy* has since functioned as the main agency responsible for suppressing any form of protest in the country. The single exception was the 1986 *amn markazy* uprising when the notoriously inhumane conditions of the conscripts, long maintained by the use of harsh punishment, finally pushed them to breaking point. The young conscripts, who were expected to suppress those protesting and fighting against the regime, were themselves seething with dissatisfaction. They finally took to the streets in their thousands, destroying property and inflicting damage on a system that had long abused them and taken them for granted. The MOI had to call upon the military to intervene and put down riots instigated by its own force.

While the dismal conditions of conscripts have only been nominally improved, the result of the riots was a substantial increase in the budget of the ministry itself. With the increasing dispossession and impoverishment of more and more groups in society due to intensive marketization, the regime became heavily reliant on the police. Requiring the police to evict people from their land and homes, to silence protestors and to terrify those who might consider resistance as an option came at a price. Since the 1990s, therefore, the MOI budget has been consistently increased relative to general expenditure, exceeding those of education and health combined (Seif El-Dawla, 2009). Financial and human resources aside, the Mubarak regime not only turned a blind eye to police excesses in dealing with society but progressively gave it free rein in the use of terror. Since the 1990s, police violence has become endemic. In its May 2004 report, the Egyptian Organization for Human Rights (EOHR) documented 292 torture cases in the period from January 1993 to April 2004. Of these cases, 20 reportedly resulted in the death of the suspect or prisoner.[18] Obviously, these figures are only a fraction of the actual total due to the under-reporting of incidents by victims and their relatives and to the obstruction of access of human rights organizations to police stations and detention centres.

The use of torture in Egypt is nothing new. Memories of Nasser's concentration camps, which held his opponents from across the entire political spectrum in the 1950s and 1960s, are still fresh in the minds and not so fresh on the bodies of the lucky ones who have survived to tell the tale. Sadat's jails continued to bear witness to the physical punishment of members of the opposition as did those of Mubarak in the 1980s. Torture was routinely employed as an interrogation method of suspects and their relatives, neighbours and acquaintances. More often its purpose was to secure confessions rather than gather intelligence. Egyptian prisons were, as they are now, crowded with convicted inmates who had signed confessions under the weight of unbearable torture to crimes which they had probably never committed. In an infamous incident in the mid-1980s, the police rounded up almost one thousand suspects after the attempted assassination of two former ministers of the interior, Hasan Abu Basha and Nabawi Ismail. The usual routine of breaking into the suspects' homes, terrorizing their relatives and using excessive torture during interrogation resulted in a swift confession by three detainees. The arrest of the 'criminals' and their confessions were hailed in the media as a victory for the intelligence services. Shortly afterwards, however, the actual culprits were arrested and the three confessors were quietly released (Abdel Aziz, 2011: 50–51). The same pattern continues to date. In fact, the Egyptian police's reputation for using extreme torture to acquire confessions has achieved international notoriety. The use of torture is so excessive that it is even regarded askance by Egypt's global partners in crime. During the regime of the euphemistically termed extraordinary rendition, Egypt enthusiastically cooperated with the CIA in the torture and interrogation of suspects in the 'war against terror'. Commenting on the Egyptian security apparatus compared to other countries in the region, a former CIA official, Robert Baer, said 'if you want a serious interrogation, you send a prisoner to Jordan. If you want them tortured, you send them to Syria. If you want them to disappear – never to see them again – you send them to Egypt' (Mayer, 2005: 47).

Since the 1990s, however, police torture has no longer been reserved for (suspected) criminals, political activists and members of the opposition. There has been an astounding escalation in torture at the hands of the Egyptian police of mostly 'ordinary' citizens. From petty crime suspects to individuals approaching law enforcement officers to mediate in minor disputes to those whose misfortune has simply put them in the path of a police officer, the 'hand' of the law was reaching ever wider. Age, region, political persuasion and religion seemed to matter little.[19] Gender, however, is a different matter. Physical and sexual violence against women, especially in the public sphere, discussed in the following chapter, was increasingly becoming a trademark of state-sponsored brutality. However, all victims of torture do have their poverty and lack of access to power in common. The police reserves its most sustained attacks and methods of collective punishment for groups most vulnerable to neoliberal policies.[20] Protests against the removal of subsidies, job losses, forcible eviction from land and a host of other grievances against the neoliberal order have gripped the country since the turn of the century. Against these protests, the police have been at their most brutal. Among the numerous sustained and targeted campaigns of punishment, few have become as infamous in the recent history of resistance to Mubarak and his police terror as the case of Sarando and Borolus villages discussed in Chapter 3. Since 2004, labour protests, which have intensified against privatization and deteriorating working conditions, have been targets of the most organized campaigns of violence. The violence against and collective punishment of striking workers at Mahalla in 2008 is a case in point.

Another marked change in policing under Mubarak was the shifting of the location of attack. Increasingly, police violence has moved from the confines of police stations, detention centres and people's private residences to public spaces. Reports of physical abuse of citizens in their workplaces, on the street, in coffee shops and even in bus stations, became widespread (Abdel Aziz, 2011: 61). This shift in the location of police violence is neither new nor unique to Egypt. With the rise of industrial capitalism, police efforts to control labour went beyond the workplace or the police station. The focus of the police quickly extended to the public sphere, especially to areas where people engaged in activities that were regarded as undermining the formal market (Gordon, 2005: 62). In Egypt, one of the groups routinely targeted with increasing violence was street vendors. Over the years, campaigns to evict vendors, especially in the capital city, resulted in bloody confrontations, injuries and occasional deaths.[21]

Modern technology and new social media were crucial to this shift in location. In the 2000s, police officers, for example, were increasingly recording the torturing of their victims at police stations on mobile phones. The recordings were circulated to the victims' families and acquaintances to send a clear message of deterrence. The objective of police violence was no longer simply to extract a quick confession, to disband a protest or to punish individuals and their close relatives. The aim had increasingly become to terrorize the 'Egyptian street'. The arbitrariness of the violence, the absence of a clear rationale for the attacks and the brutality were able to create the state of terror that the police and the regime intended.

To support the needs of an ever-expanding regime of terror, the MOI started to 'outsource' its most 'dirty' business. With increasing impunity, criminal investigation officers began to promote a new 'police force' of *baltagya* (thugs). *Baltagya* are criminals, usually with a record of violence and known to the police, who are paid to carry out duties of 'disciplining' members of the public in return for the police turning a blind eye to their criminal activities including drug trafficking.[22] The *baltagya*'s job description has expanded to include voter intimidation, beating up criminal suspects and political activists,

rape and sexual abuse, breaking up demonstrations, forcibly removing farmers from their land and much more. The advantage of *baltagya* is that they
can infiltrate any group without being easily traced to the police.

Egypt's regime of terror was intended to protect Mubarak's neoliberal
order against the dispossessed. Ironically, it helped to provide the exploited
and downtrodden masses with a focus to mobilize against the regime which
culminated in an uprising that presented the most serious challenge to
Mubarak's elite. From 2005, protestors across the country were already
expressing grievances against the MOI and often demanded the resignation of
Habib El-Adly, minister of the interior. The date of 25 January itself, with a
touch of bitter irony, was chosen by activists to protest against police violence
as it is the officially designated Police Day.

The octopus of the Nile

The Egyptian military was never a direct target of people's grievances prior to
the 25 January uprising. If anything, days into the uprising, the armed forces
quickly emerged as heroes who had presumably decided to side with the protestors against Mubarak's regime, leading to the incongruous slogan 'The
military and the people are one hand'. However, the reality is very different.
The military was deeply implicated in the reproduction of the Mubarak
regime and a willing partner in the economic order it created. While the
generals might not have been the greatest winners in the brand of crony, oligopolistic capitalism promoted by Mubarak, his son, and his son's cronies,
the military establishment was profoundly involved in instituting such a
system. The army's sprawling economic empire, while perhaps not as dominant as some exaggerated estimates would lead us to believe, has benefited
from the same system of privileges enjoyed by Egypt's new capitalist class. As
its tentacles spread to every niche of the polity, economy and society, the
military resembles the octopus, a mollusc with three pulsing hearts. Although
the military cannot claim dominance in any of these spheres, its omnipresence
has accorded it a unique position in post-1952 Egypt.

The pervasive and privileged position of the military in Egypt has roots
growing deeper than those of any other force in the country. These roots go
back to the 1952 coup staged by Nasser and the Free Officers. Nasser's
introduction of his special brand of Arab nationalism and the launching of
the slogan 'everything for the battle' in the 1950s allowed the Egyptian military to establish first claim on some of the nation's most strategic resources.
With its tentacles growing everywhere: state bureaucracy, local government,
huge infrastructural development projects, heavy and light industry from
weapon production to household goods manufacturing, land reclamation and
a wide range of activities in the services sector, the military has developed into
an autonomous middle-class entity with an industrial base. Like many post-
colonial states, the military–state complex in Egypt assumed a huge economic
role which is unparalleled in the classic bourgeois state. This role was, to some

extent, made necessary by the weakness of indigenous private entrepreneurship and the relevant social classes on the eve of independence (Alavi, 1972).

Since then, the power of the military establishment has been reflected in the number of critical top state positions held by current and retired generals. The generals also dominate local government and public sector companies. More importantly, the military has expanded its economic enterprises by exploiting its unique privileges, such as tax exemptions, favourable exchange rates, confiscation rights and preferential treatment in bidding for state contracts. The military further maintains command of considerable resources and opportunities unattainable for the civilian economy, including virtually free labour (conscripts) and huge state-owned land holdings. The army also enjoys control of its own budget without any political oversight, which has deepened its power as an organization with unparalleled independence. This last privilege has been subject to great controversy, particularly in post-uprising political debate. Even private corporations vie for the blessing of the military establishment. Like the cases of Pakistan and Bangladesh, where the military–state oligarchy dominates, big businesses in Egypt have adopted the practice of awarding profitable directorships to retiring generals.

The military enjoyed its heyday in Egyptian politics in the 1950s but over the decades, especially in the aftermath of the 1967 defeat, it has lost some of its power.[23] However, while bearing this in mind, it is crucial to understand that this analysis of the Egyptian military does not set out to prove its complete dominance of politics but to examine the way in which it has been involved in the reproduction of the regime and the establishment of a neoliberal order through its activities in the economy, society and polity.

The military's economy and society

No accurate estimate of the size of the military economy is feasible in a country like Egypt. For one thing, the term 'military economy' is fraught with methodological ambiguities, making it difficult to determine what to include and exclude in such an assessment.[24] Apart from official figures on military expenditure, which indicate a very low and not very credible two per cent of total GDP, any information on military financial and economic transactions are shrouded in secrecy and kept behind a facade of national security.[25] Furthermore, the diverse nature of the military's economic activities and the caginess which surrounds them has thrown up whimsical estimates of the military's share of the national economy ranging from a massive 40 per cent to a much more modest ten per cent and even five per cent.[26] A more accurate figure would be helpful in more carefully analysing the role of the military in the economy. However, for this analysis, the involvement of the military in the reproduction of the Mubarak economic order is the relevant issue.

The immediate post-1952 army concentrated its economic ventures in the field of weapon manufacturing. By 1984, Egypt had attained self-sufficiency in the manufacture of small arms, mortars and similar armaments. The military-owned industries exported an annual average of $191 million in the 1980s (Gotowicki, 1997). The majority of these exports were concentrated on arms sales to Iraq during the Iran–Iraq war. From the late 1970s, especially in the aftermath of the Camp David agreement, the military's production expanded into the non-armament, civilian sector. Due to falling military budgets, which was already occurring in the 1980s, there was discussion of the need for Arab militaries to seek funds from activities in the marketplace either through retired individuals or military-owned companies (Picard, 1988). Indeed, the budget of Egypt's military fell in real terms by nearly a half in the last two decades of the twentieth century while the US military aid of $1.3 billion, not included in the military budget, fell in real terms by 50 per cent (Frisch, 2001). This was an alarming situation that spurred the military to expand its economic portfolio and diversify its activities in order to compensate for its diminishing budget.

The ministry of military production had already had experience in the 1960s of manufacturing basic civilian products, such as boilers, cooking ovens, cars and other household goods. However, in the 1970s, the military embarked on a mission to build a solid base in the production of a wide range of civilian goods and services. Since then, the military has diversified into producing commodities such as pasta, bottled water and cooking oil and into running services such as taxis, cleaning, abattoirs and the construction and management of luxury beach resorts. Army manufacturing expanded under the auspices of the National Service Projects Administration, a subsidiary of the ministry of defence that was created specifically to oversee production in civilian goods and to absorb military officers who no longer had any prospect of active service. By the mid-1990s, this organization ran 16 factories employing 75,000 workers. With almost half of their production geared towards the civilian market, these factories produced numerous commodities ranging from agricultural machines to pharmaceuticals, electric cables and ovens (Frisch, 2001: 8).

The military's economic power also stretches beyond the obvious realm of production and assets. Top military officials command power over economic policy. The example of natural gas exports is a case in point. After Mubarak's ousting, investigation into the case of natural gas exports to Israel revealed that the General Intelligence Service (GIS) subsidiary company *Al-Sharq* managed the export of natural gas to Jordan. Furthermore, some of the former GIS strongmen, such as Hussein Salim, were discovered to have received credit privileges from the government to export natural gas to Israel through their private ventures.[27] More importantly, the investigations revealed the role played by Omar Soliman, head of the GIS, rather than the prime minister or the minister of petroleum, in negotiating the price of natural gas exports to Israel (Brayez, 2013).[28] Similarly, the military exerted further influence through its representation on state-owned, commercial enterprises. Retired senior officers have always been routinely appointed as board members of public sector companies. While these retired officers are in theory no longer in military service and are expected to serve in their civilian capacity, in reality this is far from the case. Many of these retired officers continue to be employed by the military on the basis of six-month renewable contracts which can go on for ten years or more (Sayigh, 2012).

The military's economic interests have been served well by the neoliberal restructuring under Mubarak. Military officers are routinely appointed as board members and consultants to a vast number of private sector companies. Contrary to the military's reputation as a 'pillar of protectionism', its projects, run by companies in which it is a shareholder, are characterized by collaboration with transnational capital. The military has repeatedly been in partnership with Gulf conglomerates such as the Kuwaiti Kharafi group, as well as Western and Asian multinationals including China's Sinopec and Italy's Breda and Eni (Marshall and Stacher, 2012). These joint ventures account for tens of billions of dollars in investment from foreign companies and banks. Even if the military's share is not huge in most of them, they are testimony to both its ever-growing influence and its enthusiastic accommodation of neoliberal capitalism.

The networks of privilege under Mubarak also included the military complex. Several high-ranking military personnel have not only been involved in large business deals but have also benefited from their political office in the service of these business interests. The case of Sayed Meshaal, a former minister of military production, suffices to illustrate this point. Before his appointment to a ministerial position, Meshaal was the head of the National Service Projects Administration which ran, among its many operations, a bottled water company that he proudly named SAFI after his daughter. At the same time, he was a member of the NDP and an MP for the Helwan district in Cairo between 2000 and 2011. Meshaal secured his parliamentary seat through the votes of the thousands of workers of the military factory 99 based in Helwan. Meshaal allegedly made a huge fortune from his multiple positions (Al-Khalsan, 2011).

The greatest privilege the military enjoys over any other economic actor in the country is the autonomy it holds over its budget and business empire. Revenues from its projects, profits from its exports and shares in companies and assets are off the national budget. They are automatically returned to the military coffers with no government accounting or tax deductions (Springborg, 1989; Gotowicki, 1997). The military's economic interests, including its monopolistic practices, its revenues and its overall budget are shielded from any form of external scrutiny in the name of national security, a justification which many critics find unacceptable. Hesham Guinena, the head of the Central Auditing Authority, for example, was quoted as saying that it was unreasonable that his agency did not have the power to audit the revenues of military-owned 'wedding halls' hired out to civilians, which he argued could not be relevant to national security.[29] However, military officers continue to reject any criticism of their complete financial autonomy. In a conference held by the Supreme Council of the Armed Forces (SCAF) on its vision for the future of economic reform in March 2012, General Mahmoud Nasr, assistant defence minister for finance, bluntly said that revenues from the military's enterprises are not the business of any other body but itself. They constitute what he described as the 'sweat of the ministry of defence'. In reference to a multi-million dollar mine-clearing operation conducted by the military in Kuwait, he insisted that the state would not be allowed to touch the millions in profits (Gamal, 2012).

However, profits derived from economic enterprises are not the only trophy secured by the military. A highly significant result of the military's involvement in manufacturing, construction and service activities has undoubtedly been its unique ability to penetrate society. Nasser's developmentalist state, like its counterparts in the post-colonial world, invested heavily in infrastructure projects. His modernization project rested on land reclamation, the building of roads, bridges and power plants and the construction of hospitals, schools and affordable housing for the country's growing population. From the early days of Nasser's republic, the military was given the task of shouldering most of these infrastructure projects. From building housing units to installing electricity grids and telephone networks to even running the national adult literacy programme,[30] the military touches the lives of almost all Egyptians, gaining it a unique position not just as the defender of the nation but also as the handmaiden of its modernization and physical development.

At a different level, the military has operated a network of petrol stations, supermarkets, hotels, beach resorts, housing complexes and function halls serving the needs of its own corps as well as those of the general public. Many Egyptians live, shop for their groceries, fuel the tanks of their cars and spend their holidays under the all-pervading banner of the military. A great many young, middle-class couples, for example, have their lives touched by the military when they hold their wedding parties at one of the nation-wide, military-owned and -run function halls. Websites, Facebook pages and newspapers advertise the competitive prices and romantic atmosphere offered by venues such as the House of Ammunition and Artillery and the Electronic Warfare and Presidential Guards Halls.

A militarized polity

Military officers, both retired and in service, occupy a wide range of positions in the state bureaucracy. They are appointed to administrative and managerial positions in academic institutions, state media organizations, hospitals, sports facilities and boards of state-owned industrial companies. In fact, some vital state institutions have been traditionally dominated by military officers. One such example is the Administrative Monitoring Authority (AMA). Established in 1958, it has since been entrusted with the responsibility of combating corruption in all state institutions except, of course, the military itself, which is above the oversight of any civilian body.[31] No institution is more central to state bureaucracy than the Authority for Organization and Administration, the body responsible for all reform, training, evaluation and restructuring of the civil service since 1964. The military has successfully managed to extend its tentacles into such a vital institution with the appointment of Major-General Safwat Al-Nahhas as its head since 2004 (Sayigh, 2012: 13).

One of the most important sites where the military has been traditionally involved in reproducing and maintaining regime power is local government, for which positions are awarded by appointment rather than election. Municipal positions ranging from the all-powerful provincial governors to village heads have always been dominated by the military and its retired senior officers. Military officers also serve as deputy governors, heads of central communication units, directors of transportation, and heads of water and sanitation companies and information centres.

Military officers control top as well as middle management positions within almost all civilian ministries including housing, transportation, environment, media and information. The military's role in the ministry of housing and its different agencies cannot be emphasized enough. As the military has unlimited access to most public land, it has always been heavily involved in construction and the real estate business. Military officers dominate the Central Construction Apparatus responsible for building housing and urban infrastructure as well as the New Urban Communities Authority. The military's control of agriculture and land reclamation projects has long been justified by the argument that national security, for which the military is responsible, relies on food security. In this regard, military officers dominate the General Authority for Reclamation Projects and Agricultural Development, an organization at the helm of large irrigation and agricultural projects.[32]

In other civilian ministries, the military presence is also acutely felt. A recent report notes an impressive 37 retired generals occupying leading positions in the ministry of environment, including some from the division of chemical warfare.[33] Even the highest state religious institutions such as the ministry of Awqaf and Al-Azhar have not escaped the encroachment of the military. The ministry of Awqaf, in charge of religious endowments and the running of mosques, has for years seen retired generals control the position of director of the central service sector in the ministry. Similarly, Al-Azhar has recently opened its doors to the generals to occupy the position of head of security. In 2010, the prestigious position of the director of the office of the grand sheikh of Al-Azhar was awarded to Major-General Ibrahim Sadeq (Al-Bahnasawi and Zalat, 2012).

Even the MOI, which has grown dramatically not only in budget but also in its centrality to the reproduction of the regime, is still relatively entwined with the military. For example, the Egyptian Armed Forces is said to 'provide a great many of the senior operational and administrative officers in the Interior Ministry and the General Intelligence Directorate' (Sayigh, 2012: 5). The same emergency law which endows the MOI with exceptional powers has also given exceptional powers to the military within similar domains. The emergency law, which stipulates that civilians be subject to military trials in certain circumstances, has meant that military courts have presided over thousands of civilian cases since the 1980s. Article 3 of the same law also empowers the military officer in charge or his deputy to monitor newspapers, booklets and other publications with the authority to confiscate them and take them out of circulation. The military thus competes with other state institutions such as the judiciary and the censorship authority.

Despite this impressive penetration of almost all aspects of society, in the final analysis, the military was not the leading economic or political victor in Mubarak's Egypt. However, the essential issue for the argument in this study is the extent to which the military complex was involved in the reproduction of the regime and the order it had created. As demonstrated above, the military has become an all-important entity for most Egyptians. The army was essential in building an independent, modern Egypt as it had the task of implementing Nasser's developmentalist project. By infiltrating and assuming important positions of power in society, the economy and the polity, the army has become a natural presence in all aspects of the lives of most Egyptians. To many, its omnipresence in the fabric of society is taken for granted. This goes a long way to explaining the high regard with which a majority of Egyptians view the military. Despite its clear complicity in the neoliberal project that was disenfranchising large numbers of poorer citizens, many Egyptians wanted to believe that the army was on their side during the 18 day uprising. Later, when confronted with the imbroglio of Morsi's presidency, an overwhelming majority of Egyptians flocked to the army as the only other meaningful political player that had the ability to liberate them from the stranglehold of the Muslim Brothers. Subsequently, in January 2014, a massive majority voted 'yes' in the referendum on a new constitution which reaffirmed yet again the army's privileges and impunity. Egyptians' hopes for a more prosperous, stable and democratic future were now entrusted to the army and its unconvincing roadmap. Yet as demonstrated by the army's tentacles penetrating to assume powerful positions in all aspects of society and the polity and its commitment to the neoliberal capitalist project, it is difficult to imagine how the inherently conservative army will do anything but staunchly defend the status quo to protect its interests.

As a political project, neoliberalism relies on a very narrow social base in terms of beneficiaries. With the exception of a privileged elite which gains from its logic of accumulation, the majority of the working classes under neoliberalism are virtually excluded from its wealth concentration. Such an order, inevitably, engenders intense discontent among the dispossessed and leads to social and political mobilization. In Egypt, as the following two chapters will show, the neoliberal order under Mubarak gave rise to intensive waves of mobilization which spanned the decade, culminating in the massive 25 January uprising. However, this order was a tightly knit network of interests bringing the military and the state-capital nexus together in an imposing edifice that was closely protected by the bulwark of a set of institutions whose function was to reproduce and protect the system. Faced with this powerful system, the overthrow of the Mubarak regime was a daunting task.

Notes

1 The American Chamber of Commerce in Egypt represents the interests of the most powerful businesses in Egypt. According to its president, in 2004, member companies accounted for almost 20 per cent of Egyptian GDP (Rutherford, 2008).
2 For a full review of the document, see Al-Ahram (2003).
3 The QIZ protocol, which was signed in 2004, allows the export of Egyptian manufactured products duty-free to the US, provided companies in specially designated zones satisfy the condition that products contain at least 11.7 per cent of Israeli components. See the full QIZ protocol at http://www.qizegypt.gov.eg/About_Text protocol.aspx (accessed April 10, 2011).
4 Sfakianakis identifies 32 businessmen whom he terms 'whales on the Nile' and who comprised the top of the business elite in the 1990s. Through their cross-cutting networks with the state elite, they built their business empires and supported the new political order.
5 The other two steel companies are Bishay Steel and Al-Garhy. For exact figures on iron and steel production, see Abdel-Fadil (2011).
6 By a tacit agreement, foreign cement plants cut prices by an average of EGP 180 per tonne, forcing domestic plants such as Wadi El Nil, El-Sweid and El Nahda to retract price increases that they had already announced. For more details, see Riyad (2011).
7 WTO members, according to this rule, cannot appeal to pre-existing domestic legislation to avoid adhering to WTO agreements; they have to amend domestic laws to abide by WTO rules or risk retaliation.
8 For detailed discussion of this and several similar cases see Adly, A. (2011a).
9 For details of the process, see Sfakianakis (2004).
10 For a discussion of methodological and ideological concerns in estimating levels of poverty, see Achcar (2013).
11 The first round of the land reform programme was implemented in 1961, restricting ownership to 100 *feddans*, while the second phase came later, in 1969, further restricting ownership to 50 *feddans* (a *feddan* is 0.42 of one hectare).
12 While article no. 33 of Law 96/1992 proposed compensating the evicted tenants with land in the desert, ridiculous as it might be, in reality no compensation was provided. Moreover, there was no mention of compensating tenants for their houses, buildings and agricultural machines that they had acquired throughout the tenancy period.
13 Hazem El-Beblawi, at the time of this interview with *Egypt Daily* on 16/7/2012, was a former minister of finance. He did not assume the position of prime minister until the ousting of Morsi in July 2013.
14 Zaki Badr, minister of the interior, in an interview with *Ibrahim*, police magazine, in 1989.
15 It is vital to realize that Egypt had been ruled by a state of emergency since 1967 with the exception of an 18-month period before the assassination of Sadat. Following the uprising, it was briefly lifted before being reinstated in another form.
16 See, for example, 'The National Initiative to Rebuild the Police: A Police for the Egyptian People'. http://eipr.org/sites/default/files/pressreleases/pdf/national_initia tive_for_police_reform_en.pdf.
17 The system of military conscription in Egypt is extremely class based. While university and other tertiary education graduates do one year of military service, those

with only a high school diploma serve two years. Conscripts without a high school diploma serve a term of three years.

18 EOHR, 'Torture in Egypt … an unchecked phenomenon' (May 29, 2004), at www. eohr.org/report/2004/re3.htm.

19 Street children and children at risk are often detained and subjected to routine beatings and sexual abuse (HRW, 2004).

20 In the industrialized West since the 1980s, the police has intensified its targeting of particular localities and populations, namely the poor, the unemployed, migrants and blacks (Bonefeld, 1993). The infamous 'stop and search' policy has given increasing discretionary powers to the police to bring into line any group which might entertain ideas about demanding rights or entitlements.

21 See Abdelrahman (2012) for a discussion of state concerns with street vendors and the informal economy.

22 'The National Initiative to Rebuild the Police: A Police for the Egyptian People'. http://eipr.org/sites/default/files/pressreleases/pdf/national_initiative_for_police_refo rm_en.pdf.

23 For a study dedicated to exploring the diminishing role of the military within Egypt's ruling elite, see Kandil (2012).

24 For a discussion of the methodological questions in estimating the size of the 'military economy', see Brayez (2013), who distinguishes between the military's share in GDP, in GNP and the total value of its assets.

25 This figure is corroborated by an estimate derived from World Bank data by Al-Naggar (2013), who uses it to counter what he regards as gross exaggerations of the size of the military economy. However, by simply relying on such a figure for the military budget, he ignores the much greater military holdings in the economy.

26 For various estimates, see Al-Naggar (2013); Al-Khalsan (2011).

27 The director of the Intelligence Service is often drawn from the ranks of the armed forces.

28 The Administrative Court later found the price negotiated to be way below market price, thus inflicting huge losses on the Egyptian economy.

29 A TV interview quoted in *Al-Balad*: 'Head of the Central Auditing Authority Wonders What the Link Is between Armed Forces-run Wedding Halls and National Security?'. http://www.el-balad.com/303191#sthash.4MZQbxLx.dpuf.

30 The Directorate of Literacy and Adult Education is headed by Brigadier-General Mahmood Abdel-Dayem, see *Al-Shab Al-Gadid* (2012).

31 Despite allegations of corruption against Major-General Mohamed Al-Touhami and his predecessor, Hitler Tantawi, both remained in their position of head of AMA for several terms at the directive of Mubarak.

32 Many of these projects, especially those with the mandate to create agricultural land in the desert, such as the multi-billion dollar Al-Salam canal carrying Nile water to Northern Sinai and the Toshka canal carrying Nile water to the Western desert plateau, have been subject to considerable criticism for wasting water resources.

33 For a detailed account of the infiltration of military officers into the country's ministries, public companies, and service projects see Al-Bahnasawi and Zalat (2012).

2   It did not start in Tahrir
Birth of the pro-democracy movement

'It did not start in Seattle' was a slogan used by activists of the Global Justice Movement to challenge the ahistorical, popular claim that the beginning of global activism could conveniently be marked by the Seattle protests against the WTO ministerial conference in 1999. The objection was that such a claim ignored the historical continuity of national and global struggles against injustice and regimes of exploitation over the decades. In the same way, it is also, at best, naïve of commentators to see the mass uprising in Tahrir and across Egypt's major squares as an isolated event with no historical lineage. In fact, a tumultuous decade of social and political protest and an intensification of political mobilization preceded the 25 January mass uprising. Not a day passed during this entire period without several incidents of collective, contentious action across the country taking place which built up to the overthrow of Mubarak. As discussed in the previous chapter, this book adopts a three-pronged taxonomy in characterizing protest against the Egyptian regime consisting of the pro-democracy movement, the labour movement and citizen-based protests. The following analysis closely examines the nature and structures of mobilization as well as the scope and content of the evolving demands of the three forms of protest and the interconnectedness between them. This chapter, in particular, examines the pro-democracy movement, whose history and tactics have significantly shaped the way revolutionary actors have been able to develop since the downfall of Mubarak.

By no means can the history of struggle against the authoritarian, exclusionary political system in Egypt be reduced to a single decade. Numerous waves of protests, uprisings and mass revolts against successive regimes took place in post-1952 Egypt. From Nasser to Sadat to Mubarak, groups as varied as university students, state security officers, industrial workers, judges and small farmers challenged authoritarian regimes and their repressive and exclusionary policies. Despite Nasser's massive popularity and charisma, as well as his absolute control of power, the 1950s and 1960s were witness to contentious action from different quarters, including the Kafr Al-Dawwar strike in 1952 and judges attempting to achieve the judiciary's independence of the regime which ended in the infamous 1969 'massacre of judges' (both are discussed in Chapter 3). Food riots shook the country under Sadat in

January 1977. Protests against Mubarak's rule started early in his presidency with police riots in 1986 constituting a significant landmark of opposition.

These different acts of protest and revolt, however, were few and far between, representing an exception to the more usual daily grinding nature of life that was characterized by subtle forms of resistance.[1] As is always the case in authoritarian systems, these protests were confronted by police or military repression that was often brutal, with the result that participants paid a high price. However, the huge reversals in Egypt's political and economic policies, discussed in the previous chapter, engendered new struggles against the regime of dispossession. These struggles, in turn, created opportunities for the development of alternative forms of autonomous politics and collective action. New forms of contentious action evolved around myriad informal political groups, activist forums, political coalitions and protest activities that were to alter the face of Egyptian opposition politics and to mobilize, and even radicalize, wide sections of the population. The sustained campaigns of mobilization by these different groups attracted more members who had never previously entertained the thought of engaging in political action and provided them with new spaces to articulate and express their grievances against the regime.

On the eve of Mubarak's downfall, the pro-democracy movement in Egypt had evolved into a network of networks, each consisting of various groups and initiatives. A loosely linked and horizontally expanding universe, it brought together groups working on diverse causes and with demands ranging from constitutional change and limiting the powers of the presidency to claiming freedoms for professional unions, lifting the emergency law, defending academic freedom and allowing more options for collective action. The aftermath of the second Palestinian Intifada in September 2000 marked the intensification of these demands and the multiplication of groups and networks behind them. The growing demands were not only targeted at challenging Mubarak's authoritarian regime and calling for more rights for particular groups, but, more radically, they were questioning both the foundations of the post-1952 state and its erosion at the hands of Mubarak and his cronies. Political freedoms, completely undermined under the corporate system of Nasser and his successors, were challenged by groups that had long been deprived of their basic rights for collective action. At the same time, the erosion of the redistributive measures at the heart of the same system, symbolic as they were, was also the target of mobilization under Mubarak.

Several aspects set the protests of the first decade of the twenty-first century apart from previous surges of struggle: new forms of organization and tactics, working outside formal political organizations, interchangeable membership of various organizations, intensive cross-ideological cooperation and pushing the boundaries of what were regarded as acceptable demands by a political opposition. However, the central defining feature of the pro-democracy movement and its constituent groups was the ability to take the struggle onto the streets and to liberate activism from the confines of underground meetings and the closed offices of formal political groups. During this decade, demonstrations, rallies, sit-ins and street blockades progressively became a daily occurrence in Egypt's main squares, workplaces, university campuses, major roads and residential neighbourhoods.

In the final analysis, on the eve of the 25 January uprising, the pro-democracy movement was able neither to produce an alternative to the Mubarak regime nor to create a strong mass base. However, it shook the regime to its core, expanded the margin of contentious action, mobilized new groups and offered a training ground for young activists. Most importantly, it provided clear evidence to a new generation that mobilization to challenge the regime was possible.

From support of the Palestinian Intifada to an anti-war movement

Periodic demonstrations in support of Palestinians against sustained forms of aggression have taken place over the decades. However, the wave of demonstrations in support of the second Palestinian uprising or Intifada, which swept the Egyptian streets in September 2000, was no ordinary show of solidarity. In retrospect, this wave of protest constituted a seminal moment in Egyptian opposition politics that continued to shape the political landscape leading up to the downfall of Mubarak a decade later. The spontaneous demonstrations which erupted in universities, mosques and even schools soon metamorphosed into a coordinated campaign of support. The epicentre of the campaign was the Egyptian Popular Committee for Solidarity with the Palestinian Intifada (EPCSPI), known simply as Lagna Sh'abia (Popular Committee). This committee was established at the initiative of human rights groups such as Al-Nadeem Centre for the Rehabilitation of Victims of Torture and Violence, the Egyptian Anti-Torture Association and several leftist activists.

EPCSPI

A first public demonstration organized by the committee on 10 September 2001 in Tahrir Square was followed by a series of demonstrations that were held in squares of central Cairo, major mosques, almost all Egyptian universities and even schools. The largest demonstration, which drew almost 100,000 protestors, took place on 1 April 2002 in the aftermath of the Israeli occupation of Ramallah and Jenin (Al-Agati, 2010: 205). All these demonstrations were marked by unprecedented participation at the grassroots level. Fund-raising campaigns were organized by the committee, allowing the financing of several medical and relief convoys that were sent to the Palestinian territories.[2] Activities also extended to organizing seminars and cultural events. New ideas were adopted by the committee, such as the campaign for boycotting US and British products. Although, at best, the boycott campaign remained a symbolic activity in terms of actual effect, nonetheless it worked as an effective tool of mobilization and stimulated public debate.

The first of many groups and networks to follow in its footsteps, the Popular Committee had two main defining features which came to characterize all groups that constituted the pro-democracy movement: broad political and ideological representation and a simple, non-hierarchical coordination structure. Although the Popular Committee was the initiative of secularist civil society organizations and leftist activists, it soon attracted Islamist activists, who joined as representatives of unions and professional syndicates that were overwhelmingly dominated by the Muslim Brothers. Nasserists followed suit and participated in the various activities of the Popular Committee as individuals rather than representatives of their political parties. The Popular Committee operated as a loose organizational structure of coordination rather than a centralized body for decision-making.

The work of the Popular Committee, and its public visibility, would not have been possible without a degree of regime approval. The emergency law would normally provide the means for crushing any street action that went beyond a brief moment of spontaneous public enthusiasm. The Mubarak regime, however, elected to tolerate the early forms of street activism led by the committee. Not only were the activists left to carry on with their activities but, in a rare incident, state television and other media actually provided selective coverage of the demonstrations. This unusually accommodating reaction by the regime could be understood as part of an attempt to halt its waning legitimacy, caused in part by the loss of Egypt's historical leadership in the Arab world. The regime hoped to co-opt and identify itself with public support, both Egyptian and pan-Arab, for the Palestinian cause.

In one analysis, the regime initially tolerated this widespread street action which it saw as an outlet for public outrage against an external force rather than against domestic targets (ibid.). If this were the case, then the Egyptian regime committed one of its most costly political faux pas. It opened the gates for further articulation of anger that eventually metamorphosed into a movement directed against the regime itself. For political activists were emboldened to seize this moment and take to the streets. Soon afterwards, mobilization in support of the Intifada turned into more popular action against the threat of war in Iraq. In the lead-up to and in the immediate aftermath of the outbreak of war in Iraq, increasing numbers of demonstrations and public rallies were organized all over Egypt, culminating in a massive demonstration in Tahrir Square on 20 March 2003 which attracted over 40,000 protestors, an unprecedented number considering the very tight security presence. In retrospect, the large numbers in Tahrir Square as well as the almost complete control that the protestors had over the square for several hours on that day, have encouraged many to think of it as a 'dress rehearsal' for the 18 days in Tahrir in 2011 (Khaled Abdel-Hamid, author interview, Cairo, June 2011).

The growing number of protests, of people joining them and of increasing levels of collective action soon became more than the regime was willing to tolerate. For one thing, the focus of protest was no longer on nationalist concerns and external enemies but the Egyptian regime itself and its regional and domestic policies. For example, the regime's role in the war in Iraq was at the centre of slogans chanted during the anti-war protests such as '*Ya Mubarak ya gaban ya a'meel el amrican*' ('Mubarak ... you coward ... agent of the Americans') and '*Ya Mubarak fouq fouq bukra el-darb fi bab el-louq*' ('Wake up Mubarak ... Tomorrow they will also bomb Bab el-louq').[3] During the Tahrir demonstration of 20 March 2003, due to this new change in tack by the regime, the police returned to its usual tactics of employing excessive force in breaking up the demonstration and arresting almost one thousand demonstrators.

The mobilization during the first two years of this century centred upon regional concerns and the global power structures which help bolster regimes of occupation and inequality in the Arab world. An important feature of Egyptian activist networks emerging at that time was their growing links with global networks of activism also struggling to expose the same global power structures, such as militarization of the global system and the economic machinery that supported it. These informal links were developed with groups working under the umbrella of the anti-war movement and the Global Justice Movement (GJM). Such links were crucial for a process of learning new tactics and the diffusion of ideas which continued to shape the whole of the pro-democracy movement in the ensuing years. Central to this process of learning and exchange was the Cairo Conference and some of the groups that it inspired, such as the Egyptian Anti-Globalization Group. Both were central to the articulation of a counter-hegemonic position to the Mubarak neoliberal order.

Cairo Conference

The imminent threat of war in Iraq galvanized Egyptian activists from different political backgrounds to organize a conference that was to serve as a focus for discussion and action against the impending war. Officially named as the Cairo Conference against Imperialism and Zionism, but usually known simply as the Cairo Conference, it played a significant role in crystallizing the struggle of activists during the ensuing decade. The conference has been credited with opening a new space for political action and debate and even for creating 'momentum for the development of a movement for domestic political reform' Browers (2009: 112). First held in December 2002, the conference produced the Cairo Declaration, which was the starting point for organizing the globally coordinated, massive protests against the war in Iraq in February 2003 that brought a total of over 16 million protestors onto the streets of many world capitals. The second edition of the conference was held in December 2003, when it saw a wider level of coordination with the global anti-war movement. It was agreed during this edition that the conference would be held annually and should strive to become an event similar to the World Social Forum (WSF).

While the issue of war and occupation sparked the launching of the conference, the main objective that gradually evolved was to demonstrate and
discuss the links between global structures of exploitation and the suffering of
people at regional and national levels. The three banners under which the
conference was held: 'No to capitalist globalization and US hegemony', 'No
to the occupation of Iraq, and Zionism in Palestine', and 'No to authoritarianism in the Arab region' served to highlight the interconnectedness of global
capitalism, regimes of occupation and authoritarian political systems. The
themes discussed during the different editions of the conference covered a
wide area including health, education, taxation, militarization and labour
rights, among many others – all within the framework of global capitalism
and dominant neoliberal policies. In 2008, a declaration of principles stated
the Conference's categorical opposition to all forms of neo-imperialism and
imperialist projects involving Arab and other peoples with the 'purpose of
exploiting them and plundering their wealth'. It also stated its opposition to
'globalization policies that aim at exploiting the poor of the world by multinationals'. The declaration made the important point which obviously reflected the mood of Egyptian activists at the time, that the struggle for democracy
and liberation could not be separated from the struggle for social justice including redistribution of wealth in favour of the poor (International Campaign
against Zionist and American Occupation).[4]

The Cairo Conference was attended by activists and delegates from across the world including the anti-war coalitions of Canada, India, Korea (All
Together Anti-war Organization) and many European countries including the
Stop the War coalition of Britain and the Scottish Palestinian Solidarity
Campaign. There were also representatives of activist groups such as the 13th
of April movement from Venezuela, as well as delegates from other Arab
countries (Cairo Conference calls for world resistance to imperialism, *Socialist Voice*).[5] Over the years, several prominent public figures participated in
the Conference including the British MP George Galloway, Walden Bello,
who was then head of Focus on the Global South, former Algerian President
Ben Bella and former senior UN representatives Denis Halliday and Hans
von Sponeck. Domestic participants at the conference have included members
of political groups such as the MB, the Al-Wasat Party, the banned A'mal
Party and the Revolutionary Socialists (RS) organization, a Trotskyist group
formed in 1995. Other participants represented human rights and civil society
groups such as the Al-Nadeem Centre for the Rehabilitation of Torture Victims, the Egyptian Association for Combating Torture, the Hisham Mubarak
Law Centre, the Arab Network for Human Rights Information, the Popular
Association for the Protection of Citizens from Unfair Taxation and Corruption, the South Group for Culture and Development and the Arab and
African Research Centre.

For most of its editions, the Cairo Conference was organized by a joint committee giving one third representation to members of three broad political camps:
the MB, the Nasserists and the left. Obviously, the equal representation of the

three camps did not reflect their actual political weight on the street or their organizational strength. The Nasserists had a far weaker organizational structure and were an inferior mobilizing force compared to the MB while the left was plagued by internal divisions and, at that stage, had an almost complete absence from the streets. However, this skewed representation was in line with the agreement to build broadly-based coalitions which characterized the pro-democracy movement, a tactic that will be discussed in Chapter 5.

Above all, the Cairo Conference served as a network of networks, an umbrella for groups of activists to connect with each other and a venue for an exchange of experiences and ideas among activists working on different causes. It also provided an opportunity for individuals to come together and create new groups and networks. One important group that appeared around the time of the Cairo Conference, and whose members were directly and indirectly influenced by ideas discussed in groups participating in the conference, was the Egyptian Anti-Globalization Group.

The Egyptian Anti-Globalization Group (AGEG)

While small in size and short-lived, AGEG stood out as an example of activism that worked on emphasizing the link between global structures of exploitation, which were reflected in a dominant neoliberal agenda, and a regime of dispossession in Egypt. More importantly, during its short life (2002–5) AGEG played a role in brokering ideas and tactics between global resistance movements and other activist groups in Egypt. AGEG was formally launched in 2002 by a group of individuals from different political and professional backgrounds who had, since 2001, closely followed the rise of the GJM and discussed the possibility of creating an Egyptian group based on similar principles. Among the founding members, and others who joined the group later, were individuals who had participated in one or more of the WSFs in their professional capacities as members of human rights and advocacy NGOs or as media professionals.

AGEG's work spanned a range of activities that aimed to disseminate information on the machinery of global capitalism as well as shed light on the connections between global and regional/national structures of injustice. The dissemination of written and audio material on the critique of corporate globalization among activists, media practitioners and a wider public was one of the main areas of AGEG's activities. AGEG members embarked upon an active mission of translating and printing documents produced by transnational groups operating under the umbrella of the GJM. This material was then distributed among youth groups and local activists from pro-democracy groups to small NGOs working more specifically on issues directly related to particular policies such as the privatization of health care and other systems of public service provision. AGEG also placed these documents on activist websites.[6] Among these were publications on the Trade-Related aspects of the Intellectual Property Rights (TRIPS) regime, agro-business and pharmaceutical multinational corporations (MNCs), the WTO, and the militarization of globalization, which aptly coincided with the war in Iraq. In a bid to show the link between global structures and local realities, AGEG members also produced their own publications, including a pamphlet on the QIZ protocol that exposed the policy's negative effect on Egyptian workers and the economy as a whole. Contrary to the sensationalist, journalistic writings on the QIZ, which were rife at the time, AGEG's work was the only critical voice that was not narrowly defined by nationalist concerns focused on the question of the normalization of relations with Israel but rather by concerns of global trade policies and their negative consequences for Egyptian workers. Similarly, AGEG organized seminars featuring guests from the GJM, such as Waldon Bello, and renowned intellectuals, such as Samir Amin. For greater outreach, these seminars were held at prominent public venues such as Cairo University, the Journalists' Syndicate and the headquarters of established human rights NGOs.

AGEG's members were also very keen to translate their critique of the global order into concrete action. This took the form of launching campaigns in support of particular groups negatively affected by neoliberal privatization policies. Examples included campaigns in support of striking asbestos workers and air traffic controllers (Molly Abaza, author interview, Cairo, August 2010). Through their professional positions in the media and civil society organizations, members of AGEG ran media campaigns highlighting the struggle of these groups and connected their members with NGOs providing legal services and advice to promote their cause.

During AGEG's short life-span, similar to many groups in the pro-democracy movement, it had a loose organizational structure, no centralized leadership, and a fluid, interchangeable membership. The fluid nature of membership meant that AGEG members were also active in other groups such as Kefaya as well as professional, political and civil society initiatives, through either their professional positions as members of advocacy NGOs or individual membership of political groups outside the scope of official politics. Gradually, AGEG ran its course as a group. Internal ideological disagreements, stretching itself over too many activities and campaigns, and its members' increasing commitment to the activities of other groups signalled the end of the group (Al-Sakkout, author interview, email correspondence, August 2010).

Was Kefaya ever enough?

Ya basta, or 'Enough', the Zapatista movement's slogan coined to articulate the movement's resistance to the NAFTA agreement became, independently of the Mexicans, the popular name for the Egyptian Movement for Change. A group whose birth in 2004 marked the launching of a sustained campaign for democratic change in Egypt, Kefaya adopted the call 'No to a new mandate, No to inheritance of the presidency' as the main focus of its campaign. In September 2004, a group of 300 intellectuals, public figures and activists from a wide spectrum of political groups and leanings came together to declare the formation of Kefaya and to articulate its daring political manifesto. In a few months, the group's declaration of principles attracted thousands of signatories and the group galvanized a substantial hub of supporters. From its inception, Kefaya represented a landmark in modern Egyptian politics. It introduced new forms of opposition politics fundamentally different in strategy and tactics from traditional opposition groups, inspired scores of young people who had never taken part in politics before, broke many taboos in Egyptian politics, and provided an example for other groups to take their demands and struggles to the street.

In addition to its two major demands, Kefaya's manifesto included ending the emergency law, overturning all laws which constrain collective and individual freedom, electing the president and vice-president from among several candidates, limiting the tenure of the president to no more than two terms, ensuring unsanctioned freedom of association, removing the state of sequestration then imposed on syndicates, and conducting fair and genuine parliamentary elections under the supervision of the Supreme Judicial Council and State Council.[7]

Kefaya capitalized on the experience of groups active in the previous four years such as EPCSPI, the Cairo Conference, AGEG, and professional groups including Democratic Engineers and 9 March Group for Academic Freedom, both launched in 2003. The group built on the experience of the members and the new tactics of these groups. Like its predecessors, especially EPCSPI and AGEG, its declaration of principles, for example, stated that the struggle for democracy should be against two great dangers which constitute two sides of the same coin and constantly interact with each other. The first is US/Zionist assaults on Arab soil while the second is the 'repressive despotism that pervades all aspects of the Egyptian political system.'[8]

Kefaya's main activity was to organize several highly visible demonstrations which broke the taboo against criticizing Mubarak and his family and cronies. It also raised the ceiling of political demands to a new level. More importantly, the demonstrations also challenged the regime's tight grip backed by the emergency law and other restrictions on freedom of association which had long held the political opposition within the confines of their offices and prohibited them from taking their demands to the street. Among the more prominent activities organized were anti-Mubarak demonstrations in February 2005, bringing together hundreds of activists from different backgrounds with the main slogan of 'No to re-election, No to inheritance (of the presidency)' and the 25 May 2005 demonstration demanding a referendum on constitutional change. While all Kefaya protests were met by brutal police repression, the level of violence used against protestors on 25 May, including sexual harassment of female protestors, went beyond anything in the past. Undoubtedly, the excessive use of police violence was a major factor in limiting the average number of demonstrators to the hundreds. Despite the huge public appeal of Kefaya's message, the numbers attracted to its rallies never reached more than several thousand and its ambition of a 'one million man' march was never realized.

The main achievement of Kefaya, however, was to provide an umbrella under which activists could launch new initiatives. Offshoots of Kefaya included Youth for Change, Students for Change, Workers for Change, Journalists for Change and Artists for Change, among others. While these groups had different agendas and worked in different areas, they shared a set of underlying principles which had at their core a call to end Mubarak's rule and to establish a legal framework to ensure electoral democracy (El-Mahdi, 2009: 3). More importantly, Kefaya inspired others to create their own groups and umbrellas, for example the groups Shayfeen.com (We Can See You) and El-Shari Lena (The Street Is Ours), developed in the aftermath of massive repression and violence against Kefaya protestors in the lead-up to the 2005 elections. Many other groups were directly or indirectly inspired by or joined in the activities of Kefaya. These included the Democratic Engineers, launched in 2003 to fight for an end to the state's eight-year custodianship of the engineers' syndicate and to defend the rights of engineers as a professional group.[9] Doctors without Rights was created in 2007 to improve the conditions of both doctors and the medical profession in face of the regime's policies of privatization and neglect.[10] Teachers without a Union campaigned against the increasing privatization of education. Other groups were Writers and Artists for Change; the Committee for the Defence of Political Prisoners; the Ma yehkomsh Campaign against Dynastic Succession; the Itkhanaqna (We are suffocating) Campaign against Environmental Damage caused by industry and business corruption; Engineers for Change; the 9 March Movement for the Independence of Universities and Doctors for Change. While Kefaya's daring political message and its ability to expand the boundaries of what was politically possible did not succeed in steering a path of political reform towards its demands, the group could be credited for its enormous effect in providing activists with a template for action. As Browers (2009: 112) argues, the group's 'proposal, rhetoric, and political activities have served to embolden other groups in the country'. Political activists, including the youth wings of traditional political parties, started taking to the streets, which became the obvious site for speaking out against the regime and for mobilizing around their different yet similar demands.

In the midst of this decade of protest, Kefaya epitomized some of the characteristics of protest movements which have swept the globe since the late 1990s: cross-ideological in composition and non-hierarchical in structure. While predominantly Nasserist, politically the group was a broad church as it was created by representatives from the left, nationalists, liberals and Islamists. It involved elements from NGOs, political parties and professional unions as well as individual activists and activists from small, informal initiatives and groups. Kefaya's first meeting was held at the house of Abu Al-Ila Madi, one of the main founders of the Wasat Party and a former MB member. Prominent members of the MB also joined, such as Essam El-Erian and Abdel Munim

Abu El-Futuh. Activities were coordinated by a steering committee comprising the different political groups which made up Kefaya: the Nasserist splinter group Al-Karama, Al-Wasat, the Revolutionary Socialists, Al-Ghad and many independent figures (El-Hamalawy, 2007). While Kefaya gained momentum, a deliberate decision was made by its members to avoid any form of traditional, hierarchical structure. The group relied on a simple steering committee for the purpose of coordinating activities and had just one position of a spokesperson/general coordinator. The first to represent the group in this capacity was George Ishaq, who occupied the position until 2007. He was succeeded by Abdel Wahab Al Messiri, a prominent intellectual and academic with both an Islamist and Communist history of activism. After his death, two more general coordinators were elected.[11]

Kefaya served as a landmark of Egyptian opposition politics between 2004 and 2006. While Kefaya has never completely disappeared from the political scene in Egypt and has continued to exist in one form or another well into the post-Mubarak era, it undoubtedly lost its momentum in 2006 after the renewal of Mubarak's term in office. Kefaya did not escape the usual weaknesses that plague all political opposition groups in Egypt, such as internal splits and generational tensions. On one hand, Kefaya managed to take on board some of the criticism levelled by its members, especially the youth. For instance, leading Kefaya members accepted criticism of their too moderate objective of reforming the Mubarak regime before eventually concluding that reform was no longer possible and realigning the group's goal to achieving peaceful regime change (Khalil, author interview, Cairo, March 2010). On the other hand, a more fundamental critique, such as the group's inability to link with workers and waves of protest by other groups struggling for social and economic rights, was more difficult to assimilate. The disenchantment felt by some members of Kefaya due to this failure to position itself within larger struggles led to the creation of splinter groups, such as Tadamon, which will be discussed in Chapter 6.

Relevant to the above critique is the defining middle-class nature of Kefaya and other groups within the pro-democracy movement. Kefaya, despite its unique position in the history of struggle leading to the downfall of Mubarak, was a decidedly middle-class movement with no mass base beyond its narrow support among urban, middle-class professionals, intellectuals and students. The pro-democracy movement was, in fact, fuelled by the grievances of middle-class professionals against a regime that had systematically reneged on the state's post-1952 social contract with its urban, educated population and by their growing aversion to the regime's increasing use of violence to protect its existence.

9 March Group for Academic Freedom

On the eve of Mubarak's downfall, Egyptian universities were a microcosm of Egypt. Mirroring the country's social, economic and political crisis, they provided mediocre education, poor quality research facilities and a stifling atmosphere due to the lack of academic freedom. The regime's response to deafening criticism of the quality of higher education was to intensify its neoliberal policy of privatization. Instead of undertaking serious reform of public universities, successive Mubarak governments embarked on an exercise of window dressing backed by international donor agencies such as the World Bank, which granted Egypt a credit line in 2002 to implement higher educa-tion reform (Kohstall, 2012). More to the point, the Egyptian government began to privatize several courses within national universities. Furthermore, the Universities Law in 1994 encouraged the expansion of new private uni-versities, whose number had reached 16 by 2010 (ibid.). Like all other public goods in Egypt, a two-tier system was being increasingly institutionalized whereby the elite paid for their children's privileged education while the mil-lions of students attending public universities were locked into a substandard education process. The same law also furthered the government's control of universities, for example by replacing a long-standing policy of electing faculty deans with a new system of appointment by the rector (Human Rights Watch, 2005: 34).

Like the rest of the country, in the lead-up to 25 January 2011, Egyptian universities were marked by high levels of political discontent and ever-increasing mobilization. At the heart of this mobilization was the 9 March Group for Academic Freedom, which was established by 25 faculty members from different universities in 2003, in the aftermath of the US invasion of Iraq, to challenge the draconian measures imposed on academics. The 9 March Group's inspiration and name come from the date when the first pre-sident of Cairo University resigned in 1932 to protest against the govern-ment's decision to dismiss Taha Hussein, the Dean of the Faculty of Arts and a renowned intellectual, to placate clerics' anger over Hussein's book on pre-Islamic poetry, which was regarded as blasphemous. In just two years, the group grew to number thousands of academics (Al-Kazzaz, author interview, Cairo, March 2010).

Egyptian universities have a long history of political mobilization. Under all post-1952 regimes, different political groups, which were unable to com-pete in a formal political space, intensified their efforts to mobilize through different *usar* (clubs) on campus and, when possible, through student union elections. At the same time, successive post-1952 regimes always sought to bring universities under their direct control in order to prevent any incipient political activity and to use universities as vehicles to advance their own political agendas. In an attempt to use universities as a launching pad to articulate an ideology for his brand of Arab nationalism and to tame Egypt's professional classes, Nasser quashed academic freedom by infiltrating the cam-puses with police informants, limiting the boundaries of academic debate and eliminating the capacity of faculties and students to wield any influence by bringing all important decisions under the Supreme Council of Universities (SCU), a body headed by the minister of education (Reid, 1990). Since 1950, the SCU has been the sole body that adjudicates on university laws and regulations, student admission policies, the appointment of rectors and deans, and the content of curricula (Hamdy, 2010). Sadat continued along the same lines but went further by playing off different political factions against each other in order to advance his political and economic project. Fearing the relative power of leftists and Nasserists, whom he regarded as a major threat to his open door economic policies, Sadat encouraged and supported Islamist students to dominate universities in order to eclipse his opponents. Sadat's regime passed a new law in 1979 allowing the government-dominated university administration to manipulate student elections by stipulating a clause requiring nominees to 'enjoy good and upright conduct and good reputation' (Human Rights Watch, 2005: 53). More compromising of academic freedom has been, undoubtedly, the constant presence of state security on campus. Appointed by the ministry of the interior, security officers on university campuses blatantly interfered in student union elections, had the power to approve faculty research and travel, vetted guest lecturers, and worst of all, had the final word on staff appointments as they required security clearance. Under Mubarak the security officers used their powers widely and stepped up the level of physical violence against student political activity, culminating in killing a student with live ammunition, blinding four others and injuring over 118 more at Alexandria University in 2002 during a student demonstration protesting against a visit by US secretary of state Colin Powell (ibid.: 63). At a different level, certain right-wing student associations were also involved in suppressing campus freedom. Horus, an *usra* sponsored by the NDP with branches in all major universities, became notorious for intimidating fellow students and spying on them (ibid.: 30).

The 9 March Group was created to confront these forms of repression. The group became active in organizing sit-ins, petitions and public statements on different issues, such as the role played by university security in staff appointments and the cancellation of some public lectures and events for security reasons. They also supported students detained on political grounds, demanded transparency of university budgets and fought corruption. The group's public profile was raised in April 2005 when a hundred faculty members of Cairo University, dressed in black gowns, marched to the university president's office to petition against security intervention on campus. Shortly afterwards, over 2000 academics rallied against the detention of a number of their colleagues on charges of being members of the banned Muslim Brothers (Shahine, 2005). The group was also very successful in stimulating public debate and bringing attention to issues of academic freedom, thereby radicalizing wider sections of staff and students. The situation of academics and their work conditions was also a focus of the group's activities. For example, a march held on 23 March 2008 to push for better pay, an adequate health care system and a resolution of problems faced by retired faculty mobilized thousands of faculty members nation-wide despite heavy intimidation by state forces (Hamdy, 2010).

The structure of the group was loose, with no real hierarchy or leadership. While Professor Mohamad Abul-Ghar evolved as a spokesman for the group, he has never been regarded as its leader. In general, the group met monthly and when there was an ad hoc need to discuss a particular issue. Decisions were always reached by a vote, with the majority opinion prevailing (Hani El-Husseiny, author interview, Cairo, February 2006). Like other groups during this decade, the 9 March Group consisted of members of different political leanings. Its individual members were also active in several other groups and networks such as Kefaya and other professional groups such as Democratic Engineers and Doctors without Rights.

The group's work was rewarded when a historic verdict by the Supreme Administrative Court in 2010, only a few months before Mubarak's downfall, ended state security presence on university campuses. The struggle also achieved several other tangible results. For example, it successfully provided support for two new staff members by organizing marches and petitions against the security's attempts to sabotage their appointment due to their political affiliation. Leila Soueif, one of the group's founders, commented that the 9 March Group, like the other movements and groups active since 2003, was part of 'the constant chipping away at the pillars of the regime' (Pratt, 2012).

The Judges' Uprising

While various professional associations were increasingly stepping up their confrontation of the regime, another battle was raging in the heart of the state itself: the judiciary. The movement popularly known as 'the Judges' Uprising' for judicial reform and independence in 2005 presented a unique moment of political mobilization. Although there had been a long history of tension between elements of the judiciary and the executive, the Judges' Uprising played an unprecedented role in the larger political struggle against the regime. The judges' threats to abandon their constitutionally enshrined role of supervising the 2005 elections, followed later by their confrontation with the regime over the electoral process and results, was regarded by many as instrumental in re-energizing the political scene in Egypt after a seeming lull in the pro-democracy movement (Browers, 2009). Some even foresaw it as a spark for the ultimate collapse of the Mubarak regime (Said, 2006).

The politicization of judges and their struggle for independence from successive regimes was nothing new in Egypt's post-1952 history. Egyptian judges, especially under the umbrella of the pro-active Judges' Club, had long stood up to efforts by the regime to infringe upon their autonomy. The 1969 'massacre of the judges', as it became known, is a landmark of this tense history. In the aftermath of the 1967 military defeat, Judges' Club members had growing fears of Nasser's vehicle, the Arab Socialist Union, whose increasing power was to the detriment of the judiciary. The Judges' Club's subsequent demands for greater freedom of the judiciary were met with a series of harsh measures by Nasser. These included the dismissal of over two hundred prominent judges and the dissolution of the Judges' Club board, whose members were to be appointed by presidential decree in the future (Brown and Nasr, 2005; Rutherford, 2008).

While both Nasser's successors, Sadat and Mubarak, generally granted the judiciary relative autonomy, as stipulated in the 1971 constitution and reflected in the establishment of the Supreme Constitutional Court in 1979,[12] the demand for more guarantees for judicial freedom never abated. The judges felt particularly disempowered in the face of the emergency law passed in 1981 that gave the government exceptional powers over detention and other issues pertaining to the rule of law. To counter the effects of this law and in support of a desire for greater autonomy, the judges repeatedly put forward proposals for large-scale legal reforms such as the 'National Conference on Justice' in 1986 and a draft law for the judiciary of 1991, which proposed reducing the role of the ministry of justice, and the executive in general, in judicial affairs. These proposals were simply ignored by Mubarak, with the result that the tension between the judges and successive governments continued to simmer. In 2004, in a new surge of activism, the Judges' Club resurrected the proposal and updated it to demand fiscal autonomy equal to that of the parliament, amending the rules over pension funds and transferring the committee for judicial discipline from the ministry of justice to the independent Supreme Judicial Council (Brown and Nasr, 2005: 2).

Against this background, the judges threatened not to oversee the upcoming 2005 elections until further guarantees were given to ensure that the judges' authority was not confined to the ballot-box process but extended to other areas which, under the prevailing law, fell completely outside their jurisdiction (ibid.: 3). Despite the Judges' Club's initial threat to boycott the elections, the judges eventually took part in the exercise. During the first and second of three rounds of elections, some senior judges, including the two vice-presidents of the Court of Cassation, Mahmoud Mekki and Hisham Bastawisi,[13] made several media appearances to condemn gross violations in the elections and to raise the alarm about incidents of direct physical intimidation of judges by NDP and police *baltagya*. Without making much effort to deny the allegations, in response the ministers of justice and of the interior made promises to improve security in the final round of elections. However, several reports showed that violence, if anything, increased in the final round of voting (Said, 2006). The two senior judges explained the situation in a letter published in the *Guardian*:

> We identified violations in a large number of electoral constituencies. We demanded the opening of investigations into election fraud, intimidation and assaults on judges who were supervising the elections. Unfortunately a large number of those assaults were carried out by the very policemen who were charged with protecting us.[14]

In retaliation for the judges making this statement to the media, the government-controlled Higher Judicial Council, a rival to the independent Judges'

Club, deprived Mekki and Bastawisi of their immunity from prosecution. The two judges, as a consequence, had to face disciplinary hearings on the grounds that judges should not be active in politics.

The huge media coverage of the judges' crisis and the public debate it created turned into a rallying point for political mobilization. The enormous respect and public support which judges traditionally enjoy in Egypt created waves of sympathy for them from both the wider public and many opposition groups. During the sit-in organized at the Judges' Club on 17 March 2006 at its extraordinary meeting and later in April during the judges' protest against the punitive action against Mekki and Bastawisi, various groups such as Kefaya, Youth for Change, 9 March, the youth of the MB, the Revolutionary Socialists and several other leftist groups came to demonstrate in support. The judges' plight became a symbol of the tyranny and injustice of the Mubarak regime. This was echoed in the chants of university students organizing rallies and protests in support of the judges across the country, such as: *Ya Qodah Khalasouna min El Toghah* ('oh judges … rid us of the tyrants') (*Al-Masry Alyoum*, 17/3/2006). In Alexandria, several parties including Al-Ghad and Al-Tagamou, and groups such as the Revolutionary Socialists, Democratic Engineers and Youth for Change, demonstrated in front of a Judges' Club branch, chanting slogans such as *El-Shab Ithan El-Shab Itzal … El-Thawra Hi El-Hal* ('the people have been insulted, the people have been humiliated … revolution is the solution'), in which the perceived humiliation of the highly revered judges was projected to represent that of the Egyptian people.

The fluidity of the pro-democracy movement and its multiple foci were clearly evident in the rallies which erupted on 17 March 2006 in support of both the judges and journalists, whose syndicate, which is located only a few metres away from the judges' syndicate, was also holding a meeting in the midst of increasing threats to the freedom of the press and the safety of journalists. In the face of ever-increasing campaigns of support, the regime resorted to its usual tactic of beating up supporters and arresting hundreds of activists on the grounds of 'supporting the judges'. At one point, representatives of all professional syndicates met to explore the possibility of a general strike in all professional sectors in support of the judges (*Al-Masry Alyoum*, 26/4/2006). Although such an idea was almost laughable under the repressive Mubarak regime, given the poor organizational capacity of professional syndicates, the sentiment it reflected set this episode apart from previous confrontations between the judiciary and the executive. Sections of the judiciary, a central branch of the state, had become an integral player in a wider societal struggle against the regime.

Leaders and icons: between El-Baradei and Khaled Said

The above review is by no means a comprehensive account of all the groups and initiatives that mobilized under the umbrella of the loosely labelled pro-democracy movement whose activities and voice have reverberated in the

Egyptian street since the beginning of the Intifada. But the relationship of all these groups to the movement resembled both new social movements, which operate outside the universe of established political parties and formal electoral politics (Edelman, 1984), and the anti-globalization movement, which Azambuja (2003) described as a:

> (dis)organization that has no hierarchical structure or operational center, consisting of just 'us', in whose interventions thousands of organizations come together horizontally to protest, in one way or another, the current world order. They can grow infinitely without anyone having to give up his individuality to any hierarchical structure.

None of the groups that constituted the pro-democracy movement had a leader in the traditional sense nor has the process of mobilization been organized around iconic figures. Not only did activists not feel the need to rally around a leader, the absence of an authoritative figure to present a tailor-made vision, lead the masses, and make all the decisions was actually regarded as a strong rallying point for many of these groups. However, during a seemingly sluggish moment in the trajectory of the pro-democracy movement, the return of Mohamed El-Baradei to Egypt in 2010 seemed to present an opportunity for revival. Not by any means an activist returning from exile, El-Baradei had lived for decades outside Egypt occupying highly prestigious positions as an international bureaucrat, culminating in his last post as head of the International Atomic Energy Agency, for which he won the Nobel Peace Prize in 2005. Although he had neither political experience nor a mass base, El-Baradei was still regarded with respect in various middle-class opposition circles for his international standing and outspoken criticism of the Mubarak regime. Like Ayman Nour before him, El-Baradei was considering running for election against Mubarak in 2011 if there were a constitutional amendment that would guarantee fair conditions. Unlike Nour, who had ended up in a Mubarak prison on trumped-up charges for his temerity in running against the president, El-Baradei could rely on his status as an international figure for protection.

To provide a structural base for his daring project of contesting presidential elections, El-Baradei formed the National Association for Change (NAC), a coalition of a broad cross-section of opposition and activist groups including members of the left, nationalists, liberals and the MB that was represented by Saad El-Katatny.[15] Interestingly, El-Baradei was not officially the head of the NAC, a fact he and members of the coalition were at pains to emphasize. In a way, El-Baradei projected himself as a figure around whom millions would gravitate but one who would defy the traditional image of a leader with a strong charisma, something he definitely lacks.

Rather than a traditional political programme, the NAC developed a seven point pamphlet that focused on legal and constitutional changes that would guarantee free and fair elections. Mobilizing to collect millions of signatures for these demands became the only focus of the NAC. The NAC did not articulate a societal or political vision nor produce long-term objectives. Instead, it framed its demand for a democratic system using the vague and all-encompassing goals of 'establishing a civil, democratic state', 'guaranteeing equality for all citizens' and 'achieving social justice' (ibid.).

The image of the sophisticated, 'respectable', technology-savvy El-Baradei, communicating with his followers through tweets, enthused thousands and sustained a wave of mobilization within the stuttering pro-democracy movement by helping to fill the vacuum left by the, then, enfeebled Kefaya. This image contrasted starkly with another figure whose representation in social media, also in 2010, sparked an even wider wave of mobilization. If indeed every revolution needs its icon, then Khaled Said was certainly the iconic image that, according to many, served as a spark for the 25 January uprising. The story of Khaled Said was strongly intertwined with that of the lives and grievances of millions of the struggling middle classes under Mubarak's neo-liberal order; a story of police brutality, humiliating daily encounters with state authorities, constant harassment in public spaces and the total absence of a reliable structure to frame the relationship between citizens and an increasingly erratic state.

Khaled Said was sitting in a cyber café in Alexandria, working on his computer, in 2010. The details are still unclear and controversial but the 28-year-old man was approached by two police officers, who dragged him out onto the street, where they beat him to death. The police later claimed that the young man had resisted arrest and died as a result of swallowing packets of cannabis which he was trying to hide during the police's attempt to arrest him on charges of theft and weapon possession. However, images taken in the morgue of Said's mutilated face and body, which showed signs of a horrific beating, clearly exposed the attempted police cover-up. The images went viral after they were posted on the Internet by his family and friends. They insisted that the police went after him for possessing videos which revealed police involvement in a drug deal (El Amrani, 2010). In other versions, Said was said to be beaten to death for simply refusing to be subjected to the random police intimidation of young men in public spaces. The images of Said and the story behind them deeply shocked and outraged the hundreds of thousands who saw them on the Internet in the following days. The deep sense of shock emanated not simply from the cruel mutilation of a young body but from the fact that Said was neither a criminal nor a political activist, the two typical victims of police brutality. The routine torture of suspected criminals and political activists had become so common in recent years that the circulation of these stories had ceased to muster any sustained reaction from a sympathetic public beyond a momentary sense of anger, fear and helplessness. However, in this case, the magnitude of the shock and the acute sense of vulnerability it engendered among the viewers resulted from the fact that Said was as ordinary a young man as you can get: the son of a middle-class family, educated, running a small business, with no criminal record and totally non-politicized. Said's story exposed the false sense of security to which millions of Egyptians had been clinging by leading a life in which they hoped to avoid any contact with law enforcement agents. Most of all, they had avoided any form of political engagement in the hope of escaping the wrath of the state. Images of the mutilated face of Said were a rude awakening: in Egypt, nobody was safe from the ruthlessness and the arbitrariness of the state and its agents.

The location of Said's killing also resonated with Egyptians' experience of public spaces. The traditional policing of urban spaces, backed by the infamous emergency law that allowed a huge police presence on the street against a backdrop of the sprawling high walls of gated communities and shopping malls, has long intimidated citizens and defined the limits of their sense of entitlement to public space. Egyptians were either physically barred from accessing public spaces or routinely harassed within them. The cyber café from which Said was dragged and the street on which he was beaten to death are spaces where a large cross-section of young Egyptians spend long hours. Said's experience, therefore, brought home to 'ordinary' citizens how vulnerable they were just going about their daily business in a hostile and threatened space.

Said's death soon became a rallying point for mobilizing large numbers of activists and sympathizers against what the event came to epitomize: regime repression. The Facebook group 'We Are All Khaled Said', for example, launched a campaign under the slogan 'No to torture, No to the emergency law'. The group was successful in organizing several off-line protests across major cities, where thousands of people came together to stand apart at regular intervals in long lines in silence to express their anger. Thanks to its unique approach to protest and the completely non-political character of the victim, within a few weeks the group's webpage attracted almost 22,000 members (El-Hennawy, 2010). On the eve of 25 January 2011, 'We Are All Khaled Said' was one of the groups which organized a call for the 'Police Day' rally.

The ebb and flow of ideas and experiences was the trademark of this phase of political mobilization in which groups drew on each other's repertoires of action, tactics, themes of contention and efforts to build public consciousness among wider sectors of the people despite the state's repressive machinery. While the experience of 'We Are All Khaled Said' was unique for the reasons discussed above, it undoubtedly built on the efforts of bloggers who had tirelessly worked on exposing police torture during the previous years. Some of the earlier blogs to appear on the Egyptian blogosphere were Nael Atef's Torture in Egypt, Bloggers against Torture and the El Wa'i Al Masry (Egyptian Awareness) by the blogger Wael Abbas (Lim, 2012). Egyptian Awareness, for example, is best known for bringing to a wide public the case of Imad Al-Kabir, a minibus driver whose beating and sodomizing with a stick at the hands of the police was captured on a mobile phone camera which reached Wael Abbas through a chain of sources.[16]

Vulnerable bodies

The themes of vulnerability, violation of the body and intimidation in the public sphere, which the case of Khaled Said epitomized, underpin the decade of struggle against the Mubarak regime. More than ever, during this period state violation of citizens' bodies was no longer confined to police stations and interrogation cells but was taken out into public spaces as an instrument of punishment and deterrence. A poignant example was the physical and sexual harassment of female protestors within the pro-democracy movement. A particular incident, which embodies this practice, occurred on 25 May 2005 and became known as Black Wednesday. This incident reflected a growing pattern of response to regime violence, as it intensified rather than curbed mobilization with the subsequent launching of Women for Democracy, more popularly known as El-Shari Lena (The Street Is Ours).

Black Wednesday started with a peaceful rally initiated by Kefaya, around the mausoleum of famous historical Egyptian leader Saad Zaghloul, to protest against a referendum on the constitution being held that day. The referendum was regarded as window dressing and simply an attempt to 'cast a veneer of legitimacy over a regime which has oppressed the Egyptian people for 24 years'.[17] As usual during these rallies and demonstrations, protestors were cordoned off by large numbers of riot police. However, for the first time, a new strategy was introduced. Female protestors and journalists were forcibly separated from the rest of the group, pushed into a side street, forced into a pharmacy, beaten up and also subjected to verbal and sexual abuse. The crime was committed by NDP-hired thugs and police officers in the middle of the day, in one of Cairo's most central locations and in front of hundreds of passers-by. For years, the police's systematic sexual harassment of women had taken place in police stations, state security intelligence offices and remote sites in different cities and villages. A case in point was the regime's strategy of targeting female relatives of Islamist militants in Upper Egypt during the bloody decade of the 1990s (El-Mahdi, 2010: 385). On Black Wednesday, on the other hand, an unprecedented level of violence against women was committed for the first time in the centre of the capital in plain view.

On 9 June 2005, a group of the same abused women and other activists, both men and women, came together to announce the launching of The Street Is Ours, a campaign intended to collect testimonies from women and men on the violence and harassment they faced in their everyday lives. The campaigners hoped that this activity would be only the first step in 'building a political movement, the core of which are women, inspired by the struggle of Egyptian women throughout history, and to constitute a strong contribution to the struggle of democracy and justice in Egypt' (ibid.). The campaign received wide support from sympathetic individuals and activist groups across the world. The group met several times during the rest of the summer, bringing together individuals from across the ideological spectrum: Islamists, nationalists, socialists and liberals. However, the group faded away soon afterwards. Like many other small initiatives, it was subsumed by larger groups such as Kefaya, while their members integrated into other networks and initiatives.

Sexual harassment of female protestors in the aftermath of Mubarak's ousting during the SCAF and Muslim Brothers regimes remained a systematic tool of repression and intimidation. From the infamous military virginity tests to raping of female protestors in Tahrir, sexual violence had one function: to intimidate women, to intensify their sense of vulnerability and to discipline and punish them for attempting to claim public space and play a role in larger campaigns of social and political mobilization. By targeting those whom it presumed to be the most vulnerable in society, the regime hoped to intimidate not only women, but also men, whose honour is traditionally perceived to hinge on their female relatives' sexual reputation.

Conclusion

Despite informal links with traditional organizations, such as professional syndicates, political parties and NGOs, the pro-democracy movement remained firmly distinct from the realm of traditional, bureaucratic political and social organizations which have time and again failed to represent the interests and concerns of large sections of the population. The budding groups, initiatives and networks aimed to be everything that these formal groups were not: loosely structured, informal, non-hierarchical and decentralized. They relied on simple committees for coordinating activities while decisions were reached through consensus or a simple vote.

A major feature which characterized the movement was the fluid and interchangeable membership between the different groups. A considerable majority of a new generation of activists in Egypt was effortlessly moving between different umbrellas and political projects. Individual activists were typically participating in organizing pro-democracy rallies calling for constitutional reform, working on a campaign supporting labour demands, advocating freeing their professional syndicate from state control, writing in newspapers to draw attention to the devastating effects of the privatization of health care and attending regional or global meetings of a women's network. Short-term, tactical, cross-ideological cooperation was another feature of the pro-democracy movement in the decade before the 25 January uprising. Almost all groups and initiatives forming under this umbrella consisted of members representing a wide swathe of political leanings including Islamists, leftists, Nasserists and liberals.

These features, allied to the absence of one clearly defined political centre or an explicit leadership, proved effective in providing activists with relatively high levels of survival in face of the state's ruthlessly repressive measures. To control the escalation of political activism organized along multiple political layers, the state had to fight on different fronts and try to contain more than one enemy, who was no longer as easy to identify. The presence of various forums for political action had offered political activists the space to move their projects and activities easily from one 'network' to another and to have different events organized under different umbrellas. The nature of networking in Egypt was essential not only for sustaining protest activities but also for allowing activists to escape heavy-handed state control. Egypt's authoritarian regimes had been very successful for decades in weakening organized political opposition thanks to a twin strategy of co-optation and violent repression but were often flummoxed when confronted with a Hydra of opponents.

Social and political change, whether along radical or reformist lines, does not arise from a vacuum. It is a result of a long process of accumulation of experience, mobilization, networking and the evolution of a different, more inclusive political culture. Movements and groups almost always build on the experiences of previous groups and can, in the process, be absorbed into larger or newer projects. The Egyptian pro-democracy movement, as a whole, built on the experiences of earlier waves of struggle during previous decades but the individual groups discussed in this chapter also drew on the experience of other groups working for similar yet different causes. In many ways, the accumulation of experience and the learning process aided by exchange between activists was one of the main achievements of the pro-democracy movement. We know that the success or effect of social movements cannot be confined to the sphere of visible results or immediate, measurable outcomes alone. The global justice movement, for example, cannot be judged a failure for its inability to transform global financial institutions or arrest the unchecked power of MNCs. Movements, it is argued, play a more subtle and indirect role in shaping society at large (Reed, 2005; Cohen and Rai, 2000; O'Neill, 2004). Reed notes how 'Beneath the more studied level of formal ideologies, or even elaborated cognitive "frames", are levels of ... socially meaningful layers of consciousness' (2005: 310). This diffused, indirect way of shaping politics and political culture at large is insufficiently acknowledged, and movements which contribute to eventual change in this way are rarely given adequate credit. In the same vein, the contribution of the pro-democracy movement was to create a new political sphere which has potential for social and political transformation and where new identities could be developed and new demands articulated.

Notes

1 See Bayat's concept of 'Quiet encroachment of the ordinary' (2009).
2 EPCSPI newsletter: www.eocities.com/solidarity_palestine/Support.htm (accessed October 2005).
3 A district in the heart of central Cairo.
4 www.ahewar.org/eng/show.art.asp?aid=448 (accessed 1 August 2011).
5 http://mrzine.monthlyreview.org/2007/riddell260407.html (accessed May 2011).
6 For example Fathet Kheir, Islamonline, z.net and kefaya.net.

7 http://www.harakamasria.org/node/2944 (accessed 23/4/2009).
8 ibid.
9 'Democratic Engineers: Who are they and what do they want?' http://groups.
yahoo.com/group/takadom/message/4733 (accessed June 2013).
10 Doctors without Rights http://atebaabelahokook.blogspot.co.uk/2007/05/blo-post.
html (accessed June 2013).
11 Abdel Galil Mustafa agreed to act as interim coordinator until the end of 2008 and
was succeeded by Abdel Halim Qandil.
12 For a history of the Supreme Constitutional Court and its role in Egyptian politics,
see Tamer Moustafa (2007).
13 Hisham Bastawisi later ran as a candidate in the first post-Mubarak presidential
elections.
14 May 10, 2006 'When Judges are Beaten', *Guardian* www.guardian.co.uk/commentis
free/2006/may/10/comment.egypt (accessed 15/8/2011).
15 At the time, Katatny was an MP and member of the Guidance Office. Later, he
became the spokesman of the post-Mubarak, short-lived MB-led parliament.
16 The video on the blog served as crucial evidence in the trial of the officers involved
which, to the surprise of most, found the officers guilty.
17 Journalists' Syndicate Press Statement, 2005, consulted in documents compiled by
The Street Is Ours Organization Committee.

3 Workers, farmers and almost everybody else

The pro-democracy movement, with groups such as Kefaya at its helm, was able to attract media attention both regionally and internationally due to its technology-savvy, middle-class character. The similarities it shared with several other protest movements across the world from Thailand to Argentina and Russia had inspired academic researchers to focus on the dynamics and alternative politics of these groups. Conversely, the massive wave of labour protests by millions of workers, which spread across Egypt like wildfire during the same decade, was paid little heed as a significant political force. Moreover, the growing ferment in the labour struggle, which dwarfed the pro-democracy movement, both in terms of the size of mobilization and intermittent victories won, was not generally recognized for the crucial role it played in the lead-up to and during the 25 January uprising. The importance of this role was, however, still recognized by some observers, who in fact argue that worker strikes in the final days of the 18 day uprising were a decisive factor in the downfall of Mubarak (Beinin, 2012; Naguib, 2011; Land Centre for Human Rights, 2011).

Enthusiasm in the academic literature in the last two decades for the rise in social movement-led protests has been accompanied by equal dismissal of the role of organized labour in projects of political transformation. In most quarters, the academy confidently declared the decline of class politics and the diminishing role of organized labour in post-industrial societies. Castells (1996: 354), for example, pronounced collective labour organizations as passé 'political agent(s) integrated into the realm of public institutions' which are no longer able to operate in the networking society using the logic of the information age. Decline in labour union membership as a result of the nature of global capitalism and the changing nature of production – flexibilization, relocation, outsourcing, temporary jobs, etc. – was taken as evidence of the end of class-based politics (Beck 1992, Giddens, 1990). This arrogant, Northern-centric analysis, however, ignores the role of labour both in global networks of activism such as the GJM and in political struggles in the more industrialized nations of the global south such as South Africa, Brazil and South Korea (Moody, 2005). Both traditional unions and more informal labour groups were at the forefront of national struggles in these countries;

a testimony to the continual presence of class and labour politics. The rise of new forms of unionization, in particular, is evidence of the dynamism of labour within radically changing global production structures (Upchurch and Mathers, 2011).

As Beinin (2011: 181) poignantly puts it, Egyptian workers seem not to have 'received the message that class struggle is unfashionable'. Indeed, the decade leading to the downfall of Mubarak saw the expansion of probably the most sustained wave of labour protest in Egypt's recent history. This chapter argues that class politics and the role of Egyptian labour in politics are far from over. Workers, farmers and large groups of the dispossessed were at the forefront of the struggles against the Mubarak order and are still at the heart of Egypt's long revolution.

Corporatism and its undoing

Egyptian workers have a long history of struggle and have, equally, experienced a long history of repression. The post-1952 regimes employed a two-pronged strategy of co-optation and violent repression to contain and undermine the labour movement. Since his early days in power, Nasser's populist regime was eager to build a mass constituency in the labour movement. He therefore used a strategy of introducing many progressive labour reforms such as Law 165 of 1953, discussed in Chapter 1, granting job security and other social and economic privileges (Bianchi, 1989). However, granting such privileges, which actually surpassed any previous labour demands, came at the expense of crippling trade unions and banning all strikes as described by Beinin and Lockman (1998). This undermined significantly the potential for collective action of future generations of Egyptian workers. Nasser's attitude towards labour unions exemplified his aversion towards any form of organized action outside his control. Only months after the Free Officers coup, several strikes broke out in a number of unionized textile factories in the Delta, demanding the right to create their own unions and the removal of managers still loyal to circles of the ousted king. While the latter demand was swiftly met by the new government, four workers were summarily arrested for their role in inciting the strike. Soon afterwards, four workers were shot during an exchange with police attempting to crush a strike at Misr Spinning Company in Mahallah while a series of military tribunals of striking workers were held across the country in the following months. Nasser wasted no time in showing his unbending opposition to workers' strikes irrespective of the nature of their demands (ibid.: 420). His actions demonstrated clearly to all workers that he had no qualms about using the violence necessary to quash any form of strike.

Unlike his strategy of banning all political parties, however, Nasser implemented a corporatist arrangement which strengthened and selectively co-opted working-class organizations instead of crushing them and excluding them from the political process (Bianchi, 1989: 126). Immediately after the Free

Officers came to power in 1952, unions were reorganized into 'singular, non-competitive, hierarchical organizations' sanctioned by the authority of the state, while 'at the regional level a single labour confederation was to enjoy a monopoly of representation for the union movement as a whole' (ibid.: 431). The regime in fact followed a textbook policy of corporatism, defined as:

> A system of interest representation in which the constituent units are organized into a limited number of singularly, compulsory, non-competitive, hierarchically ordered and functionally differentiated categories, recognised or licensed (if not created) by the state and granted a deliberate representational monopoly within their respective categories in exchange for observing certain controls on their selection of leaders and articulation of demands and support.
>
> (Schmitter and Lehmbruch, 1979: 13)

The essential element of this definition is the role played by the state in reorganizing interest associations along controlled, corporatist lines. In this connection, Offe (1981: 173) explains that the state attributes public status to interest organizations by providing them with resources that may take the form of direct subsidies or tax exemptions, or by defining the range of areas in which they may operate and their potential membership. This describes precisely the creation of the Egyptian Trade Union Federation (ETUF) in 1957. Inspired by the Soviet model, the ETUF leaders were drawn from the ruling party and their actual mission was to control and regiment the working class rather than defend its interests (Achcar 2013: 155).

The changing economic realities of the 1970s and 1980s, together with continuous repression and co-optation strategies, combined to aggravate the weakening of the labour movement. Massive waves of labour migration to the oil-rich states of the Gulf partially shifted the conflict between labour and capital away from Egypt as well as provided the cash needed to cushion the negative effects of the early policies of privatization on workers' living standards. These factors 'perpetuated the disorganization of the working class' (Beinin and Lockman, 1998: 460). However, despite systematic state repression, an effective strategy of co-optation and the total monopoly of the ETUF over labour representation, sporadic labour action never completely disappeared under Nasser and his successors. Examples of this action include the strikes of the iron and steel workers in 1968, textile workers in Shubra Al-Khaymah and Mahalla, transport workers and iron and steel workers in 1975/76 and the prominent participation of workers in the 1977 food riots. While such actions might not have had much weight in winning rights or negotiating workers' relations with the state, they proved that the continuing presence of the working class as a historical actor could not be eliminated (ibid.).

As early as the late 1980s and early 1990s, several voices were already questioning the potential sustainability of the 'social compact' put in place by Nasser. Goldberg (1992: 159) echoed many studies which predicted the eventual end of this compact as the regime, as a result of its neoliberal privatization programme, would eventually have to remove subsidies, revoke laws granting permanent job security and restructure wages in relation to productivity or institute piece rates. These measures already started to gather pace in the 1990s with the passing of Law 12 of 1995, which made official strikes virtually impossible, leading some observers to expect an eventual increase in informal and wildcat strikes (Pousney, 1993). Beinin and Lockman (1998) argue that the 1984 Kafr al-Dawar textile workers' strike and riots signalled an end to the period of relative economic peace and labour quiescence. Indeed, a few years later in 1988, almost 20,000 Mahalla Misr company workers took to the streets carrying a coffin with Mubarak's picture, protesting against the government's decision to cancel workers' educational allowances. Egyptian workers were becoming a force to be reckoned with.

A tidal wave of protests

At the dawn of the new century, out of a total wage labour force of almost 27 million, the ETUF could claim a membership of only 3.8 million, the majority of which was drawn largely from the public sector. Despite its traditional role of controlling and disciplining mainly public sector workers, the ETUF was no longer capable of containing a tidal wave of labour action as early as the late 1990s. Considering that most private sector labour is not unionized, a large sector of Egyptian workers was not hamstrung by the co-opted official unions. Concomitantly, changes in the regime's economic policies and the launching of the Nazif government's neoliberal policies emboldened more of them to join the struggle. According to one estimate, between 1998 and 2010, between two and four million workers took part in as many as 3,400 to 4,000 forms of collective action (Beinin, 2010: 3). The intensification of strikes, demonstrations, occupations, hunger strikes and sit-ins across various sectors was a response to reduced wages and deteriorating working conditions under the growing weight of neoliberal-inspired privatization. The breakdown of Nasser's social compact and the inevitable escalation of workers' contentious action was everywhere to be seen, from Alexandria in the north to Aswan in the south, both in urban and rural areas, from the public to the private sector, affecting even the informal economy. Collective action spread even to factories and companies owned by the military establishment and increased dramatically among both blue and white collar workers. This action covered almost all sectors from textiles and iron to petroleum, cement and food processing as well as service sectors such as transport and telecommunications.

Like their counterparts across the global south, successive Mubarak governments aggressively vied for the prized trophy of FDI, removing every obstacle which could conceivably deter foreign investment from coming to Egypt. To achieve this singular objective, laws were passed and regulations implemented to favour the interests of (transnational) capital and crush any workers' rights that might discourage it. A series of legal and administrative steps in this direction culminated in the enactment of the infamous Law 12 of 2003, which signalled the end of Nasser's policies protecting workers. The law allowed employers to hire workers indefinitely on the basis of fixed-term, temporary contracts, thus depriving workers of their job security that had been enshrined in previous laws requiring employers to grant workers permanent positions after a fixed period of probation. The law also gave employers the right to dismiss workers at their discretion. Furthermore, enforced early retirement schemes, hiring freezes and the privatization of half of all public sector companies, reducing the number of workers in this sector from 1.3 million in 1985 to 400,000 in 2002 (Clement, 2009: 105), resulted in a severe deterioration in the living conditions of many workers. The appointment of the Nazif 'businessmen' government signalled a relentless programme of 'reform' heralding a divestiture of state assets which, during the government's first two years in office, was greater in scope than the cumulative total of all previous privatization undertaken since the beginning of such programmes in the 1990s. The sharp increase in FDI by 82 per cent from US$6.1 billion in 2005/06 to US$11.1 billion in the following year was claimed as a triumph for government policies.[1]

The spreading and mushrooming of labour action reached new levels with the landmark strike by 24,000 workers of the El-Mahalla al-Kubra Spinning and Weaving Company in 2006. The factory complex, which is the largest in the whole of Africa and the Middle East, employing more than one quarter of all public sector textile workers in Egypt, was the site of the most important event in the workers' struggle and mobilization in the decade preceding the 25 January uprising. The strike erupted in response to the failure of the Nazif government to deliver on its promise of a significant increase in the public sector workers' annual bonus. On 7 December 2006, the strike was ignited by 3,000 female workers marching through the massive factory complex, calling upon male workers to join them. The three-day strike by about 24,000 out of a total workforce of 27,000 led to the factory's closure and brought production to a halt (Clement, 2009). The scale and force of the strike compelled the government to agree to the full bonus increase and other demands including increased allowances for transportation, medical care and day-care centres as well as an investigation of corrupt management. The strike ended with threats to resume action if all demands were not fully met (Naguib, 2011).

While the government was true to its promises and most of the economic demands were met, the workers' anger towards the regime, the co-opted unions and the corrupt management continued to simmer. The momentum continued to build and workers were emboldened to take their struggle to another level. In March 2007 over 5,000 workers in the Mahalla Misr Company resigned from the state-controlled Textile Workers' Union in protest at its failure to support their strike earlier in 2006 (El-Mahdi, 2012). Subsequent to this action and building on its success, the Mahalla strike committee of 2006 called for another strike on 6 April 2008 to demand a national minimum monthly basic wage of EGP 1,200 (Beinin, 2012).[2] The Mahalla Misr Company has always been central to the Egyptian labour struggle not least due to the concentration of large numbers of workers, its long history, job continuity within generations of the same families and the fact that the whole city is in one way or another connected to the industrial complex. Therefore, as De Smet puts it: 'Whenever Mahalla workers won an industrial victory, this led to a general upturn of industrial action in the whole of Egypt' (2012: 257). This proved indeed to be true in this round of the labour struggle. The strike movement that began at Mahalla in December 2006 spread in an unprecedented manner. Only weeks later, workers in the Helwan cement factory started an occupation followed by a hunger strike. They were followed in January 2007 by drivers of railway engines, the Shibin al-Kom Spinning and Weaving Company, and in February by a massive strike of 11,000 workers in the Kafr al-Dawar Fine Spinning and Weaving Company. Labour action spread from the public sector to the private sector to the civil service and from old industrial areas to the new towns, in all provinces. It spread from the textile sector to engineering, chemicals, building and construction, transport, to teachers and civil servants. As labour activist Fatma Ramadan put it: 'we saw a strike infection, where workers suddenly realized that industrial action actually paid off' (author interview, Cairo, June 2011). This was reflected in a huge 212 per cent increase in contentious action from 222 recorded incidents in 2006 to 692 in 2007, following the Mahalla strike (see Table 3.1). The strike played a major role in generalizing and strengthening the culture of protest which had been gripping Egypt since 2000.

Workers in major urban centres, such as Mahalla, Suez, Kafr El-Dawar, Port Said, Alexandria and Cairo among others, with their long history as

Table 3.1 The development of contentious action from 2000 to 2010

Year	No. of incidents
2000	102
2001	132
2002	96
2003	86
2004	266
2005	202
2006	222
2007	692
2008	447
2009	478
2010	530

Source: Adapted from Al-Merghany (2013)
Note: There are often discrepancies in figures for contentious action by labour depending on the source, as the definition varies according to which activities are included. For example, the Land Centre for Human Rights estimates 198 incidents in 2006 and 474 in 2007. Regardless of the source, however, the dramatically upward trend is irrefutable.

industrial centres and sites of labour action, were able to draw on the experience of labour leaders who had been active since the 1970s and on the collective memory of labour protests deeply embedded in the consciousness of generations of workers. However, a new industrial policy from the late 1970s resulted in a geographical shift in the concentration of new industries to satellite cities isolated from old industrial centres and from each other. Law 59 of 1979 offered investors huge benefits and tax holidays for locating their factories in these satellite cities, such as the 15th of May, 6th of October, 10th of Ramadan, Al-Sadat and others.[3] The increasing relocation of industrial production and hence labour to these new cities had implications for the ability of workers to organize and protest. Moreover, the capital-intensive nature of industries in the new cities meant that they employed relatively fewer workers, in some cases no more than fifty in one factory (Centre of Socialist Studies, 2007). Hardly any of these workers were unionized or had experience of organizing collective action. They not only had to find their own way in organizing collective action but also had to resist the efforts of formal unions to weaken their resolve (Haytham Gabr, author interview, Cairo, April 2011).

While the main rationale for moving industries to new cities was to ease the pressure on already congested urban centres, isolating workers from their traditional centres of collective action was also a bonus for capital and the regime. Indeed, attempts to isolate workers from their historical centres had been pursued in the past as an industrial policy specifically to control workers. Beinin and Lockman (1998: 453) argue that in 1927, the Mahalla Misr Company deliberately opened its textile mills in the Nile Delta away from the heart of traditional labour collective action in the urban centres of Cairo and Alexandria. The physical isolation, scattered numbers and absence of collective memory or organizational skills in these new industrial cities led many to assume that they would escape the protest fever that was taking established urban centres by storm (Gabr, author interview, 2011). However, as early as 2000–2001, workers in several companies in both 10th of Ramadan and 6th of October were already protesting against the aggressive exploitation by capital in these new investment zones. The impressive eight-month-long strike of Egyptian–Spanish Asbestos Company (Aura) workers in 10th of Ramadan City in 2004 was a clear sign that any assumptions about the weakness of the labour movement in these localities were unfounded.[4] The victory of Aura workers led to an explosion of industrial action across many of the city's 1,430 factories and hundreds of small workshops and inspired similar protests in several new cities (Bassiouny and Said, 2008).

Official statistics heavily underestimated the actual numbers of workers employed in the new cities by failing to account for temporary and unregistered workers, who constituted a large part of the workforce and who experienced the worst forms of job insecurity. This, in turn, underestimated the potential numbers of workers who could be called upon to act collectively. Furthermore, the lack of historical experience of labour protest was often actually an asset for workers in these areas as they were free from the dele-terious influence of official trade unions and from the negative experiences of internecine struggle among workers in other areas (Gabr, author interview, 2011).

The state of violence

The Mubarak regime initially tolerated public protest in support of the second Palestinian Intifada in 2000 in an attempt to identify itself with over-whelming public sentiment in favour of the Palestinians and hence shore up its waning popularity. However, this move backfired badly by unleashing a massive wave of protests against the regime itself, demanding democratic reforms and ultimately regime removal. Similarly, the regime showed a moderate willingness to negotiate with labour in the same period instead of employing its usual policy of brutally repressing any collective action. Traditionally, the form of corporatism used in Egypt had always been backed by brute force, which provided successive regimes with a tool to enforce its social compact with labour. In light of their historical experience of this state violence, Mahalla workers in 2006 braced themselves for what they anticipated was the inevitable attack by security forces. However, they were surprised by the regime's willingness to negotiate and 'its flexible, paternalistic public discourse on the strike' in which it made reference to 'our sons, the workers' (Centre of Socialist Studies, 2007). Moreover, Mahalla was not the first case in which the regime actually showed a willingness to negotiate. In fact, earlier labour action had been successful in yielding concrete results, such as a threefold increase in wages in some severely underpaid sectors (Clement, 2009). More-over, the threat of further labour protest in some cases saw the government attempting to pre-empt action by granting better pay to workers in certain sectors or in companies where it hadn't even been demanded (ibid.: 113).

This change of strategy can be understood in light of faltering social wel-fare itself and of a shift in labour policy under the later Mubarak govern-ments, especially the 'businessmen' government of Nazif. The advent of a new variant of capitalism in Egypt saw the rise of a different type of business owner who employed cost-benefit analysis in labour relations rather than knee-jerk repression. These capitalist owners calculated the cost of every strike in terms of the immediate effect on production and the long-term effect on labour's ability to organize in relation to the cost of meeting workers' immediate demands (Bassiouny and Said, 2008). El-Mahdi (2012) concurs with Bassiouny in stating that the new power-holders in the cabinet and the policy committee of the NDP under the leadership of Gamal Mubarak were unlike the hardliners of previous governments who would have considered negotiating with workers both a sign of weakness and unnecessary as they could put down any strike by naked violence. Furthermore, new members of the regime had also become painfully aware of the cost of media exposure of its violent labour practices and the possible ensuing international condemnation from international rights and advocacy groups. In fact, the ILO, on several occasions, had put Egypt on its blacklist of countries that violate labour rights, a reputation which the regime perhaps feared for its effect on FDI (Fatma Ramadan, author interview, Cairo, April 2011).

Despite this relative willingness to negotiate with labour on its demands, the Mubarak regime still used violence, especially when strikes were beginning to threaten the status quo or have an influence on labour outside a local area. The intensification of labour protest reached its peak in 2007, when 400,000 workers took part in one form of contentious action or another. This rise could no longer be tolerated as it was gathering a momentum which might lead to the birth of a fully-fledged labour movement. Furthermore, the demand of Mahalla workers in 2008 to increase the national minimum wage was also a step too close to linking local grievances with a national policy which would have far-reaching consequences for all capital. Finally, when there was a call for a general strike on 6 April 2008, the government felt it had to step in. Hence, the strike was subverted by a combination of co-optation, mass dismissals, the moving of workers to jobs in other locations and violent repression. The time-honoured tactic of members of official unions infiltrating the ranks of the strikers in order to undermine any action was also used on many occasions (ibid.).

New forms of organizing

The pro-democracy movement and its constitutive groups worked outside formal political organizations that had largely become irrelevant. One of the movement's stronger rallying points was undoubtedly its alternative, non-hierarchical, loose organizational structures. Similarly, labour protesters worked outside formal labour organizations but they also had to contend with the state-dominated trade unions directed by the ETUF. Furthermore, unlike the pro-democracy groups and their steering committees, which functioned simply to coordinate activities, strike committees, which developed at the heart of every strike and contentious action, had a much more onerous role. According to Bassiouny and Said (2008), one of the characteristic features of labour strikes from 2006 was their duration, as they lasted anywhere from a few days to a few weeks and even a few months. Thousands or tens of thousands of workers occupying factories for weeks on end, for example, meant that strike committees had to organize meals and sleeping quarters for the occupiers, secure both machines and buildings to prevent infiltrating *agents provocateurs* from causing damage that would be blamed on strikers, organize shifts of striking workers occupying the factories and negotiate with the management and state representatives before reporting back to their fellow workers. This was a great organizational challenge that many workers, who had no experience, had to come to terms with very quickly. In some cases, workers showed an ability not only to manage a strike but even to self-manage production in factories which had already received official orders to be liquidated. For example, workers of the Amonsito Textile Company, owned by Syrian-American tycoon Adel Agha, who had fled the country in 2007 leaving behind massive debts, managed to keep production going to avoid closure. This required great organizational skill and the experience of workers and managers with a long work history (ibid.). After the inevitable factory liquidation, they kept up the struggle by continuing to demand legally required termination pay that the creditor, Banque Misr, was refusing to pay (Fathi, 2011).

The case of the Mahalla strike, in particular, was a feat of organizational ingenuity and professionalism. The strike was not only an exercise in challenging the state, but, more importantly, set an example to other workers and dissident groups. The elected striking workers' committee showed it was possible to work outside the official co-opted unions, while simultaneously resisting their spoiling tactics, and still operate democratically by regularly reporting back to mass meetings of thousands of strikers on the progress of negotiations (Alexander, 2008: 56).

Despite the impressive work of the mushrooming strike committees, a ground-breaking step in Egypt's history of labour organization was yet to come. In 2007, a sit-in on the road in front of the ministry of finance by over ten thousand real estate authority tax collectors employed by local governments was backed by strikes of thousands more of their colleagues across the country. They were demanding salary parity with tax collectors employed by the ministry of finance, which determines the salary scales of all tax collectors. The sit-in, which lasted over ten days, set an important example for other striking workers and protesting groups across the country by providing a sophisticated model for coordinating action across many governorates that was characterized by advanced negotiation skills and the crucial role played by female employees. The sit-in was concluded after successfully securing the strikers' demands, including a 325 per cent salary increase.[5] The strike committee, led by Kamal Abut Eita,[6] however, had the much greater ambition of taking a step toward restructuring the whole of state–labour relations. Further mobilization and continuing struggle by the real estate tax authority employees over almost two years was crowned by the launching, in April 2009, of the Union of Real Estate Tax Authority Employees (URETAE), the first independent union to be formed in Egypt since 1957, with a membership of 37,000 out of a total of 52,000 employees.

As will be discussed in the next chapter, strike committees – impressive as their achievements were – remained localized and offered neither national leadership nor a political programme. The effect of industrial action in certain sectors, such as transport, could have been far more damaging to capital and the government, had national coordination taken place (Gabr, author interview, 2011). Nonetheless, numerous strike committees together with the landmark URETAE inspired the creation of several independent unions in the months that followed the launching of the tax collectors' union. The culmination of these efforts was the formation of the Egyptian Federation of Independent

Trade Unions (EFITU), which was launched only days into the 25 January uprising in Tahrir Square.

Beinin (2012) argues that the launching of the URETAE was an unusual development on several counts, including the fact that tax collectors are not 'real workers'. Indeed, tax collectors are not workers in the same sense as those at Mahalla and other industrial workers. They are, in fact, civil servants, cogs in the machinery of state bureaucracy. Like the judiciary, tax collectors and their protesting fellow civil servants in other sectors, from telecommunications to information, transport and education, were yet another example of sectors of the formerly privileged bureaucracy turning against the state in the lead-up to the 25 January uprising. This phenomenon was a particularly interesting feature of labour protests during the 2000s – the widening base of protestors. Protestors now included not only the traditional factory-based industrial workers but their numbers were swelled by a vast range of civil servants who were adversely affected by privatization policies that targeted them in the same way as industrial workers. Changes brought about by the restructuring of production under global capitalism meant that the old binaries of white and blue collar workers were often no longer relevant in analysing labour reaction to neoliberal policies. Precarious employment, in particular, did not only affect the traditional working classes but, increasingly, large sections of the professional middle classes.[7] Both categories of worker were increasingly subject to the same job insecurity, the chipping away of their social benefits and rising unemployment. As El-Mahdi (2012: 389) puts it, both blue and white collar workers came to share 'common objective conditions, and similar subjectivity and relational positions within the neoliberal matrix, in opposition to the new ruling elite of "technocrats" and business-owners'.

In the years before the 25 January uprising, the pro-democracy movement expanded to include new categories of participants. Similarly, labour protests began to embrace more sectors, new geographical locations and categories of labour that had not traditionally been organized. However, labour protests and leadership, in the form of strike committees, were not based on the cross-ideological cooperation which characterized the pro-democracy movement. The majority of the wildcat strikes and other forms of contentious action developed their own natural, local leaders who mostly did not have any political affiliation. The few who did were often from the ranks of the Nasserists or the left. Historically, and with the exception of a few local and partial cases, the MB were never able to establish a stable base within the working class.

This was largely due to the group's paternalistic approach to labour and its aversion to trade union militancy, which they regarded as a cause of social conflict among Muslims (Beinin and Lockman, 1998: 452). At the core of Islamist discourse on social and labour relations is the express wish to avoid any conflict and insist on harmony that can only eventuate when different social groups realize they have distinct roles to fill and are able to accept principles of harmony and cooperation. The approach to labour struggle engendered by this principle did not change over the years. Gabr, a labour activist, argues that:

> It would be naïve to assume that MBs are completely absent from labour action. They are there among workers in many locations. However, the way the group has used workers for its own benefit: to gain votes, win elections, dominate unions, etc., rather than extending support to the workers' struggle based on a conviction about the role of workers as a force for change, makes workers generally unwelcoming of the MB.
>
> (author interview, Cairo, 2011)

The inability of the MB to build a base within the working class was compounded by the nature of the class base of the group itself. Several key MB members are big business tycoons who in fact own some of the factories in which many of the strikes were taking place. Already in his seminal study of the group, Mitchell (1969) demonstrated the MB involvement in private business as a means to build an economic basis for financing their activities, especially their network of welfare services. Echoing these two historical factors, Kamal Abu Aita argues that:

> their factories, which are crucial to financing the group's business empire, have experienced strikes during recent years. The MB factory owners behave like any capital owner: exploiting workers, denying them rights, punishing striking workers and, above all supporting laws which weaken and marginalize workers. The best the group seems to be capable of in terms of supporting the recent workers' struggle is to provide food and other services to striking workers in some locations. These are the same methods the group uses to support the poor and the needy. The group, however, will never help workers to organize to demand their rights.
>
> (author interview, Cairo, 2010)

This situation actually led to confrontations between striking workers and some MB leaders. The most illustrative example came in 2007, when the MB MP for Mahalla, Said Husayni, a businessman himself, was physically barred from entering a textile mill in his bid to show support for the striking workers. Initially, Husayni had supported the workers when he mediated during the 2006 strike by taking their demands to parliament but workers regarded this of little consequence in comparison with the absence of genuine MB support for the workers' movement in general (Gabr, author interview, Cairo, 2011).

After a full decade of sustained struggles, workers moved to take part in the uprising on 25 January 2011. Throughout the ensuing 18 days of the uprising, workers were present in Tahrir and all other occupied squares across the country especially after the government sent all public sector employees on indefinite leave in early February. Workers participated in the uprising in their individual capacity rather than as an organized force. However, the last few days of the uprising saw a wave of mass strikes by workers in over 60 factories across key sectors of the economy including the textile, petroleum, iron and steel, cement, telecommunications and public transport sectors. According to Saber Barakat, from the Land Centre of Human Rights, 'the government stupidly ordered the closing down of all factories on 26 January, which allowed massive numbers of workers to come out on the streets in their towns and cities and mingle with the protestors; it then compounded this mistake by reopening the factories in early February after the same workers had become quickly radicalized into a revolutionary mode and were eager to go on strike' (author interview, Cairo, 2011). The strikes spread across main industrial cities and zones from Alexandria in the north to Aswan in the south. One of the key cities which witnessed huge strikes was Suez, where 6,000 workers in the Suez Canal went on strike on 8 February before becoming involved in intense street battles with the security forces. A major development during this period was the spread of strikes into military-owned factories that were usually run with iron discipline by Egypt's generals (Naguib, 2011).

Citizens' protests

During Egypt's decade of protest, the pro-democracy movement and workers, white and blue collared, were challenging the regime in a relatively organized, albeit horizontal, loosely structured, fashion. Concomitant with these waves of protests, more spontaneous, dispersed forms of contentious action were sweeping the Egyptian streets. The participants in this form of protest were marginalized citizens, some of whom worked in the informal sector and some of whom did not work at all as they had lost any ability to access the labour market or restructure market relations in their favour. Everywhere, in shanty towns and small villages, government offices and local markets, a sustained range of protests and acts of civil disobedience were carried out by diverse groups from taxi and *tuk-tuk* drivers, shop owners, street vendors and small farmers to the unemployed and housewives demonstrating against rising food prices and a rapidly disappearing sense of entitlement. Blocking roads, burning tyres, jamming entrances to government buildings and marching around in the streets became a daily practice in both rural and urban areas. These marginalized groups left no space where their anger was not expressed. These forms of protest were often small in numbers and tended to erupt and dissipate quickly, materializing around specific, immediate injustices in people's living and working spaces. Acts of dissent along these lines usually flared up to protest about the almost total breakdown in the provision of basic services such as water, electricity, education facilities, health care and housing, which characterized the second half of Mubarak's rule. They tended to break out when groups of angry citizens reached a point where they could no longer accept the daily injustices and humiliation inflicted on them by state and market institutions. In a way, this type of protest constituted a more immediate reaction to the inability of increasing numbers of people to enjoy their basic rights as citizens. This inability to access housing, potable water, health care, basic foodstuffs and loans, among other services and goods, was again the outcome of privatization and the withdrawal of the state from its traditional role of provider for low-income groups.

These marginalized citizens also flocked to the streets as did the more organized workers, civil servants and middle-class professionals. While doctors and nurses were striking and protesting inside hospitals, families of patients were blocking roads around them. In 2008, a demonstration by hundreds of virus-C patients erupted at the steps of Al-Kasr Al-Aini, the largest public hospital in Egypt, protesting against repeated delays in delivering their weekly treatment. The majority of poor patients had to travel hundreds of kilometres from villages to this hospital at great cost (Nader, 2008). While teachers were protesting against miserable working conditions, parents were storming schools to demand a better learning environment for their children. The government's failure to organize effective collection of rubbish from the streets of Giza, due to large-scale corruption, became a subject of public outrage. In 2008, a particular case saw rubbish accumulating on some streets of Faisal, a Giza neighbourhood, until it actually blocked the entrance to a secondary school. The parents of hundreds of students and the school administration, having failed in their endeavours to get a response from the government, urged the students to protest on the streets until the local municipality or any official body took notice of their plight (*Al-Masry Alyoum*, 12/2/2008).

Female workers often took the lead in strikes and sit-ins among factory workers and civil servants. Similarly, housewives and female heads-of-household were also prominent in the less organized protests due to the nature of the division of labour within the household and the increasing burden on women under economic restructuring. For example, 400 people who had been living in 'temporary' shelters for twenty years were led to protest against the partial collapse of these shelters by 15 female heads-of-household (*Al-Masry Alyoum*, 26/1/2008).

Like civil servants and factory workers, who often framed their struggle in language which appealed to the government and even to Mubarak to respond to their demands and deliver justice (Ali *et al.*, 2009), most of the protestors discussed here also shouted their demands and signed petitions in which they called upon the government to ease their daily suffering and humiliation. In some cases, however, the protestors used a different language in which the government was portrayed no longer as a potential saviour but an adversary. In 2007, for instance, 300 families from the Basatin neighbourhood in Cairo organized a march to contest a proposed forced eviction from their homes before a court case for demolition of their properties had been concluded (Gabr, 2007). During the march, the protestors distributed pamphlets with the title 'A declaration of war', which portrayed local government institutions as the enemy and their struggle as a matter of life and death.

None of these protestors regarded themselves as activists or as involved in a political struggle to challenge the state. Their activities did not have the sustained energy or articulated ideology of social movements. However, these protests were not part of what Bayat (2009) described as 'non-movement movements' either. The citizenship-based protests, to some extent, are non-movements in the sense that they constitute collective action by non-collective actors. However, unlike the non-movements, which are part of the practices of everyday life and survival strategies where the poor struggle by 'quietly impinging on the propertied and powerful' (ibid.: 15), citizenship-based protests in the decade leading up to the 25 January uprising constituted forms of collective action against the system which had forced them to resort to such survival strategies in the first place. By raising their demands, they were anything but quiet. They were in fact non-movements that had evolved to a point where they undertook contentious action.

Due to their small numbers, extremely localized focus, and mostly short life-span, this form of contentious action is the least documented among all forms of protest. If no journalist, activist or publicly-minded individual happened to be present during the event and managed to report it to independent media or human rights centres involved in the documentation of protest activity, the event was lost to the outside world as most of these protests were spontaneous. These protests, however, were paramount to the process of mobilization of previously unpoliticized citizens and for emboldening more groups and individuals to confront the state in new spaces and employ a new language to describe their situation. By its very nature, this category of protest saw the least evidence of organization. The bitter struggles by these marginalized citizens, however, did not develop into community groups like those which had spread in Latin America and other parts of the global south, such as community organizations in South Africa (civics) or Chile's shanty town movement. The Egyptian experience of this type of protest was entirely disjointed and fragmented with no core or even an embryonic structure which could guarantee their sustainability or potential to evolve into a larger-scale movement. The loose organizational structures of both pro-democracy and labour activism meant that there was no framework to allow these dispersed struggles to be included within a broadly-based coalition.

Farmers' struggles

Accounting for almost one third of the national labour force, Egyptian rural areas began to reverberate with expressions of protest from the late 1990s in response to government policies that were systematically impoverishing its overwhelming majority of small farmers and landless peasants (Ayeb, 2012; Bush, 2012). The initial wave of protests broke out in 1997, when the Agricultural Development and Credit Bank in Beni Suef refused to extend any loans to farmers from villages across the governorate in anticipation of the application of the new tenancy law discussed in Chapter 1. The bank refused to give loans without an explicit guarantee from landlords that the farmers' tenancy contract would be renewed. As a reaction, over 3,000 farmers jammed all entrances to the city, blocked the main highway and sabotaged railway tracks (LCHR, 2002).

This initial outburst was followed by similar forms of action, such as sit-ins in front of agricultural banks and cooperatives and the blocking of roads across the country. Farmers quickly started holding informal meetings to discuss their future and possible courses of action. Like workers, civil servants, and marginalized citizens across the country, farmers hoped to garner support from the government and they sent thousands of letters and petitions to the president and minister of agriculture. The hope of a sympathetic reaction to their plight was soon dispelled when the government in fact reacted with brute force. These farmers' protests were met with police arrests, detentions and torture in police stations, forced evictions and the mass punishment of whole villages and families of protestors (ibid.). The ramifications of the law continued to fuel farmers' protests for years to come. In December 2006 for instance, 130 families, whose members had been evicted from their rented land, demonstrated in front of the governorate's office in Daqahlia in the Delta, demanding compensation that the government had promised them since 1997. Similarly, hundreds of farmers protested in front of the headquarters of the ministry of agriculture with similar demands (LCHR, 2007).

Protests across rural areas have not ceased since their eruption in 1997. An expanding repertoire of contentious action has reflected the heightened level of suffering and desperation experienced by small farmers and landless peasants. For example, the first six months of 2008 witnessed 61 forms of recorded contentious action across rural areas, resulting in the arrest of 1,394 small farmers (LCHR, 2008). Protests were often staged against injustices related to the shortage of irrigation water which led to crop failure, increased rents by land-owning ministries such as Awqaf, confiscation of rented state-owned land that was sold to foreign investors and the increasing shortage of drinking water, leading to a 'revolution of thirst' by residents whose villages were cut off from drinking water for months on end.[8] Furthermore, it was remarkable that violent protests against the erection of mobile phone masts became widespread across the countryside, showing a heightened sense of awareness of environmental and health hazards (Saad, 2008). In addition to the usual actions including road blocks, demonstrations, signing of petitions and sending telegrams to officials and the media, farmers also violently attacked and attempted to tear down the masts, attacked communication engineers and workers present at the mast sites and torched the houses and belongings of the owners of land on which the masts had been erected (ibid.). The level of violence used by the police against rural protests was unparalleled in any other sector, resulting in 270 cases of death in 2010 alone (LCHR, 2011).

Some villages have become iconic in this recent history of rural resistance as well as emblematic of police terror. In 2005, the Delta village of Sarando was witness to the collaboration of capital and police against small farmers. The Nawar family, which owns the majority of land in the village, decided to kick out tenants who had farmed and invested in the land for decades. The police stormed the village, attacked farmers, including women and children, and *baltagya* were deployed at the village entrances to imprison the residents. The police and *baltagya* attacked homes and arrested and beat up farmers, especially women. The violence used against women in particular was unprecedented in previous confrontations. Women were tied together by their hair, their faces trampled on by shoes and their veils forcefully removed. The violence led to one case of miscarriage of a young pregnant woman and the death of another.[9] The Borolus Delta village was also immortalized because of the levels of police violence used against protesters in 2008. The removal of subsidies on basic food commodities, in this case on bread, created widespread riots in Egypt. Residents of the Borolus village, mostly working in fishing, were enraged by the government's decision to deprive them of subsidized wheat. In response, they blocked the main highway going past their village, burning tyres and stopping traffic. In response, the police conducted one of its most violent campaigns during that decade, in which tear gas and birdshot were used, leading to injuries and hundreds of arrests, especially of women and minors. The injured were reportedly removed in ambulances, not to hospitals but directly to police stations and state security offices.[10]

Protests in rural areas lacked any form of leadership or organization. The links some of these protests had with any political groups were negligible and were limited to support received from human rights groups, such as the Land Centre for Human Rights, and committees of Nasserists and the leftist parties such as Tagamou. The MB did not play an active role in rural protests but, significantly, took a pro-government stance on Law 92 of 1996. This came after years of MB MPs keeping mostly silent during the parliamentary discussions on the potential law during the 1980s (Utvik, 2006). This silence, interpreted as endorsement by some, hid varying individual views on the issue. However, the official MB stance was finally made clear when the MB supreme guide, Al-Houdieby, came out in strong support of the law on the grounds that it is in agreement with sharia law. The supreme guide went even further by warning labour not to protest against the implementation of the law, which could result in justifiably strong reactions by the landlords (LCHR, 2002).[11]

Rural protests were highly dispersed, spontaneous and almost totally unorganized. They had no leadership and lacked any organizational structure. The rudimentary village committees that developed early in 1997 were quickly eliminated by the regime, leaving no room for the development of any organization. The relentless violence by the regime and landowners against protesting farmers failed to quell these protests but was effective in crushing their potential to develop into a movement.

The 'normalization of protest' over a decade

This section examines the process of 'normalization of protest' which developed in the decade before the 25 January uprising. The process and its dynamics refer to the groups examined in this and the preceding chapter. The term is employed here in a totally different way from the way that it is usually used in classic literature on new social movements. It is used, more specifically, in contradistinction to other terms that have been loosely bandied about to explain the presumed sudden change in protestors' behaviour.

For example, many journalistic writings on the Arab uprisings have excessively used the term 'breaking the fear barrier' to refer to the new willingness of ordinary citizens to take to the streets in the face of authoritarian regimes employing violence. However, this language evokes deterministic, psychological explanations which tend to reduce a long, complex process to isolated moments and events. While the 25 January uprising was undoubtedly a unique moment, it is nonetheless one which could better be understood as part of a larger process in which a culture of protest, political mobilization and contentious action developed consistently and incrementally in the face of all odds over a long period. The decade of struggle against the Mubarak regime saw a process that could be described as one of 'normalization of protest'. During this decade, demonstrations, rallies, strikes, sit-ins and street blockades progressively became a daily occurrence in factories and workplaces, on major roads, in residential neighbourhoods, university campuses and government offices. Increasingly, the number of Egyptians taking part in protests expanded to include myriad social groups with a wide scope of demands and grievances. Gradually, subversive action was no longer seen as an exceptional moment regarded with awe and incredulity by the larger masses but part of everyday lived reality.

The notion of 'normalization of protest' is used in the literature and in traditional theories of new social movements to describe protest activity that becomes 'normalized' in the sense that it moves from the margin to the mainstream (Norris, 2002; Gamson, 1990; Verhulst and Walgrave, 2009), thus becoming simply 'another form of conventional political participation in modern democracies' (Moseley, 2010). The concept of a 'movement society' coined by Meyer and Tarrow also refers to the same phenomenon, where social protest becomes institutionalized in Western democracies as an 'instrument in the realm of conventional politics' (1998: 4). In this movement society, not only does protest become more common and frequent but it also begins to draw citizens away from traditional forms of political participation such as electoral politics (Koopmans, 1993; Crozat, 1998).

Obviously, in the Egyptian context, and under any authoritarian rule, the normalization of protest means something completely different. It is used here to refer to a process of the accumulation of experience by which protest becomes a lived daily reality to the extent that people involved in protests, as well as those observing them from a (close) distance, begin to accept them as part of everyday existence. Far from being 'normal', in the sense of classical new social movement theory, participating in protests under Mubarak in fact represented an 'exceptional' act of bravery. Protesting did not represent a lawful option to political participation to which individuals and groups with grievances could resort in addition to, or in place of, participation in formal political institutions. Protest action was criminalized and always met with disproportionate violence, resulting in protestors' arrest, torture, loss of employment or disappearance. Moreover, as Egypt had no legal channels for genuine political participation in the first place, protest was not at all an alternative to institutionalized opposition politics. On the contrary, protest in Egypt was the *only* form of meaningful political expression.

The process of normalization of protest in Egypt was facilitated by a number of factors, such as the rise of independent and new media and Egypt's high population density, the effects of which are intensified by its choked road networks. The rise of new, independent media outlets, for instance, played a significant role in the normalization of protest. While most analysis of the 25 January uprising emphasizes the role of new social media in facilitating new forms of activism, it is even more important to recognize the role of the newly established, privately owned newspapers and TV channels during the same decade. The launching of independent daily newspapers such as *Al-Masry Alyoum* in 2004 and *Shorouq* in 2009, as well as that of Dream TV and ON TV among others, resulted in invaluable coverage of the burgeoning protests, which remained almost completely ignored by state-owned media. Ironically, neoliberal policies had opened the media market, allowing business tycoons such as Ahmad Bahgat, Salah Diab and Naguib Saweeres, to name but a few, to venture into the lucrative media business. Their coverage of protests gave them a competitive edge over state media. The wish to exploit this comparative advantage to raise their market share became a significant contributor to an increasing awareness of the protests among an audience that had traditionally been kept in the dark by state media and was now eager to learn what was really happening. The complete absence of coverage of any forms of contentious action had been a successful method used by successive regimes over many decades to isolate and marginalize such action. The market logic of profit, pushed by the regime, now turned against its authoritarian logic and dealt a massive blow to its tight grip on information dissemination.

Although satellite TV channels and independent newspapers targeted a more literate, middle-class audience, these outlets still spread awareness of protests beyond the educated middle classes. However, irrespective of class or education, all Egyptians experienced the rising protests first hand in their immediate locales. Egypt's high population density, its choked road networks and nightmarish traffic, especially in large cities, meant that ordinary citizens experienced protests or the effects of them in the course of their daily life. While some groups of protestors resorted to directly blocking roads and halting traffic on main roads, any form of street protest – whether a sit-in on the steps of the Journalists' Syndicate demanding an end to Mubarak's rule, a group of factory workers staging a march in front of their company's headquarters or farmers protesting against accumulated debt at the doors of an agriculture bank in any city in the delta – brought the streets of Cairo and other major cities and towns to a standstill. People's daily routines were disrupted by major traffic jams and many had to plan their day and routes according to news of scheduled protests. Contentious action thus became an ordinary sight on the streets of Egypt. The inevitable presence of disproportionate numbers of riot police and armoured personnel carriers always made matters worse and was a reminder to all passers-by of the nature of the deepening crisis and rising conflict between the state and its citizens. As a consequence, regime defiance was not only a news item one read about in a newspaper; it was out there on the streets for everyone to see: passers-by as well as media reporters and camera crews. The majority of Egyptians, while not taking part, nevertheless became hugely aware of intensifying protest.

At one level, this awareness and close proximity to protest encouraged more people to join the protestors. Despite the heavy police presence and frequent brutal repression, protestors kept coming out, admittedly in small numbers at first and often in support of local issues but more regularly and persistently than ever before. Protest was no longer the domain of 'professional' activists, but one for 'ordinary' citizens who did not in fact see themselves as activists or attach a political label to their actions. For those who participated in protests, a process towards a 'participatory state of mind' was set in motion (Verhulst and Walgrave, 2009: 458). However, unlike the deterministic, psychological explanations of protest which emphasize personality traits as factors for making some individuals more prone to protest than others (Lipset, 1981; Davies, 1962), we can still definitely speak of a process in which individuals, through observing protest action and joining it, develop an internalized 'activist identity' (Melucci, 1989).

More importantly, however, news of protests and strikes across the country created an intense public debate and contributed to a process of politicization. The debate was not always profound; it often included the discussion of banal details such as the effect of protest activities on the flow of traffic in cities and on major roads. However, it mostly focused on the justice of the protestors' causes, on the regime's disastrous economic policies, on corruption and on the violence and humiliation that had become the trademark of people's daily existence. Contentious action, for many Egyptians, was not necessarily discussed either as an act of heroism or as criminal behaviour. The discussion focused on the reasons behind protests, government policies, regime corruption and the possible outcome of these protests. Slowly, a process of politicization of formerly apolitical citizens was beginning to take root.

Notes

1 Achcar (2009) reminds us, however, that this increase in FDI was in fact a result of a boom in global oil prices which was reflected in a huge increase in Gulf Cooperation Council (GCC) capital outflows to Egypt.
2 This was equivalent to about $200, which represented a huge increase over the prevailing rate of about $23 and the official rate of $6.50 set in 1984.
3 See Soliman, S. (1999) for a discussion of the law and the advantages granted to investors in new cities.

4 For details, see, for example, Laurie Kazan-Allen (2005) 'Victory for Egyptian Asbestos Workers'.
5 For a detailed account of the sit-in, see Ali et al. (2009).
6 Eita is a well-known labour leader who later, and to the dismay of many of his colleagues, became minister of manpower in the July 2013 military-backed interim government after the ousting of Mohamed Morsi and his government.
7 For the debate on precarious employment both in the industrialized North and the global South, see Kalleberg (2011); Lee and Kofman (2012) and Adler and Webster (1999).
8 A number of state institutions own a large percentage of land in Egypt. The ministry of agriculture, the ministry of Awqaf (religious endowments) and the Egyptian military are among the largest owners of land in the country. According to some reports (e.g. Saber, 2006) the ministry of endowments was just as implicated in the use of arbitrary and illegal procedures to evict farmers from their homes by confiscating their possessions, imprisoning them or arresting their wives and children.
9 For details of this account, see LCHR (2006).
10 For more details, see Nahdet Masr (2009).
11 This view concurred with that of other Islamist parties including Al-Gama'a Al-Isamiya and Al-Azhar as well as Muslim scholars. This was no surprise as it reflected Islam's emphasis on the sanctity of private property and the limited role of the state in the economy.

4 Praising organization?

Egypt between activism and revolution[1]

Mubarak's ousting was a momentous event, crowning the breathtaking 18 day uprising which itself was the culmination of a much longer struggle by the Egyptian people. The overwhelming sense of euphoria and the ease with which Mubarak had been deposed briefly masked for many Egyptians the glaring reality that bringing down Mubarak was one thing but 'bringing down the regime' was another entirely. Soon enough, however, it became clear that the fall of Mubarak had not created a power vacuum that would eventually, let alone necessarily, be filled by the seemingly triumphant revolutionary forces. On the contrary, the well-entrenched ruling elite, including the powerful military, the security forces and the state–capital nexus, on the one hand, and the patient, well-organized, political hopefuls of the Muslim Brothers, on the other, were about to embark on a sustained process of counter-revolution. Nonetheless, on 11 February, the die had not yet been cast. In one of those rare moments in history, the balance of power in Egypt was in fact relatively open to contestation between old and new actors. Obviously, the former were heavily advantaged by their access to state power and their ability to quickly draw up the rules of a game that they had played before.

Within days of the uprising, SCAF declared itself the effective ruler of the country and set in motion a political process which it claimed was intended to achieve a liberal democratic transformation. This process, which took place during an ever-expanding 'transitional' period, saw SCAF carefully orchestrate a marathon involving two rounds of presidential elections, ballots for both the upper and lower houses of parliament and two sets of constitutional referenda over two years. The Muslim Brothers exploited every opportunity provided by the dramatic removal of Mubarak to secure for themselves as much power as possible in this period. The result of this process, which ensued largely from a tacit agreement between the two major actors, reaffirmed the privileges and power of the military in both the economy and state institutions in return for assuring the dominance of the MB in both houses of parliament and the triumph of their candidate for the presidency.

By contrast, activists who in the years before the uprising had bravely challenged an increasingly repressive regime, occupied Egypt's main squares for 18 days, risked their lives and taken the brunt of brutal state violence were quickly shunted to the margins of this power struggle. The problem was that these activists, over the course of only a couple of weeks, found themselves unexpectedly transformed from protestors, demonstrators and strikers into 'revolutionaries'. These newly minted revolutionaries were now suddenly expected to take part in renegotiating state power and to provide a vision for the future that would transform both polity and society – a task for which they were woefully unprepared. In fact, Egypt's new revolutionaries had no plan for the day after, grand or otherwise.

The fast-moving events of the transition period strongly confirmed the strategic strength of both the military and the MB as players with which the heterogeneous revolutionary forces were unable to engage to their advantage. The potential of activist groups to carry out the transformative tasks expected of them was seriously put into question by the form into which their organizations had developed on the eve of Mubarak's downfall. The absence of a centralized organizational structure, which had allowed the mobilization of the previous decade, quickly became a liability in dramatically different circumstances. The activists and protestors were suddenly dragged into a political process that was reduced to electoral politics, for which centralized organization is paramount and specific skills and tactics essential. They had neither.

The complex issue of organization is key to explaining the process that unfolded both before and after the uprising. However, the following analysis of organization is neither a prescription for an ideal 'model' that revolutionary forces should take nor an elegy for the failed potential of a massively supported movement. Such an approach would be far too deterministic for the objective of this book, which is to understand the evolution of political actors in the specific context of Egypt's ongoing revolutionary process and to explore the future of protest movements in their struggle against global neoliberalism.

The centrality of organization in the history of movements during revolutionary moments is not unique to the case of Egypt. Authors such as Charles Tilly (1978), for example, argue that during the phase after the fall of an old regime or at least its heads, political arrangements either for assuming power or for setting the basis for a transitional period require some form of organization. In his words: 'The presence of a coherent revolutionary organisation makes a great difference ... An organisation facilitates the initial seizure of control, spreads the news, activates the commitments already made by specific men (*sic*)' (1978: 208). In another historical overview of class–vanguard relations in the 'great revolutions', Walzer takes the case of the Jacobin republic in eighteenth-century France to demonstrate the relevance of organization in revolutionary moments. He argues that the Jacobin republic had a short life precisely because it lacked the necessary history of organization. In his words:

> Organisation requires more than competence, however; it also requires practice ... In the years immediately following 1789 ... the radicals were

compelled to innovate on the spot ... [The Jacobins] lacked trained and disciplined cadres and members ... The short life of the Jacobin republic, and its failure to leave any significant institutional residues, has to be connected with the short history of Jacobinism before the republic was founded.

(1998: 131–32)

Similarly, Petras posits that the history of political activism and its dynamics has a huge bearing on the emergence of organizational structures during revolutionary processes. As such, he argues that one of the key influences in shaping a revolutionary process is:

the origins and initial organisation of the revolutionary party ... the political culture in which it is embedded ... The insertion of the embryonic party into an ascending mass movement or within a politicized population is crucial in the creation of the collective experiences within which the cadres will frame their revolutionary programmes.

(1978: 31)

Walzer's analysis could be seen as deterministic, in that it ascribes an almost exclusive role to the history of organization in shaping the outcomes of a complex political experience. Furthermore, reference to a 'revolutionary party' is not pertinent to the case of Egypt or to the forms of activism discussed in the previous chapters. Such analysis, nonetheless, underscores the vital role of the provenance of political actors and their past experience in shaping their ability to accommodate to changing historical circumstances, which might mean playing a leading role in the aftermath of a major uprising.

Days into the 25 January uprising, while SCAF and the MB were quickly drawing on their vast organizational structures and power bases, groups of activists who had occupied Tahrir Square and made Mubarak's ousting possible frantically began to create 'revolutionary' networks and coalitions in an attempt to represent the millions who had risen up against Mubarak and to negotiate on their behalf. The history of these activists and their experience with political organization, as well as their conception of the notion of political power, significantly moulded their ability to assume the task of a revolutionary spearhead. During the preceding decade of intense activism, no group or network had entertained the thought of assuming state power. As a consequence, they had neither experienced any need to create institutions that could mobilize potential revolutionary forces leading towards the capture of power nor, more importantly, worked on articulating a set of political objectives as a part of a long-term political project involving such a prospect.

Brothers and generals

The main political power which has dominated the post-Mubarak political process has been the military, the most sophisticated organization in Egypt's modern history. The centrality of the military in post-1952 politics, discussed in Chapter 1, leaves no space for doubting the crucial and controversial role of the powerful military establishment, not only in formal politics but also in its penetration of both society and the economy. With its tentacles reaching into all sectors of the economy, the military has developed into an autonomous sector with a substantial economic base. The power of the military establishment reflected in the number of critical top state positions held by current and retired generals is only reinforced by its unique privileges, such as tax exemptions, preferential exchange rates and free labour. The Egyptian military has developed into a class in the Weberian sense with interests and resources which have made it relatively autonomous from other state institutions. This relative autonomy explains how members of SCAF, despite having been handpicked by Mubarak, played an instrumental role in his ousting. Realizing the impossibility of continuing its support for Mubarak in face of the rapidly intensifying massive popular uprising in January 2011, SCAF made a strategic decision to side with the protestors against Mubarak.

The Nasser era adage that the 'fate of the military and the nation' are inseparable lives on in the post-Mubarak era. Presiding over the transitional period, SCAF has managed to mould the political process in its favour. By engineering a complicated and flawed electoral law and manipulating the constitutional drafting process, Egypt's generals have secured an outcome that resembles a military dictatorship, according to many. The constitutional declaration of June 2012, for example, gave SCAF wide-ranging legislative powers in the aftermath of the dissolution of parliament, including complete control over its budget and military appointments.[2] The 2012 constitution, approved by 63.8 per cent of the popular vote later that year, only confirmed this constitutionally approved power. Article 195, for example, explicitly enshrined the principle that the defence minister must be a military officer. Similarly, article 197 stipulates that military officers should always form a majority within the National Defence Council, a clause which effectively gives the military veto power over any national security or critical foreign policy issue (Ashour, 2013).[3] The 2014 constitution, which received a majority approval in a referendum, reaffirms these rights. It goes a step further than the previous constitution in making the appointment of the minister of defence conditional on the approval of SCAF, for the first two presidential terms following the constitution being formally approved. Moreover, all post-Mubarak constitutions have protected the military's right to control its budget and try civilians in military courts.

On the eve of the 25 January uprising, the MB was the most organized political group outside the state. Founded by Hasan Al-Banna in 1928, the Muslim Brothers have been legally banned for most of their history and have mainly operated as a clandestine organization. However, the group's relationship with successive regimes, especially in post-1952 Egypt, has been a complex one. While most regimes banned the group and criminalized its activities, it has sometimes been expedient for a regime to grant the Brothers some degree of freedom. The group's main phase of re-consolidation of its organizational power, which had been lost under Nasser, began in the 1970s, when Sadat allowed members of the MB to participate in parliamentary elections as independents and take part in professional syndicate and student union elections. This was a strategy to counter leftist and Nasserist opposition to his de-Nasserization project. Sadat also released MB members arrested by Nasser, while allowing those exiled in the Gulf to return to Egypt. Sadat exploited rising Islamist sentiment and a surge in new forms of religiosity inspired by Wahabi ideas brought back by Egyptians working in the Gulf, to raise the profile of the MB.

The organizational power of the MB was honed through the participation of what became known as their 'middle generation' in student activism in the 1970s and later in the leadership of most professional syndicates in the 1980s (Baker, 2003; Browers, 2009). In professional syndicates, MB members learned to acquire higher levels of professionalism, competence and pragmatism than had ever been expected of them before (Wickham, 2004: 17). In the absence of any other strong political group, the 'Islamic trend' achieved impressive electoral victories within almost all professional syndicates including physicians, engineers and pharmacists. The value of this experience in organizing the affairs of professional syndicates, after having taken over university student unions in an earlier phase, was to enable the growing 'Islamic counter-elite' to develop its overall leadership capacity, promote an 'Islamic sub-culture' and widen its support base among the middle classes (ibid.: 179). At a more grassroots level, the MB developed a highly sophisticated and wide-reaching network of social services across the country. Based upon a system of private mosques and NGOs built up over several decades, the MB and other Islamist groups, such as the Salafis, provided education, health care and employment to wide sectors of the population that had been abandoned by the state.

On a different level, while the Brothers was still an illegal organization, MB members had participated in parliamentary elections as independent candidates. Despite regime repression and the violent targeting of their members and their voters, the MB managed to secure seats in several parliamentary elections from the 1980s to 2010. Their most impressive performance was in 2005, when the Brothers achieved an unprecedented 88 seats – over 20 per cent of the total seats in parliament – compared to 14 seats for the legal opposition. When the moment came after Mubarak's downfall for a liberal democracy-style political contestation, the MB were therefore more than ready to take on the task. The group deployed all its resources, under the umbrella of a strong organizational structure, to compete in the only game in town: electoral politics that were to shape the political process in the immediate post-Mubarak era. In three elections and two referenda, the MB in the form of their Freedom and Justice Party (FJP) were victorious. Since the fall of Mubarak, and until Morsi's ousting from power in July 2013, the FJP was easily the largest party in every single national election held in Egypt.

The FJP won 43 per cent of seats in the People's Assembly (November 2011–January 2012) and 58 per cent of seats in the Shura Council (February 2012), while Morsi secured his presidency with 51.7 per cent of the votes in the second round in June 2012. However, a closer reading of these results reveals more than first meets the eye. The low turnouts and tactical voting to keep out the Mubarak regime candidate in the second round of presidential elections shows that the popularity of the MB was far from overwhelming (Wade, 2013). Nonetheless, the experience of the MB in both electoral and ex-parliamentary politics allowed them to emerge as the main electoral victor, albeit briefly.

Without a doubt the main feature that has guaranteed the survival of the MB for eight decades under hostile regimes and campaigns of intense persecution has been the legendary strength of their organizational structure and the supremacy of the organization over any other consideration. A heavily centralized decision-making body with a hierarchical, pyramid-shaped edifice tolerating no dissent, the group has an organizational strength unique in Egypt's political landscape. Despite occasional internal ideological differences and generational tensions, the MB have managed to retain their organizational unity over the decades, except for a few waves of resignations (El-Houdaiby, 2013). To illustrate the potency of the organization, Tammam (2006) describes the following structure:

> The project of the MBs was reduced ... to building a strong, iron-clad organisation ... capable of achieving an Islamist project for change ... the organisation was modelled along that of the [Egyptian] state in all its details. The Guidance office mirrored the cabinet, the Shura Council mirrored the parliament and the administrative office mirrored the system of governorates. The geographical distribution of the group was a replica of official electoral units ... The [MB] organisation became a state within a state, short of a military and a security apparatus.

Such a level of organization managed to control the almost half a million 'card holding' members of the group during the worst crises. It also provided a solid base from which to participate in any nationwide elections. In another account of how the organization became an absolute, El-Houdaiby (2013) explains how through a process of centralizing decision-making and decentralizing implementation of decisions

> the Brotherhood sought to maintain internal unity and efficiency. Unity was fostered by narrowing the decision-making circles (until former Chairman Mahdi Akef stepped down in January 2010, these circles were comprised primarily of the group's 'historical' leadership, that is, those who had personally known its founder, Hassan al-Banna), thus reducing room for disputes and disagreement. The Brotherhood was able to sustain this system by substituting members' need for empowerment with a strong sense of duty.

Moreover, the MB is also a closely knit group held together by networks of business and economic interests, marriage and family relations and regional loyalties.[4] Allied to these interweaving networks, the ultimate strength of the MB as an organization is, in great part, based on ideological and political convictions and unquestioning loyalty to the leadership, which has the final say in all aspects of the organization.

Having said that, it would seem that the power of centralized organization is best suited to particular contexts. In certain instances, the dominance of the organization can prove detrimental to the attainment of a project. This has been, to some extent, the case of the MB in power and their subsequent demise at the hands of the military. The supremacy of the organization over all other considerations and the consequent suppression of all disagreement or dissent, though being instrumental in the group's survival over eight decades, contributed to sealing the fate of the MB once they came to power. When the FJP was launched after the fall of Mubarak, it was immediately seen by many critics of the group as merely the political arm of the MB, who went to great efforts to deny it. However, the dominance by the MB guidance council and the supreme leader of both the party and the presidency was quite evident, confirming the worst fears of the group's critics and, as ultimately transpired, a large section of the Egyptian population, including many who had initially voted for Morsi. In a blatant example, supporters were mobilized on the streets by the MB to cheer the wide-reaching powers that Morsi had granted himself even before the constitutional declaration, which embodied these powers, had been made public. To make matters worse, in response to the announcement of Morsi's infamous constitutional declaration, Mahmoud Ghozlan, official spokesperson of the Muslim Brothers, and not a member of government, described it to journalists as a 'revolutionary decision' (Ahram Online, 2012). The perceived blind obedience of the MB followers to Morsi's decisions and the unapologetic meddling of Muslim Brothers representatives in issues of government caused further cynicism about the sectarian nature of Morsi and FJP rule, thus alienating large numbers of Egyptians. The FJP was unable to become a political party independent of the movement that created it. The failure of the MB to create a genuine political party which could function in the Western sense, showed that the group's legendary organizational power was a double-edged sword.

The two political forces of the military and the MB, although vastly unequal in terms of power, realized that they needed to create an alliance in order to secure their common interest in reproducing the Mubarak order and to dominate the political process in the post-Mubarak era to achieve this end. In order to secure its position, suppress revolutionary aspirations and co-opt the undiminished popular mobilization, the military temporarily entered into an uneasy marriage of convenience with the MB, whereby the military accepted the MB presidency and their accession to political power. The brief alliance was successful in one respect: it reduced a revolutionary process characterized by demands for radical social and political transformation into a narrowly

defined, limited version of liberal, procedural democracy and electoral politics. Egypt's new revolutionaries suddenly felt obliged to compete in a game
for which they were ill prepared and which dissipated their energies over
multiple initiatives for little reward. The question of organization, not simply
in the narrow sense of a political party, but as a platform for developing
political and societal visions, remains at the heart of the future of Egypt's
revolutionary forces.

Pro-democracy activists: from New Social Movements to revolutionary process

The myriad informal political groups, activist forums, political coalitions and
protest activities which have formed the core of the pro-democracy movement
have been analysed by many commentators within a framework of New
Social Movements (NSMs) under authoritarian regimes (El-Mahdi, 2009;
Shehata, 2009; Munson, 2001; Abdelrahman, 2009; Beinin, 2011). These
studies emphasize a number of features that characterize new social movements including decentralized, loose organizational structures, a rejection of
traditional hierarchical leadership and a reliance on members themselves to
initiate activities. In Egypt and across the globe, NSMs have been celebrated
as horizontal networks needing no leader, capable of organizing without a
central authority and based on a diffuse notion of power. However, NSMs are
fundamentally distinguished from 'old' social movements not simply by their
tactics and mobilization structures but in the fact that their political objective
is not to capture the state. In revisiting his earlier analysis of anti-systemic
movements, Wallerstein draws our attention to deep suspicion of the state and
state-oriented action as *the* defining feature of NSMs. He argues that in the
two-staged formula of old social movements, by which capturing state power
was to be followed by transforming the world, committed activists usually
ended up discovering that

> state power was more limited than they had thought ... the cadres of a
> militant mobilising movement became the functionaries of a party in power.
> Their social positions were transformed and so, inevitably, were their
> individual psychologies ... the militant, syndicalist tactics that had been
> the daily bread of the social movement became counter-revolutionary.
>
> (2002: 23)

It is this perceived betrayal of the movements' goals and the inability of
revolutionaries/new rulers to resist the corrupting influence of power and
party politics that has created this deep suspicion among members of later generations of social movements. Their objective, therefore, is no longer to take
over state power but to challenge the boundaries of traditional politics and to
establish decentralized alternatives. The image of a Leninist revolutionary party
involving a rigid hierarchy, centralized power and the imposition of iron discipline

under the leadership of a professional elite, which had dominated most of the twentieth century, furthered activists' aversion to centralized organizations. Such a model was perceived as profoundly antithetical to the spontaneity, innovation and even radicalism of activists and protestors (Pratt, 1978: 117).

Wallerstein's analysis contrasts new social movements with old movements, such as nationalist movements of independence which swept parts of the world in the second half of the twentieth century. More recently, cases of what would be considered 'new social movements' have come to reinforce the suspicions among an even younger generation of movements about the perils of competing for and capturing state power. The last decades of the twentieth century abound with cases in which new social movement activists progressed to become part of a new order, once they had achieved their objective of bringing down at least part of the old regime. A comparative study (Grodsky, 2012) of several cases, such as Solidarity in Poland, the Congress of South African Trade Unions (COSATU), South African National Civic Organisation (SANCO) and a host of coloured 'revolutions' elsewhere, records the sense of betrayal and disillusionment felt by members of these social movements at the hands of their former friends and comrades once the latter had acceded to state institutions. Such experiences have further deepened the misgivings of a new generation of social movements in the twenty-first century about considering long-term plans which might involve engaging with formal state power.

Furthermore, under the repression of successive authoritarian regimes it is not surprising that Egypt's pro-democracy activists were unable even to conceive, let alone entertain the possibility, of capturing state power. In their struggle to challenge the regime and its policies, they also set out to challenge all formal institutions which constituted part of the political landscape associated with the state. Activists within the movement rejected all formal institutions, including political parties which were regarded as thoroughly co-opted by the regime, rife with corruption, dominated by ailing leaderships and which had, time and again, betrayed their constituencies. Even when engaging with more formal organizations that were not part of the state apparatus, such as professional syndicates, the aim of activists was to transform the existing structures and create alternative models of unionization. As discussed in the previous chapters, the absence of a formal, traditional organization became one of the strongest rallying points for the pro-democracy movement. According to a leading Kefaya activist:

> We celebrated Kefaya and all its sisters for its new 'form': horizontal, non-hierarchical, loose and flexible. This was everything that traditional political parties were not. We rejected structures which suffocated new ideas and were typically undemocratic. We were not just trying to make a point. These forms, in fact, were at odds with what we were trying to achieve: challenging hierarchy and oppression in social relations between classes and genders.
>
> (Khalil, author interview, Cairo, May 2009)

Centralized structures were regarded, by definition, as embodying principles of repression and hierarchy. However, rejecting hierarchy and oppressive centralization was only one reason for activists' choice of more loose models of organization. Egyptian activists had also developed a very fluid notion of 'power' which in a way necessitated loose, horizontal structures. Although many of the pro-democracy groups had a seemingly narrow focus, such as academic freedom, independence of professional unions, changing the constitution or even the much greater objective of regime change, they situated the analysis of their specific targets within much broader frameworks which emphasized larger structures of oppression. While the Mubarak regime was the target of mobilization, activists understood their critical analysis as encompassing a larger system of exploitation in which global and regional actors and processes were at play. The absence of academic freedom, the failing health care system, the systematic torture of prisoners and arrest of critical journalists were understood as manifestations of a wider system of hierarchical and exploitative relations. Groups such as AGEG and the anti-war movement led campaigns that were levelled at global institutions such as the WTO and the World Bank (WB), and against the increasing militarization of superpower political power in addition to focusing on action against the increasing disenfranchisement and impoverishment of the Egyptian people by the state–capital nexus. By their work at multiple levels, these groups were engaged in redefining power not as 'something out there' to be captured but as a diffused and plural system to be addressed and challenged at different levels. The multiplicity of demands and targets that constituted the agenda of the pro-democracy movement meant that struggles for change were no longer necessarily focused on the takeover of political power nor on a simple demand for larger representation in a narrowly defined, formal electoral system. As such, activists in the movement regarded centralized structures and rigid blueprints for change as irrelevant to their vision of social transformation. The greatest good for pro-democracy activists during the decade leading up to the ousting of Mubarak was to widen the scope of mobilization and to take the struggle to the streets. Their aim was to re-appropriate political activities for the general masses from the grip of professionals, or what della Porta (2005: 192) calls the 'emphasis of participation (versus bureaucratization), the attempt to construct values and identities (versus managing existing ones)'.

However, a debate about the sustainability and effectiveness of loose networks of activism was starting to resonate among some activists towards the end of the decade. The absence of an organizational form that could mobilize people on a larger scale, instead of the few hundreds or at best thousands, and better harness the enthusiasm of protestors, was beginning to be seen as a weakness by growing numbers of activists. Some were realizing the limitation of transitory structures such as steering committees and coordination boards that were focused on events rather than long-term strategies. The same Kefaya member elaborated upon this point:

The problem now is that Kefaya does not exist beyond the event. In other words, Kefaya is very successful at organizing a rally or a demonstration; it attracts people, emotions rise high. However, once the event (demonstration) is over, there is nothing left. Those newly mobilized, especially the youth, who are so inspired, full of energy and desire to do something, really have nothing to do ... no homework, no ongoing activities and responsibilities to make them feel connected to a movement.

(Khalil, author interview, Cairo, 2007)

The pro-democracy movement was hence facing a major challenge on the eve of 25 January: to find an organizational set-up that allows spontaneity and lack of rigidity and at the same time ensures sustainability. For some members the movement lacked the tools to coordinate its activities and reach out to different groups while creating a more coherent front which all necessitated a different organizational form. Developing from a protest event or even a series of events to a movement while finding this requisite organizational form was becoming the main challenge for Kefaya and other pro-democracy groups. Of course, this challenge is not unique to Egypt and has, indeed, been highlighted in various contexts where the survival of a revolutionary process requires institutions that can pose alternatives to the existing system. But these institutions must not develop a dominance that necessarily ends up freezing the dialectic of this process 'in a totalitarian bureaucratic monolith' (Pratt, 1978: 197).

Pro-democracy activists did not regard political parties as having even the potential to constitute the organizational form needed. Indeed, the possibility of transforming a movement such as Kefaya into a political party was either never discussed or completely dismissed. Veteran political activist and Kefaya member Karima El-Hefnawy was typical in her view that political parties were antithetical to the inclusive nature of the pro-democracy movement (author interview, Cairo, April 2007). The main shortcoming of political parties is not only their hierarchical structure but the fact that they work on the basis of fixed ideologies which target only specific sectors of the population while alienating others. For El-Hefnawy, this was a luxury the movement could not afford at that stage. According to her, the movement needed to create a more inclusive umbrella for all shades of activists who, under the repression of the Mubarak regime, would not have been able to stand alone as political factions. This sentiment was dominant among most activists, as will be discussed in the following chapter.

The life-span of pro-democracy groups was also a significant factor in shaping the organizational structure of the groups activists formed. In general, protest movements with a longer history are more able to fall back on their experience and knowledge when developing tactics and methods of sustainable organization. Unfortunately for the groups constituting the Egyptian pro-democracy movement, one of their main features was their short life. The fluidity and ability to move activities from one umbrella to another, for groups to coalesce, metamorphose, dissolve and be reborn, was highly necessary for survival, amongst other advantages. However, the ever-expanding foci of protest and the rising needs for more mobilization structures meant that most groups, such as AGEG and The Street is Ours, had short life-spans. They either outlived their initial energy or their members decided to change their focus and join other existing forums or create new ones. Even the umbrella group Kefaya was active for no more than two years, despite the fact that it was never actually dissolved. While activists carried their ideas and experience from one forum to another, institutional memory was undermined and long-term planning was almost completely missing.

On the eve of 25 January, the majority of activists were mostly content with the organizational situation of their groups and with the tools and tactics they had developed which were in line with protest movements active both at the global level and in the global South. Few were tussling with the predicament of finding sustainable organizational structures while maintaining the flexibility of their autonomous politics. Moreover, under relentless police repression and state security harassment, activists did not have the luxury of exploring new forms of organization that would accommodate both needs at the dawn of a new phase of the revolutionary process. The considerable shift in political alignments sparked by the uprising and the sudden emergence of unprecedented potential to participate in this process in effect forced the activists at the forefront of the uprising to rethink their position on questions of power and political strategy as a matter of urgency.

Days into the uprising, activists began forming coalitions that were intended to coordinate the disparate groups occupying Tahrir Square, prioritize demands and later negotiate with SCAF on behalf of all protestors. The Revolution Youth Coalition (RYC), which was one of the earliest to be formed, comprised representatives of different political leanings, including groups such as the youth wings of the MB and liberal parties, leftist groups and cross-ideological groups and networks such as the Youth for Justice and Freedom Movement (El-Guindy, 2012). The RYC and other coalitions that followed did not manage to create a broadly based alliance or to give rise to any other form of organization that could claim a meaningful degree of representation. Their main weakness was their inability to offer a workable plan for operationalizing the goals of the uprising: bread, freedom and social justice. Their members fell back on tactics with which they were familiar. The RYC adopted strategies that had characterized the previous decade of mobilization. Among them was building a cross-ideological coalition, a tactic that was beleaguered with a host of challenges, including coordination difficulties and a deepening of intergroup rifts (Abdelrahman, 2009). While this tactic, despite its shortcomings, had served activists' needs during the Mubarak era, replicating exactly the same model when moving forward to the next phase of the revolutionary process proved quite inadequate.

At the grassroots level, numerous initiatives continued to be developed by veteran as well as newly mobilized activists, within both established and newly created networks, around various causes emanating from the goals of the uprising. The Popular Committees for the Protection of the Revolution, for instance, grew spontaneously from the early days of the uprising, following the withdrawal of security police from the streets. They were formed by local residents in almost every neighbourhood across Egypt's main cities to provide security and other services in the wake of a near-complete collapse of all state services. These committees were the closest that citizenship protests, discussed in the previous chapter, came to any form of organized structure. In the months that followed, most of these committees disappeared under the weight of police repression.

The 'Let's write our constitution' campaign developed as a nationwide initiative in 2011 to shadow the forthcoming formal process of drafting the constitution. One of the campaign's main objectives was to study the experience of other countries in drafting constitutions in transitional periods. More importantly, it also aimed to draft a popular constitution, parallel to the official one, based on widespread polls and popular discussions, which could be used as a tool to influence the framing of the official constitution. Another campaign is 'No to the World Bank and IMF loans', which has been working since the early days of the 'transition' period to expose the dangers of 'generous' aid packages offered by these institutions to help the country through this period. 'The generals are liars' was another campaign which marched the streets of major cities, screened films documenting the military's abuses since the uprising and demanded more transparency from all powerful institutions. Numerous other groups and networks continue to rally to the cause of the marginalized and launch initiatives to locate economic and social rights at the heart of the ongoing political struggle. These initiatives have been essential for keeping the revolutionary spirit and struggle alive but they have had little effect on the formal process which has been reduced to an exercise in electoral politics.

With the lifting of restrictions on the formation of political parties, many activists, who only months before had been deeply suspicious of this political model, were suddenly confronted with a perceived need to adopt a longer-term strategy. In particular, in order to contest parliamentary elections at the end of 2011, they had to create new political parties as a matter of urgency. In a mad rush, over 40 new parties were founded in the months leading up to the elections but only 23 actually took part. Realizing their weakness and unpreparedness for electoral politics, many of the newly founded parties joined forces in coalitions including the Democratic Alliance, the Egyptian Bloc, the Islamist Alliance and the 'Completing the Revolution' Alliance. Bringing together the most unlikely bedfellows, most of these coalitions soon splintered because of ideological and tactical differences as well as power issues. For example, the Democratic Alliance, which began as a broadly based coalition of liberal, leftist and Islamist parties, was soon riven by ideological differences that led to the withdrawal of the leftist Tagamou party, the liberal Wafd and most of its other 34 secular parties as well as all Islamist parties except for the dominant FJP. The breakaway parties soon joined a swathe of other coalitions.[5] These abrupt shifts were symptomatic of the new actors' severe inexperience and lack of clarity on their role in the new process. In fact, at that time, the newly formed political parties resembled more what Goldberg (2012) described as 'debating clubs' than genuine parties. Not surprisingly, almost all of the newly created parties, with the exception of the Salafi Nour party, only managed to get a handful of votes. The majority of seats in both the upper and lower houses of parliament were secured by the FJP and Nour parties.[6]

Workers: rebels without a movement

The post-Mubarak political elite has worked on ensuring a smooth continuity of the political and economic system established under Mubarak. This has been reflected in successive governments' commitment to existing policy and their failure to declare a policy envisioning any change in the future, let alone commence any policy initiative to change the status quo. Neoliberal policies and directives have been 'business as usual', with the result that continuing privatization of public sector companies and increasing anti-labour legislation has caused labour unrest to grow. In 2012, the country witnessed a dramatic increase in labour action, reaching an all-time high of 3,817 incidents across all sectors (see Table 4.1). This was a 452 per cent increase from the 692 incidents reported for 2007, which was the highest of all years of the previous decade. Much more significantly, the number of incidents of labour contentious action in 2012 exceeded the total of all recorded incidents from 2000 to 2010 (El-Merghany, 2013: 2). In the first quarter of 2013 alone, there were over 2,400 protests by blue and white collar as well as informal workers (Aboul Enein, 2013).

Since the 25 January uprising, labour has continued to focus on multiple demands, at the heart of which has been the right to organize outside the long co-opted ETUF and to challenge its monopoly over labour (mis)representation. The landmark launching of the first independent trade union by the municipal tax collectors in 2009 (see Chapter 3) and the numerous strike committees which were set up to represent the demands of protesting workers across the country

Table 4.1 Labour contentious action during 2012

Sector	Number of incidents	%
Public	1,355	35.5
Private	393	10.3
Public business	221	5.8
Self-mployed	192	5.0
Others	1,656	43.4
Total	3,817	100

Source: Adapted from El-Merghany (2013)

were admirable achievements under the repressive Mubarak system. However, unlike Poland's Solidarity and South Africa's COSATU, which developed into broader movements, Egypt lacked labour organizations that could mature into a cohesive movement, let alone a wider, more inclusive movement with national leadership potential. For many workers and union activists, creating a movement of this nature under Mubarak was the real struggle.

While moving the struggle to a wider level was beyond labour at this stage, one positive development was a huge surge in newly created, independent unions. Emboldened by their role in the 25 January uprising, the Egyptian Health Technologists' Syndicate, the Independent Teachers' Syndicate and the Pensioners' Federation joined with workers across the country to form the Egyptian Federation for Independent Trade Unions (EFITU), launched in Tahrir Square only days into the uprising. Soon afterwards, and following a large strike in February, the Cairo transport workers launched the Independent Union of Public Transport Authority Workers in March 2011. In the months that followed, the floodgates opened and a huge number of requests to form independent unions were supported by the EFITU (Totonchi, 2011: 273). By 2013, there were no fewer than a staggering 1,000 independent trade unions set up across all sectors and regions. Seen from the perspective of a Gramscian analysis, Egypt's workers have not been seeking state power but pursuing a process of revolutionary development rooted in ongoing struggles which is intended to culminate in a qualitatively new 'network' of proletarian institutions (Gramsci, 1971).

Creating independent unions is one thing. Coalescing workers' efforts into a movement that could play a leadership role in Egypt's revolutionary process is quite another. Moreover, the nascent union 'movement' has been beleaguered by both internal and external challenges. For one, the union movement soon became plagued by internal splits. The one thousand new unions have split into those affiliated with the EFITU and others which have joined the umbrella of the Egyptian Democratic Labour Congress. The latter broke away from the EFITU, with the Centre for Trade Union and Workers' Services (CTUWS), the oldest and most outspoken NGO in support of labour, at its helm. While personality clashes are often cited by activists as a possible cause of this split, the divide between the two groups runs much deeper. The anticipated form of workers' organization and its role is at the heart of this break-up.[7] As early as 2010, the Revolutionary Socialists had already split precisely over this issue. The Popular Democratic Movement for Change, *Hashd*, and the Socialist Renewal Current stood on opposite sides of a schismatic debate on whether organization should precede action or vice versa. In an interview only months after the 25 January uprising, Mohamadain, a leftist labour activist, described the growing rift among activists as follows:

> The main debate now is about creating organizations. The majority of activists, like the EFITU people, insist that we must use the current atmosphere to grab the opportunity to create as many independent

unions as possible. Other activists, and I am with them, argue that this is unwise, considering how small in membership numbers these new unions are. Instead, we argue that mobilization and creating a mass base among workers is the first step. Organizations will naturally evolve afterwards.

(author interview, Cairo, April 2011)

Following the second strategy means first and foremost widening and deepening the radicalization of workers. More workers need to be won over and their awareness raised in regard to confronting the state–capital nexus. In this process, workers' demands will develop from a focus on salary increases into fighting for minimum wages and an overhaul of all labour laws (ibid.). Fatma Ramadan, a prominent labour activist of EFITU, on the other hand, does not mince her words when she describes the need to build unions in the post-Mubarak era as a 'matter of life and death for workers' (author interview, Cairo, June 2011). The overwhelming energy demonstrated by workers and their desire to create independent unions needs to be encouraged and the momentum maintained at any cost (ibid.). The main problem, according to Mohamadain, is that both strategies require financial and human resources, enabling representatives to visit workplaces, meet and discuss with people, train cadres, coordinate activities and much more (author interview, 2011). However, these resources are simply not available. This unresolved debate on whether building unions is the best way to harness workers' efforts and mobilization, or whether deepening and radicalizing the struggle is the only guarantee for the evolution of sustainable structures, continues to imperil the future of the movement.

These diametrically opposed visions and the ensuing competing strategies, which have spawned different camps within the same movement, are taking place within a much more complex and hostile environment. The relationship of workers to new unions and the old ETUF is very problematic. The minister of labour and manpower, Ahmed Al-Bourai, encouraged the launch of independent unions during his brief tenure in the immediate aftermath of the uprising. However, after his quick dismissal from government, his draft law of August 2011, which granted new unions a legal identity, was quietly shelved.[8] New unions' lack of a legal identity makes workers' decisions to shift from the ETUF a risky step. Leaving the ETUF and joining an independent union is not a difficult ideological choice for most workers. The ETUF has always been a repressive arm of the regime and a tool for containing and disciplining labour more than a representative of their interests. In fact, some of the major protests by workers in the decade leading up to the ousting of Mubarak were directed against the corrupt management of the ETUF. On more practical grounds, however, severing one's links with the ETUF can prove a costly sacrifice that not everyone is prepared to make due to the very significant financial consequences. Large sectors of Egyptian workers, such as those employed by the massive Mahalla Misr Spinning and Weaving Company, employing almost a quarter of all public sector manufacturing workers, are heavily reliant on the ETUF, to which their pensions, health care and other subsidies are tied. As Beinin (2013) puts it: 'Leaving the state-run federation while this linkage remains enshrined in law would entail a prohibitive loss of money they believe belongs to them ... [they] find themselves trapped under its umbrella'.

However, the main threat to the development of an autonomous labour movement remains the increasing violence the state is willing to employ to quash any moves in this direction. Like the Mubarak regime, successive (interim) governments under SCAF and the MB were all willing to accommodate some of the demands raised by workers during their unrelenting waves of protest. Nonetheless, like their predecessor, and of course like Nasser before them, SCAF and the MB could not tolerate the threat of an autonomous, organized mass labour movement. They employed every tactic to abort any such development. It is hence no surprise that one of the early actions taken by SCAF was to decree Law 34/2011, which criminalized any form of strike and protest that curtails production. The law applied very heavy fines and prison sentences upon workers who participated in, called for or publicized strike activity (Human Rights Watch, 2012). After the ousting of Morsi in 2013, the military-backed interim government passed Law 107/2013, which put further restrictions on strikes and protests and increased the penalties against violators.

The adoption of such repressive legislation in a post-revolutionary moment is not unique to the Egyptian experience. The Le Chapelier law, for example, passed by the French Constituent Assembly in 1791, similarly prohibited any form of association based on occupation or profession. Violators of the law were punished by hefty fines and even by the staggering 'suspension of citizenship rights' for one year (Sewell, 1980). While the Le Chapelier law was justified on the grounds that under the regime of liberty, no intermediary bodies were necessary between the state and the individual (Rimlinger, 1977: 212), the Egyptian Law 34/2011, followed by Law 107/2013, defended banning labour strikes on the grounds of their threat to the production process and the national economy. In both cases, however, workers were left completely vulnerable at the hands of their employers, who were backed by the state.

And the state did not hesitate to use the law to employ violence against workers. Numerous examples include the sentencing of five union leaders at the Alexandria Port Containers Company to a lengthy three-year prison sentence for their role in organizing a strike of 600 workers in September 2012 (*Egypt Independent*, 12 October, 2012). This was followed by a suspended sentence of one year in prison for five workers in the Egyptian oil company Petrojet in July 2011, the arrest and torture of striking workers at the Somid company port in March 2012, and indiscriminate shooting by riot police which caused serious injuries among striking Mahalla El-Kubra Samoli company workers (*Socialist Worker*, 2012).

In another move, Morsi approved Law 97/2012 to amend the infamous Law 35/1976 which allowed the replacement of former NDP members of the

ETUF board, who had reached retirement age, with MB cadres while maintaining the repressive structure of the federation (El-Merghany, 2013: 10). Fatma Ramadan, executive board member of the EFITU, feels this is very significant: 'Morsi's first decree, following his complete takeover of state power on 22 November, was a labour decree. This is a clear indicator that Morsi is seeking to monopolise the labour movement by first "Brotherhoodising" the ministry of labour and manpower, and now the ETUF' (Charbel, 2012). In the same year, the highly controversial constitution, which came into effect in December 2012, re-affirmed the existing law that gives the state a monopoly over the formation of trade unions. One of its central planks was to maintain all measures that sabotage workers' rights to organize and engage in collective action.

Another option for labour activists beyond the creation of unions is the launching of political parties that represent the interests of workers. Echoing this possibility and its centrality to the labour struggle, Sameh Naguib (2011) of the Revolutionary Socialists argues that 'Our enemies are organised. They have the backing of the bourgeois media. Only an organised revolutionary party that is strong enough in numbers, and that is capable of propagating its ideas for revolutionary action among the masses, can hope to win this battle.' Debating the virtue of a Leninist vanguard party model is one thing, the reality of politics in Egypt is another. In Egypt, the law governing political parties, fortified by the military junta's constitutional declarations and the 2012 constitution, continues as a barrier to the formation of any political party based on labour or class in general. This is a huge impediment to workers' ability to muster any political strength as activists argue that all current political parties, founded both before and after January 2011, continue to ignore labour issues. One labour activist complains that these parties 'provide us with no assistance or support during our struggles. Other than lip service, they offer us nothing' (Charbel, 2012). Egypt's political parties, even those laying claim to a progressive agenda, have so far been incapable of building mass constituencies among workers and more marginalized groups. As a consequence, both labour and the more vulnerable in society remain unrepresented while political parties with a progressive or revolutionary agenda stay insignificant and isolated.

This chapter has examined the issue of organization within the context of Egypt's ongoing revolutionary process. It argues that, in the phase following the downfall of Mubarak, revolutionary forces suffered due to their particular organizational forms. The established elite and groups with more centralized organizational forms were able to dominate a 'transition' process that favoured such structures. In the final analysis, however, it is clear that while the form and nature of an organization is an important factor in creating sustainable platforms for launching transformative projects, it is not sufficient for the success of such a project. In fact, particular types of organization and the nature of organizational strength could adversely affect the achievement of a political project. The experience of the Muslim Brothers, discussed earlier, is a powerful case in point. It should also be borne in mind that a revolutionary process is never a pre-designed series of events following a clearly devised plan of action. This is more in the style of reformist projects in the transition to liberal democracy or some other limited outcome. Uprisings and protests, on the other hand, erupt without those involved in them necessarily knowing what the outcome will be and how the process will evolve. The rise of a revolutionary subject and project could well be born out of these events rather than give birth to them in the first place.

Notes

1 Part of this chapter was originally published in *Development and Change* 44(3): 569–85, May 2013.
2 Only two days before the presidential election run-off, the Egyptian supreme constitutional court passed a ruling that the entire Islamist-dominated parliament should be dismissed on the grounds of misapplication of rules for independent candidates during the elections.
3 The National Defence Council, according to the constitution, is responsible for decisions to declare war or send armed forces overseas. More crucially, it is responsible for the military budget.
4 To get a glimpse into this network, see El-Kharabawi (2012).
5 For a review of all the political parties and coalitions which were created during this period, see Carnegie Endowment (2012).
6 The Nour party was the Salafis' first foray into organized formal politics in their history. However, they had a clearly structured organization going back many decades, similar to that of the MB, which allowed them to garner a substantial share of the electorate.
7 See Beinin (2013) for a discussion of the personality clashes between Kamal Abbas and Kamal Abu Eita.
8 The submission of the draft law to SCAF for discussion encouraged the International Labour Organisation (ILO) to remove Egypt from its blacklist of countries that do not respect trade union freedoms. However, the shelving of the draft law by SCAF for months on end, despite pressure from workers and labour activists, led the ILO to return Egypt firmly to the same blacklist once more in May 2012. Two years later, despite MB governments and the interim government appointed by the military in July 2013, the draft law was still collecting dust.

5   On coalitions

Revolutionary and otherwise

The single-mindedness of Egypt's Tahrir Square protestors during the 18 days leading up to the ousting of Mubarak was all the more remarkable given the absence of a unifying ideology. Not only was there no one predominant political group leading the protestors and articulating their demands, it almost seemed that there was a tacit agreement among protestors to downplay the role of any one ideology in the revolution. The 25 January uprising was clearly not inspired by Islamist, nationalist or Marxist sentiment and world views. More importantly, the 'vanguard' of the Egyptian revolution was undoubtedly the millions of ordinary Egyptians who had never before taken part in politics and who, in most cases, had never subscribed to any political ideology. Furthermore, those who had a history of political activism and took part in the mass revolts all over the country represented almost the entire Egyptian political spectrum, although some only joined much later in the day. In fact, preparations and planning for the 25 January 'day of rage' were coordinated by youth groups from different ideological backgrounds, including the 6 April Movement, Youth for Justice and Freedom,[1] the Youth of El Gabha Party, the El-Baradei campaign and the MB Youth as well as the Facebook-based 'We are all Khaled Said' group. With the exception of the last two, the other groups themselves were examples of cross-ideological cooperation, consisting as they did of members of divergent political camps. Quickly, and in response to the unexpected developments of the uprising and the perceived need to establish a body providing some form of representation, the Youth of the Revolution Coalition was formed on 6 February with two members from each of the above six groups. This stratagem of broad representation was a legacy of the previous decade of activism, in which cross-ideological cooperation dominated the pro-democracy movement. Despite this experience of forging alliances and experimenting with coalition-building before the uprising, the post-Mubarak era has been characterized by the inability of revolutionary groups to create any sustainable broadly-based coalitions. This, arguably, has rendered these groups vulnerable to the forces of the counter-revolution that are working to derail the revolutionary process.

This chapter argues that the nature of coalitions forged under Mubarak: pragmatic, tactical and short-term, while serving an essential function of allowing broad mobilization under a repressive regime, was of little value for the formation of a sustainable revolutionary coalition after the uprising. The history and character of the activism that marked the Mubarak period, such as the nature of organizational structures discussed in the previous chapter, continue to influence the fate of the revolutionary process unfolding in Egypt. Hence, this chapter examines the conditions under which disparate political groups such as elements of the left, Islamists, Nasserists and liberals attempted to work during this historical period and how the global, regional and local contexts engendered new strategies including tactical cooperation with 'historical enemies'. The rise of the pro-democracy movement, discussed in the previous chapter, is mirrored in the history of cross-ideological cooperation between the traditional adversaries of Egypt's political opposition. The following analysis, therefore, focuses on the pro-democracy movement, where such cooperation dominated, rather than labour protests and other forms of activism.

As with the discussion of organization in the previous chapter, it is important to note that the absence of a broadly-based revolutionary coalition is not discussed here as a regrettable failure, or on the grounds of any *a priori* assumption regarding the progressive value of such a strategy. The aim is to trace the history of this strategy and locate it within current debates on the potential course of Egypt's revolutionary process.

Coalition building: a short history

The increased politicization engendered by action in solidarity with the second Palestinian Intifada created spaces in which representatives of diametrically opposed political groups found themselves able to experiment with the forging of tactical alliances. However, this cross-ideological cooperation has an earlier provenance in the efforts of university students which began in the mid-1990s.

Cooperation between students from different political backgrounds is not new to Egyptian university campuses. Ahmed Abdallah, author of the most important work on Egyptian student movements, notes that 'Whenever nationalist feelings ran high enough to involve the large masses of independent students, the leaders of the different political factions found themselves compelled in haste to create a common organization to direct the uprising'(1985: 69). The number of student committees created in the 1940s, reflecting not only cross-ideological cooperation among different political groups but also cross-sectorial coalitions between students, workers and professional unions, is testimony to the vital role of students in creating such coalitions.[2] More recently, university campuses have begun to see new forms of cooperation. Starting in the late 1990s, students from the Revolutionary Socialists (RS) and other individual activists on the left, for example, began to have isolated exchanges with MB students on university campuses. These developed to the stage where MB students invited leftist activists at Cairo

University to speak in rallies held against the US airstrikes on Iraq in 1999. Leftist students were eager to grab the opportunity, which represented significant recognition by the overwhelmingly stronger MB. The Free Student Union (FSU), formed in November 2005, was a landmark in joint student cooperation due to its institutionalized form. Established as a parallel body to official student unions, which were under the tight control of state security, the FSU brought together students of different political shades, especially at Cairo-based universities. While not accruing a mass membership, the FSU, nonetheless, started to become a space where a new generation of students learned to overcome bitter ideological divides and work together tactically by offering mutual support. One example was the solidarity expressed by FSU socialist members in Helwan University with female students expelled from hostels for wearing the niqab. Another was a solidarity campaign against the expulsion of more than 400 students for alleged membership of the MB (El-Hamalawy, 2007).

Outside university campuses, the launch of the EPCSPI in 2000, which became the marker for the start of a decade of protest movements, came at the initiative of a number of left-wing activists and non-governmental organizations that were soon joined by Nasserists and some members of the MB. The metamorphosis of the pro-Palestinian support movement into an anti-war movement campaigning against the war in Iraq saw the intensification of co-operation through joint demonstrations, rallies, boycott campaigns, public statements and support convoys. Further, the Cairo Conference was shown to be a microcosm of all shades of the political spectrum. Several Egyptian groups, including the RS, utilized the conference to rally support for 40 MB members who were facing military trials in 2007. Similarly, Kefaya was initially formed as a predominantly Nasserist movement with representation of leftist groups and the Muslim Brothers. Other initiatives and groups, such as the Movement in Solidarity with Egyptian Judges, 9 March Movement, Youth for Justice and Democracy, AGEG and the NAC, became opportunities for intense collaboration between individuals and groups from diametrically opposed ideological positions.

For a period of ten years, the public squares, university campuses and professional syndicates of Cairo and other major cities became sites for demonstrations at which banners of the banned Communist Party jostled alongside photographs of Nasser and copies of the Quran held high. The fast-changing regional and domestic events and the broadening of protest along new lines maintained the momentum of activists in this period. State security, in attempting to control protests, no longer differentiated between liberals, leftists or Islamists. Facing the same police brutality during demonstrations and often sharing the same detention cells was important in consolidating efforts at co-operation and even in creating a sense of 'comradely' or 'brotherly' solidarity among some.

Just as the pro-democracy movement itself was a fluid, loosely structured amalgamation of several initiatives and groups, cooperation across ideological

lines was also far from being a closely structured, unified process. Cooperation in organizing joint activities did not evolve into a united coalition
representing the official line of certain political parties and groups, nor was it
always blessed with the explicit approval of the leadership of the left, liberals,
the Muslim Brothers or the Nasserists. Resurgent activism on the Egyptian
street derived from loose networks of members and subgroups within the
various opposition streams as well as independent sympathizers. While
mother organizations such as the Tagamou, Nasserist and Al-Ghad parties
and the MB often participated in joint events, the core group which led sustained efforts of cooperation came from dissident groups and the youth wings
of these organizations as well as groups which developed independently of
their grip. Often disillusioned with the rigidity of their leadership and radicalized by new events and spaces for actions, individuals and splinter groups
sought to break away from the mould, at least in terms of mobilization
strategy.

For example, the representatives of the Nasserist group, who were the most
actively engaged in cooperation, came from the Karama Party, a splinter
organization that broke away from the Arab Democratic Nasserist Party in
1997. Hamdin Sabahi, founding leader of the Karama Party, described it as a
'nationalist, progressive party with a Nasserist touch, based on a programme
of social justice and Arab nationalism' (author interview, Cairo, June 2008).
Sabahi, who came third in the first round of presidential elections in 2011,
argued that what really set Karama apart from the traditional Nasserists was
the fact that it actively sought cooperation with other political streams. Even
within its own ranks, Karama comprised members with political leanings that
differed from hard-core Nasserism. For example, a small number of members
had either Islamist or communist tendencies, something that the Nasserist
Party would never have tolerated (ibid.).

While the decision to participate in activities and launch initiatives with
other groups would never have been possible without at least the tacit endorsement of the MB leadership, there was a clear generational divide within the
MB regarding this process of cooperation. Members of the MB 'middle generation', including prominent figures such as Esam Al-Erian and Abdel
Munim Abu al-Fotuh, took the lead in forging new alliances with leftist, liberal and Nasserist political groups.[3] The middle generation also trained the
youth wing of the MB (Shabab el-Ikhwan) in the same tactics. The MB youth
wing, a group of university students and graduates who had in the previous
decade challenged the MB leadership on several issues, was at the forefront of
the footwork in building alliances.

The initiative on the left for cross-ideological cooperation came from
quarters of the so-called 'new left', which comprised various elements ranging
from newly formed leftist groups such as the RS, to human rights groups such
as the Hisham Mubarak Law Centre and the Nadeem Centre for the Rehabilitation of Victims of Violence, to individual members of the more traditional left such as Nabil El-Hilali and others who had become disillusioned

with the stale politics of their organizations and the latter's failure to gain any popular support. A process of redefining their position towards Islamists and Nationalists was at the heart of this cooperation and came often at the cost of accusations of opportunism and selling out by comrades who disagreed with this strategy.

Neither brothers nor comrades

Members of the divergent political groups who took to the streets, risked their lives side-by-side, shared the same prison cells and worked together regularly, were able, at least temporarily, to put their deep historical rivalries to one side. However, the history of political opposition in Egypt has always been marked by profound divisions and intense antagonism between the rival political groups which is deeply rooted in ideological differences. This antagonism has, at certain times, been more extreme between the different opposition enemies than between the opposition and the regime, which was consequently often in a better position to manipulate and undermine any serious political challenge to its rule. Recalling this history is all the more important in appreciating the efforts of the various groups in reaching common principles of cooperation and in understanding the difficulties they faced in maintaining this fragile cooperation. Of these rivalries, the most long-standing has undoubtedly been that between the MB on one hand and the Nasserists and the Egyptian left on the other – despite the great animosity that also exists between the latter two.

Volumes have been written on the acrimonious history between the Nasserists and the Muslim Brothers, which has been characterized by decades of deceit and brutality. The hostility goes back a long way to the period immediately after power was seized in 1952 by the Free Officers who, having no popular base among the masses, relied on the support of the MB to underpin their coup. However, Nasser, who could not tolerate any strong, political organization outside his control, soon excluded the Brothers from the political arena and outlawed their activities. After an alleged assassination attempt by the Brothers on Nasser in 1954, several leaders of the group were executed and thousands of its members imprisoned in a systematic wave of elimination. In the decades that followed, members of the scarred MB remained deeply suspicious and antagonistic towards Nasserists. This animosity was more than reciprocated.

The bitter rivalry between the left and the Muslim Brothers goes back even further. In the 1940s, the MB collaboration with King Farouk in breaking labour strikes and their resistance to the mobilization of workers sparked the beginning of long-standing hostility.[4] The embourgeoisement of the MB during their exile in Saudi Arabia to escape Nasser resulted in an increased conservatism of the group, particularly in its stances on social and economic issues. Subsequently, Sadat's ploy to use Islamist groups as an ideological weapon in his battle against the left and the Nasserists, especially during his project of 'de-Nasserization', cemented the MB position within the capital camp. It is no surprise, therefore, that the MB sided with Sadat's government during the January 1977 food riots. Mass demonstrations protested against the Sadat regime's removal of subsidies on basic commodities which had caused a dramatic increase in the prices of staple foods that were essential to the poor. The ensuing riots were blamed on the left, which Sadat himself accused of fomenting what he called *thawret el-haramya*, or 'the thieves' revolution'. Significantly, the MB, as well as members of other Islamic asso-ciations, swiftly adopted the government's line by referring to the demonstrations as a 'communist conspiracy' (Harman, 1994). Sadat's tactics for weakening the left and the Nasserists also included allowing Islamist groups to play a larger role in associational and public life. During this period, repeated attacks by Islamist university students on activities and events organized by leftist and other secular students became a regular feature (Abdallah, 1985).

This unambiguous behaviour led to virtually universal condemnation by the Egyptian left of all Islamist groups as fascist. Leftists and the secular opposition in general, therefore, had no qualms about the Mubarak regime's concerted campaign against Islamists during the 1980s and 1990s. With the exception of a few leftist lawyers, such as Nabil El Hilali and Hisham Mubarak, who actually defended Islamist detainees (El-Hamalawy, 2007), the left either turned a blind eye or tacitly endorsed the regime's persecution of Islamists. Among occasions when the secular opposition, including the left, explicitly sided with the regime against the Muslim Brothers was its welcome of the 1993 Unified Law for Syndicates. The Islamists had demonstrated their mounting influence in these syndicates in the 1991 and 1992 elections. The government hence passed this law, which allowed it to suppress the MB by intervening directly in the internal elections of professional syndicates. Fur-thermore, alleged deals between the government and Tagamou Party, as well the general conciliatory position of the party towards the Mubarak regime, were construed by many to be part of the left's position towards Islamists (Naguib, 2009). Silence in face of the wave of arrests and military trials of leading Islamist syndicate figures in 1995 was justified by the left in the name of protecting a promise by the regime to allow more democracy in the future (Baker, 2003: 187–88).

However, changing realities can lead to changes in a political position, albeit tactical and short-term. Historical enemies can learn to work together when the opportunities that this cooperation affords are seen as beneficial for their struggle and long-term objectives. Social movement theory explains cross-ideological cooperation as a response to rising threats or opportunities in which informal organizations tend to come together to derive the most from a certain situation by making use of the information and material resources available to them. Several authors argue that under authoritarian political systems, in particular, opposition movements often consist of loose coalitions comprising diverse social and political groupings (Goodwin, 2001; Schock, 2005). This multivariate nature of opposition movements is the necessary response of weakened civil society and political groups as no single group is sufficiently powerful on its own to resist the regime (Almeida, 2005). This has definitely been true in the case of the Egyptian opposition, whose different streams were largely motivated to cooperate by the realization that they could not independently of each other counter the repression of the regime.

The following two sections focus on the position of the left and the MB in regard to joining forces with each other and with other ideologically opposed groups such as the Nasserists and the liberals. The relationship between the first two groups is singled out for detailed analysis not only because of their historical animosity and fundamentally irreconcilable political projects, but for their active participation in intellectual debate on issues of cross-ideological cooperation, moderation, radicalization, and tactical and strategic thinking prior to and during the actual experience of cooperation. Both camps produced interesting, albeit fragmented, sets of publications which articulated their position on these issues. Neither the Nasserists nor the liberals engaged in such a reflective analysis.

Did the left go right?

From the mid-1970s, the Egyptian left started to become a thoroughly marginalized political force in the country. With Sadat's tactical manipulation of the forces of Islamist resurgence and his policy of alternating between encouraging and repressing Islamist groups, the left became divided between those who sided with the regime and others who simply withdrew from active politics, thus quickly losing its mass support (Howeidy, 2006). The left in Egypt had never managed to present a unified front and by the late 1990s it was divided into several strands, including the Tagamou parliamentary opposition party,[5] the banned Communist Party, the Revolutionary Socialists, El Sha'b (The People), and the Democratic Left. The emergency law had rendered all opposition political parties irrelevant by prohibiting any street gathering. Without the means of establishing any mass base, the left's role in Egyptian opposition politics had thus become negligible. Furthermore, by allegedly striking deals with the regime, Tagamou, the only leftist parliamentary party, further tarnished its image and that of the left in general, thus alienating many potential and actual sympathizers.

It is no small marvel then that despite waning popularity, a lack of credibility and fragmentation, the left still managed to play an active and visible role in the protest movements which swept Egypt from 2000. Leftist activists were at the forefront of marches, sit-ins, rallies and other activities and were also part and parcel of the organization of groups such as EPCSPI, Kefaya, the Cairo Conference and the 9 March Movement among many others. In all these events and forums, they had to coordinate closely with their historical adversaries, including the MB. While the entire spectrum of the Egyptian left participated in the protest events during the decade leading up to the

25 January uprising, the actual task of coordinating activities with the dreaded MB was spearheaded by only a few activists. The RS took the lead in this process under the banner 'With the Islamists, sometimes. With the state, never'. They were accompanied by a number of individuals, such as journalist Adel El-Mashad, the legendary communist lawyer Nabil El-Hillaly and members of the Hisham Mubarak Centre.

A new approach to 'cooperating' with the MB was undoubtedly born out of the opportunities afforded by the return of street politics, burgeoning mobilization and the necessity of sharing the streets with other political groups. Growing unease among members of the left with the 'secular' opposition's silence on the regime's record of violating political liberties and ignoring human rights in curbing the power of Islamists was also a motivation. This new tactic of cooperation was supported by a more conscious analysis of the role of Islamist groups in the political life of the country and a concomitant reappraisal of the relationship of the left with these groups.

In the case of the RS, this analysis drew on Harman's *The Prophet and the Proletariat,* published in 1994, as the basis for revising their theoretical position and strategy in relation to the Islamists. Harman's analysis of the left's perceived 'failure' to deal effectively with the Islamists in the Middle East in general, and Egypt in particular, identifies two opposing approaches. The first is the left's view of Islamism as a fascist movement and a necessarily reactionary force, a position endorsed by many leftists in Egypt and Algeria, for example. In his words, a significant part of the left has regarded the Islamists as 'the most dangerous of all political forces, able to impose a totalitarianism that will prevent any further progressive development' (Harman, 1994: 18). In contrast, another strand within the left in the Middle East has regarded the Islamist revival and the spectrum of organizations promoting an Islamic vision of society and politics as constituting 'progressive' and 'anti-imperialist' movements in favour of the oppressed. This was mainly the position of the left in Iran during the events leading up to the Islamic revolution.

Both approaches, according to Harman, are flawed and mistaken in so far as they 'overrate(s) the cohesion of Islamism and ascribe(s) to it an ability to dictate historical events which in reality it does not have' (ibid.: 70). The major predicament of the first approach is that it often led the left to side with the ruling elite and the regime in repressing these Islamist groups. On the other hand, some leftist analysis of political Islam that naïvely regards Islamist movements as necessarily progressive forces in the struggle against imperialism, fails to offer a critique of these movements. Consequently, as in the case of Iran, the left has sometimes given Islamist movements unconditional support, which has been detrimental to the interests of the working class and other disadvantaged groups in the Middle East. The conclusion which Harman reaches is that the left can neither uncritically support the Islamists nor ally itself with the repressive state against them. However, the left cannot take a neutral stance towards these groups either. Harman (ibid.: 23) articulates the need for a third position in the following passage:

But this does not mean we can simply take an abstentionist dismissive attitude to the Islamists. They grow on the soil of very large social groups that suffer under existing society, and whose feeling of revolt could be tapped for progressive purposes ... many of the individuals attracted to radical versions of Islamism can be influenced by socialists – provided socialists combine complete political independence from all forms of Islamism with a willingness to seize opportunities to draw individual Islamists into genuinely radical forms alongside them.

This analysis was mirrored in the writings of Sameh Naguib (2006, 2009), a founding member of the Revolutionary Socialists, who argues that the Egyptian left had committed a serious mistake in historically regarding Islamists as a static, homogenous, reactionary group fundamentally averse to modernity and democracy. In *The Muslim Brothers: A Socialist Perspective* he even goes so far as to describe the left's alliance with the regime to prevent the MB from attaining power at any cost as 'political suicide' (2006: 40).

On a more pragmatic note, the RS and some other leftists began to argue that they only stood to benefit from working with the more popular Islamists, who had been able to cultivate mass grassroots support from the 1970s. Many leftists became aware that the left could no longer afford to lose even more ground to its opposition rivals by persevering with failed political tactics. The crippling weakness of the left in recent decades was seen as partly the outcome of its absence from the street, while the street presence of the Islamists, and to a lesser extent the Nasserists, has been one of their strengths. The idea was that the left could enhance its popularity by working with the Islamists and Nasserists while simultaneously competing with them for mass support. 'Working alongside these groups gives us visibility and access to the masses ... . If we insist on working on our own, we will remain isolated and irrelevant', explained and warned Yehia Fikry, a founding member of the RS (author interview, Cairo, June 2006).

Leftist activists involved in the process of cooperation went to great lengths to differentiate between their accommodation of the MB as an opposition force on one hand, and their critique of Islamist groups and their conservative project on the other (Naguib, 2006). This, however, did not prevent the opening of a huge rift between the already divided strands of the left. *Bosla*, the newsletter of the Democratic Left, for example, devoted many articles to elaborating a critique of the essentially non-democratic nature of the MB and the threat the group posed to genuine revolutionary movements. The publication contained both implicit and explicit critique of the RS and their approach.[6] Other groups, such as the Maoist Communists, used a much more unforgiving language in criticizing the RS and their cooperation with the MB. In one account, the RS are described as 'agents created and manipulated by the MB in the latter's effort to establish the state of the Supreme Guide'. In another, the RS are seen to 'lead protests not to acquire power – they are incapable of this – but to hand it to suspect and malign forces ... all in the name of democracy and under the banner of power to the people'.[7] Summing up the way RS were perceived by even the most moderate of their critics, De Smet (2012: 247) states that 'in their fervor to correct what they perceived as the sectarian attitude of the "anti-religious" Left, the RS seemed to have bent the stick too much to the other side'.

The MB and the rest

Sadat's strategy of marginalizing Nasserists and leftists, whom he perceived as the main opponents to his neo-liberal economic policies and new political alliance with the US, involved supporting Islamist political forces which had been crushed by Nasser and historically spurned by the left. Islamist groups, including the MB, hence experienced a revival during the 1970s, when they enjoyed relative freedom, enabling them to regain their mass base through building networks within civil society organizations and actively engaging in student politics. After Sadat's assassination, Mubarak's regime continued to alternate between violent repression and relative accommodation in dealing with the MB. As a consequence of this two-pronged approach the MB, in order to evade state repression and seek legitimacy, were pushed to work with groups from different ideological backgrounds by joining alliances. The MB thus found themselves having to work with a larger, more diverse constituency that went well beyond the MB supporters in the professional syndicates that they had dominated since the 1980s.

The regime's crackdown on both rank-and-file members and the leadership of the MB from the early 1990s onwards weakened the group. A wave of arrests and the freezing of assets of the major MB financiers in the 2000s dealt a further major blow to the Brothers. Hence, they hoped to work in the shadow of other groups that enjoyed more legitimacy. Already in the 1980s this had taken the form of electoral alliances. In a bid to gain new ground and enter formal politics, the group cooperated with the liberal Wafd Party and won eight seats in the 1984 parliamentary elections. Later, in 1987, the MB formed a tripartite alliance with the Islamist-oriented Labour Party and the opposition Al-Ahrar Party, with which they shared a joint ticket in parliamentary elections, thereby managing to secure an unprecedented thirty-five seats. However, this option was subsequently closed to the Islamists in 2000, when the State authorities froze the activities of the Labour Party and closed down its newspaper.

The activism of the extra-parliamentary opposition that burgeoned from 2000 was quickly identified as the next space where the MB could forge new alliances. In the elections of 2005 the Brothers achieved an impressive victory, securing 88 seats, over 20 per cent of the total. Nevertheless, leaders of the group insisted that they still needed to work with other smaller opposition groups inside and outside parliament to act as an 'effective democratic opposition force'. According to Ali Abdel Fattah, a leading member of the MB in charge of most cooperation work, it was precisely because of the group's showing in the 2005 parliamentary elections that it needed, more than ever, to find allies in other political opposition groups in order to secure its power as a meaningful opposition force (author interview, Cairo, May 2009).

Some elements of the left articulated an ideological position towards working with Islamists before it was first put to the test during protests in the 2000s. On the other hand, for the MB, the actual involvement in student and associational politics in the 1980s and 1990s was the driving force behind their pragmatic approach to working with members of other political groups. In discussing the MB change in discourse to a language of democracy, pluralism and citizenship in the 2000s, Mona El-Ghobashy argues that this shift mostly came from involvement in actual politics. According to her 'the rules of political engagement hold powerful sway over the behavior and make-up of political actors' (2005: 391). Wickham (2004: 216) concurs with this view and argues that: 'The Islamists initially seized new opportunities for electoral participation not out of a commitment to democracy, but as a means to further their goal of establishing an Islamic state.' Although Wickham goes on to elaborate on how this initial pragmatism evolved into actual moderation through participation, the Muslim Brothers' brief period in power after Mubarak's downfall raises serious questions about this claim. It is true, however, that during this period the MB members became adept at playing the democratic game through the participation of their middle generation in student activism in the 1970s and in most professional syndicates in the 1980s (Baker, 2003; Browers, 2009). This middle generation differed greatly from the older generation, or the 'prison generation' as it is often called, in their outlook and approach. They came to age in the 1970s in the new atmosphere of tolerance towards the group's presence on university campuses; they were spared the prison experience of the previous generation and they had the opportunity to work openly within universities. Wickham (2004: 182) further notes that 'once elected to leadership positions in student government, they successfully cultivated the image of competent administrators'.

While members of the middle generation did not produce an alternative model which could challenge the MB leadership's main positions, they were responsible for the publication of a new, ad hoc literature on democracy, political pluralism and women's rights (Rutherford, 2008; Shehata, 2009). These publications produced a change of discourse that was also motivated by pragmatism. In anticipation of a changing political climate that might allow the MB to form a political party, the group circulated a document outlining its comprehensive socio-economic and political programme in 2004.[8] A running joke among many non-Islamist intellectuals at the time was that most of the group's manifesto was nothing but 'cut and paste' from the ruling NDP programme. While this was meant as a scathing criticism of the MB and their perceived conservative social and economic policies, it was also a reflection of the group's growing use of the language of democracy, freedom and women's and minority rights.

One example of this new discourse was a quote in the London-based *Al-Hayat* newspaper by a leading figure of the MB Guidance Office, who stated that, in the current situation, the main priority was not sharia but democracy and that 'the gravity of the situation has reduced rifts between different political trends to this old-new common ground' (Naguib, 2006). A 2003 report by the International Crisis Group showed similar arguments used by the Brothers. In a public lecture at the American University in Cairo in 2006, Mohamed Habib, deputy supreme guide, stated that the MB believed in the right of all political groups, including communists, to take part equally in open political contestation and to create their own political parties. This change of discourse was also used very strategically. The middle generation leaders of the MB realized that they stood to benefit from transforming their discourse to a more inclusive one. Ali Abdel Fattah explained how broadening the slogans under which the group worked meant that the group could get much wider support for its cause beyond its immediate supporters:

> For example, campaigning against police torture as a matter of principle meant that activists from across the political spectrum could join and create a larger, more effective political campaign. But since we are the ones who suffer most from police torture, we would be the first to benefit from such a campaign, although it is not articulated specifically to support the MB.
>
> (author interview, Cairo, May 2009)

The intellectual debate which formed the background to this change in discourse, and it remained at the level of discourse, was reinforced by the rise of the 'New Islamist Trend', which represented a group of Islamist intellectuals who regarded their school of thought as an outgrowth of the centrist Islamic *Wasateya*, or middle ground. In doing this, they attempted to distinguish their position from extremist Islamist tendencies (Browers, 2009: 49). One of their leading figures, Kamal Abu al-Magd, published what came to be the group's manifesto, a pamphlet entitled *A Contemporary Islamic Vision*, in 1991. Other members of this loosely formed group, such as moderate Islamist thinkers Howeidy and Omarah, articulated their ideas in widely distributed Egyptian newspapers. They engaged with the concept of democracy which they regarded as offering the best means of achieving justice in the modern world (Baker, 2003: 171). More significantly, they also articulated a view of community that goes beyond the traditional understanding of an *umma* consisting exclusively of Muslims to one that creates space for accommodating liberal notions of democracy, pluralism and citizenship (Browers, 2009: 5). Strongly influenced by the New Islamist Trend, as well as other non-Islamist writers, the Wasat (Centre) Party was formed in 1996 by members who broke away from the MB, Copts and individuals from other backgrounds. The party's ideas were more in line with the New Islamic Trend, which contrasted with mainstream, conservative MB politics.

This intellectual debate, the formation of the Wasat Party and more importantly, the experience of the middle generation within student unions and professional syndicates were all precursors to the cooperation between the MB and other political groups in the protest movement of the 2000s. While the growing cooperation with other political streams since the second Palestinian Intifada would not have been possible without the endorsement of the MB leadership, it was the Brothers' youth generation that pioneered this facet of the new MB political strategy. Tutored by the middle generation and adopting its pragmatic approach, members of the youth generation, who became active in university politics in the 1990s, took the initiative in sowing the seeds of this cooperation. At the encouragement of their 'supervisors', the MB students started to seek out students from other political groups, which initially proved difficult due to the almost total invisibility of politically active non-Islamist students. Towards this end, the MB students developed a coordination committee which was solely responsible for cross-political coordination. The first group which the MB approached was the Revolutionary Socialists but later coordination continued with Nasserists, the Al Ghad Party, Kefaya and 6 April. Mohamed Osman, MB supervisor of Cairo and Ain Shams university students, sums up the reasons for this experience:

> We were encouraged by our university leaders to seek this form of cooperation for a very pragmatic reason: to lessen the relentless pressure of the state security on our students. However, for us, we saw it as a means for creating a more moderate wing and as a tool to isolate more radical voices in our midst. We could afford to be the ones to take this initiative because we were much larger and stronger than any other student activists. They could not in any way pose a threat to us and we had nothing to lose from going down this road.
>
> (author interview, Cairo, May 2011)

After graduation and with the outbreak of protests in Egypt, the youth of the MB continued to be at the forefront of the coordination. The more typically conservative attitudes of the leadership also led to the rise of a growing critical voice articulated by the youth which continued well after the January 2011 uprising. Many reports of dissension within the Muslim Brothers started to come into the open after 2000. For example, one Muslim Brother resigned from the organization, blaming the stifling of free thinking and progressive ideas, while another member published an article in which he attacked the, now late, supreme guide Maamoun Al Hodeibi on similar grounds. In 2002, an open letter to *Al-Hayat* published by a group of young MB members questioned the leadership's compliance with state security and demanded more involvement of the organization in public events and street protests (Naguib, 2006).

Apart from the efforts of the MB youth, the pragmatism of the MB in modifying their public discourse should not be taken as a genuine commitment to the principles of democracy and inclusiveness it proclaimed. The group's leadership remained firmly intolerant of any form of dissent. Members who wished to propose a different approach to the group's general line were forced to resign from the group and to seek alternative forums. This was the case, for example, for those who founded the Wasat Party. Later, the youth wing of the MB, which took the lead in participating in the 25 January uprising, was expelled from the MB for its criticism of the leadership. It subsequently formed the Tayaar Masry (Egyptian Current) political party and participated in the 2012 elections as part of the Revolution Continues coalition.

Unlike the left and the MB, other political actors, such as the Nasserists and the liberals, for example the Ghad Party, had not articulated an analytical position on cooperation. They were willing to cooperate out of the simple pragmatic realization that under the repressive measures of Mubarak's regime and the ensuing stifling political environment, no political group could succeed in challenging the regime alone. For example, while the Nasserist Karama members expressed major reservations regarding the Brothers' stances on women, Copts and issues of social justice, their leader argued that 'we have to work with them because at this particular moment in history, no individual faction can work on its own in fighting for the nationalist demands that we all have in common, such as democracy' (Hamdin Sabahi, author interview, Cairo, May 2006).

Principles of cooperation: between consensus and independence

The wave of cooperation in the 2000s was characterized by a conscious, pragmatic view of its participants of the short-term, tactical nature of working together. None of the participants entertained ideas of a long-term, broadly-based coalition. Precisely because of this naked realism, cooperation was able to survive in the multiple networks and umbrellas of activism. The space created by the political opposition with its myriad protest activities from 2000 never in actuality witnessed the formation of a coalition of political forces acting together in unity. Even so, cooperation between the traditional enemies of the political opposition was no easy process. When analysing global protest networks, Mayo (2005) notes that a generally agreed goal and a common enemy do not *per se* help in bridging the varying perspectives or organizational styles of the participating groups. This was certainly true in the case of Egypt, where principles of cooperation had to be agreed upon after difficult negotiation and then tightly monitored by all involved.

Two basic principles underlay any negotiation of joint activities: consensus and independence. In the organization of any form of action, such as a demonstration, a conference or the issuing of a statement, representatives based their final agreement on consensus and not on the view of the majority. For example, activists preparing for a demonstration had to follow the rule of thumb that all sectarian slogans had to be avoided. Only chants and slogans that did not openly disparage the ideas or even offend the sensibilities of any of the participants could be adopted. For instance, the well-known slogan of the Islamists: *Khaibar Khaibar* ('Oh Jews, Mohammed's army will be back'), which was often enthusiastically endorsed by the nationalist Nasserists, but deeply abhorred by the left, was eliminated at all jointly organized demonstrations. The contentious issue of suicide bombers was, for a time, another theme which had to be resolved through consensus. Wael Khalil, of the RS, explained that:

> since there could be no agreement on this issue (some regard Palestinian suicide bombers as martyrs and heroes while others see them as detrimental to the Palestinian people's cause) and no consensus could be reached, we agreed not to include it in any of our slogans, statements or public discussions. We only do what we can agree upon even if the majority wants to advocate a particular position.
>
> (author interview, Cairo, June 2004)

Earlier on, within the EPCSPI, another divisive issue was how to respond to the events of 11 September. A leftist activist and founding member of the committee, Adel El-Mashad, explained in an interview with *Al-Ahram Weekly* in 2002 that

> after 9/11 some of us felt we should issue an announcement extending our condolences to the families of those who died and explaining the general context of the crisis. Others among our ranks opposed the idea. In the end we issued nothing.

Many issues which could undermine the fragile alliance and the possibility of further cooperative work had to be dropped. Avoiding these important issues could be very frustrating to many participants, who did not always want to compromise on their priorities. In the same interview, El-Mashad points out that this problem is not unique to Egypt:

> Many international movements – such as the anti-globalisation movement – face this quandary. Either to limit their ranks to like-minded people, or to open up and incorporate all different views and live with the difference. We have chosen the second option, and we feel that it is more productive, even if on certain issues we are unable to take a collective stand.

The second principle of cooperation was that all groups, while seeking consensus, would maintain their independence. One of the major tactics that these global coalitions adopt, and which clearly applies to the Egyptian case, is the development of a means of ensuring 'cooperative differentiation', whereby they 'maintain a public face of solidarity towards the movement's

targets while differentiating themselves in communications with their constituencies' (Bandy and Smith, 2005: 10). This allows for diverse political
groups with different ideological leanings, class interests, and long-term projects to work together. Such alliances usually begin, and often continue, as
short-term, ad hoc collaborative efforts with specific aims (ibid.: 3).

For leftists, the experience was explained in terms of working 'alongside'
rather than 'with' the Islamists or the Nasserists. Naguib, of the RS, stressed
that the objective of joint activism is not 'programmatic cooperation' or
reaching a 'third way' (author interview, Cairo, May 2006). According to
Sabahi, the aim was to undertake 'coordinated work for particular short-term
missions and specific demands' (author interview, Cairo, June 2006). In all
jointly organized demonstrations of recent years, the participants consistently
emphasized this principle of independence. While activists chanted the same
slogans during demonstrations, individual banners and pamphlets distributed
by each group expressed their different politics. A telling motto of the activists
was 'one voice and similar demands but diverse political programmes'.

Cooperation not conciliation

Managing cooperation in joint action was a very time- and energy-consuming
task for activists. Simple, logistical steps in the planning of demonstrations,
rallies and conferences, such as the order of speakers, the choice of slogans
acceptable to all, and male/female separation in some demonstrations, could
become highly contentious terrain. However, these were mere nuisances. Serious conflict within the process of joint coordination was of a much more
fundamental nature.

The most divisive issue over which even short-term, tactical coalitions
stumbled was the desired level of confrontation of the regime and its security
apparatus. For the left, the Nasserists, and youth groups from across the
political spectrum, the radicalization effect of the Second Palestinian Intifada
and the ensuing revival of street politics was an opportunity to expand the
boundaries of confrontation with the regime. Activists seized the chance to
increase the ceiling of political demands and to take their struggle out onto
the streets. The MB, on the other hand, is an organization with a track record
of political horse-trading and behind-the-scenes deals as part of its concilia-
tion with the Sadat and Mubarak regimes. Members of the group were much
more reluctant to openly challenge the government by taking to the street at
every opportunity. This fundamental difference in strategy raised any number
of tensions between the MB and rival groups. For instance, during a number
of pro-Palestinian protests in 2000, when groups of leftist activists clashed
with the state security and burned a number of police vehicles, members of
the MB denounced this action as 'socialist sabotage'. In subsequent events,
Islamist university students often attempted to physically restrain classmates
from marching outside campus walls (El-Hamalawy, 2002). Similarly, in 2002,
the Committee for the Defence of Democracy, which spearheaded a petition

campaign against renewal of the emergency law, consisted of five human rights organizations and four opposition parties: the Wafd, the Nasserists, the leftist Tagamou and the banned Communist Party. The MB were conspicuous by their absence. The Brothers' absence from one of the committee's conferences was blamed on the group's lack of commitment to the common cause.[9] On another occasion, the MB enraged other activists by taking part in an 'official' demonstration at the Cairo stadium which had been sanctioned by the government during the first week of the war in Iraq. The Brothers participated in full force in the event, accepting the government's condition not to raise any anti-government banners or slogans that demanded political freedom.

Members of the MB denied all allegations of complicity and pointed to the extremely high price they had paid throughout their history. They explained their reluctance on some occasions to take to the streets and to join in chants against Mubarak by name on a number of grounds, including the reformist philosophy of the organization and the particular training they receive which is inspired by Hassan El-Banna's ideas. As Sameh Al-Barqi, an active member of the MB youth wing during the 2000s, explains:

> We believe in reform and gradualist change. This is the core of the MB philosophy and we translate it into action by calculating the steps we take in our battles. Other groups, like Kefaya, wanted immediate change. It is not always useful for the cause to create unnecessary confrontations. We also receive a very strict training in the ideas of El Banna which discourage attacking the person of an individual. We conceive of a battle against systems and not individuals.
>
> (author interview, Cairo, June 2011)

But as the struggle intensified and protests multiplied and expanded, the youth of the MB put more pressure on their leadership to become more engaged with street protests and to show more commitment to the joint struggle. Al-Barqi continues to argue that the MB, under pressure from their youth, 'were much more flexible than we got credit for; we later joined in in open condemnation of Mubarak as the head of the system'.

For their part, members of the MB often complained about the way they were treated by their supposed partners in the struggle as ready 'contractors' who could be relied on to bring large numbers to rallies and protests. 'Without being involved in the preliminary preparations for events, whether they were rallies or protests, we would be given short notice when asked to show up for the day and mobilize our members to participate' said Ali Abdel Fatah (author interview, Cairo, April 2010). Considering the weight of the MB as a political group, this attitude was regarded as an affront, while claims that the Brothers were cooperating as equal partners were doubted by more suspicious MB members who harboured reservations about this cooperation in the first place.

Tensions over fundamental principles within joint activism also arose between leftist activists and their Nasserist counterparts. According to Yehia Fikry (author interview, Cairo, September 2006), the main problem the RS encountered in its dealings with the Nasserists was that:

> they are all replicas of Gamal Abdel Nasser. They want to run the world around them like Nasser did; to have one large coalition under their control with only symbolic and meaningless representation of other political and social forces.

The annual Cairo Conference was a good example of these attempts by the Nasserists to dominate the opposition movement. The conference, which had been co-organized for five years by Nasserists, leftists and the Muslim Brothers, was a site of intense disagreement and difficult negotiations revolving around power struggles. For instance, the Nasserists always pushed to have one of their representatives give the opening speech while also trying to get some of their members who had Islamic leanings to represent the Islamist camp instead of members of the Muslim Brothers. In the predominantly Nasserist group Kefaya, Nasserists were seen to take advantage of their majority in the group to marginalize supposed partners, mostly the Brothers. According to members of the RS, the Nasserist Karama group wanted all forms of protest and activism to be under the banner of the Nasserist-dominated Kefaya – an all-too-painful reminder of the workings of the Arab Socialist Union (ASU) that had been established by Nasser after he had banned all political parties. The main concern of Nasser's regime was to achieve national unity. This notion of unity precluded any form of organization in society other than the government-directed party, which was viewed as the living symbol of the unity of the nation (Choueiri, 2000; Dessouki, 1994).

> While the limited participation and representation granted to the left in Kefaya was a good achievement for the left considering its relatively small presence on the ground, it was laughable for the Muslim Brotherhood in light of their massive popularity and ability to mobilize the Egyptian street.
>
> (Fikry, author interview, Cairo 2006)

Agreeing with this analysis, Mohamed Osman from the MB argues that the heart of the matter is that Nasserists 'hold on to bygone days of power and mental frameworks' (author interview, Cairo, April 2011).

Members of the Nasserist Karama Party found it easier to work jointly with the leftists and the communists, whom they regarded as closer to their own programme and principles in terms of ideology and modes of thinking. Conversely, the experience of coordinating with the Muslim Brothers was very frustrating not only because of the totally different and conflicting political programmes and policies but largely because the Karama regarded the

Brothers as fundamentally 'authoritarian in their work, having no room for differences, blindly obeying the leadership, and being very rigid in their thinking and dealings with the outside world' (Siham Negm, author interview, Cairo, June 2006). Members of the Karama deeply believed that the participation of the Brothers in a broad coalition movement needed to be restricted. They feared the disastrous effects that the Brothers dominating the movement could have, in particular helping to bring them to power. Karama members further believed that the political repression which Egypt experienced under the Mubarak regime would be much worse if the Brothers were actually to gain power. In any case, the Nasserists regarded a theocracy as dictatorial by definition because of the theological references which the Islamists would use to justify their unilateral actions and to suppress their opponents once in power (ibid.).

A significant effect of the joint activism was to deepen internal rifts within the ranks of the different participating groups. On the left, the old guard, certain groups and individuals became increasingly critical of comrades who were seeking to cooperate with the Islamists. Members of most leftist groups, such as the Democratic Left and the Egyptian Communist Party, had never been reconciled to the presence in a progressive coalition of the Muslim Brothers, who they viewed as a reactionary bastion and the antithesis of democracy. Similarly, a considerable number of MB leaders and activists did not see the advantage of working with groups so different in their ideology and political outlook. Members of the old guard were split on the issue of cooperation and many regarded it as potentially threatening to the group's unity and power (Mohamed Osman, MB youth activist, author interview, Cairo, May 2011). The MB continued to organize their own political activities without extending an invitation to other political groups and even held events parallel to those organized jointly by the left and other groups. One example is a demonstration organized on 15 February 2003 by the banned Labour Party and the Muslim Brothers, which had previously been electoral allies, to protest against the imminent US war in Iraq, while at the same time, another broadly-based demonstration was held on the other side of Cairo protesting on the same issue.

From short-term cooperation to broadly-based alliances

The short-term, tactical cooperation between unlikely bedfellows served a clear function during the last decade of Mubarak's rule. Where successive authoritarian regimes had for decades successfully weakened political opposition forces through a mix of tactics including co-optation, divide and rule, repressive legal measures and the use of naked violence, the divided and weak opposition could only sustain protest movements against the regime by swelling their numbers in the form of alliances. For example, Kefaya's ability to transcend traditional boundaries and break taboos in Egyptian politics would not have been possible had the group relied on a narrow ideological base to mobilize supporters. Similarly, the visibility achieved by elements of the left, which was greatly disproportionate to their actual numbers of supporters, would have been unlikely had they continued to work in isolation. Furthermore, the evolution of professional groups such as judges, engineers, nurses and civil servants into such stout critics of the regime, as discussed in previous chapters, would have been negligible had they relied on the support of members of a single political stream. The confluence of energies of different political groups made it possible for activists to muster sufficient strength to create the context for the eventual downfall of Mubarak.

These coalitions, however, were short-term, tactical formations rather than long-term strategic alliances. They did not demand any meaningful compromises over fundamental issues or require working together towards long-term strategic goals. With the downfall of Mubarak and the advent of a new political phase, mostly dominated by the military, these old coalitions became irrelevant. Only days into the January uprisings, new coalitions and alliances between unexpected players were quickly being forged.

The MB and post-Mubarak alliances

As discussed in the previous chapter, after Mubarak's downfall the MB managed to win a majority in every election bar one – the first Lower House election, where they needed the Salafis' support to constitute a majority. The Islamists' control of the presidency and both houses of parliament confirmed them as the dominant political force. Once in power, and emboldened by its electoral victory, the MB promptly shunned all their former allies and refused to engage in any meaningful consultation on fundamental issues. The Brothers ignored calls to create a broadly-based consensus that could result in the creation of a new political force capable of representing wide sections of Egyptians. Applying their usual pragmatism, the MB quickly sought new allies whom they regarded as more useful in promoting the Brothers' interests and cementing their power. After February 2012, the MB swiftly turned towards new and, in some ways, even more unlikely bedfellows: the Salafis and the military.

The most unusual alliance the MB undertook in the post-Mubarak era was that with the Salafis, an umbrella of several factions and groups, with which they shared more mutual animosity than the common Islamist label could hide. After historically being vehemently opposed to participating in formal politics, Salafi groups rapidly became politicized in the aftermath of the 25 January uprising, forming several political parties.[10] The Nour Party, in particular, won a considerable number of seats in both houses of parliament. They cooperated very closely with the MB for a short period during the drafting of the 2012 constitution. However, the fragile partnership buckled very quickly as the MB swiftly marginalized their unlikely new partner, causing its leader, Younis Makhyon, to publicly accuse the MB of implementing a 'Brotherhoodization' of the state – a term used to describe attempts by the MB to take over state institutions while rendering all other forces irrelevant (Al-Anani and Malik, 2013). The two groups became locked in a vicious media campaign for months in which each tried to undermine the other. As a result, the Nour Party was more than willing to support the military coup in the summer of 2013 that ousted President Morsi and to agree to its complex roadmap (ibid.). In doing so, the Nour Party leaders were hoping that this support would secure their future as a political player in the next phase and enable them to emerge victorious as the leaders of the Islamist camp.

While it was under SCAF that thousands of members of former jihadi groups, such as al-Gamaa al-Islamiyya, were released from prison and returned from exile (Adib, 2011), the MB also extended a hand to these groups. Some of the former jihadi leaders, such as El-Zomor, who was involved in the assassination of Sadat, actually became regular participants in public debates and television talk shows during Morsi's abortive term in office. However, this warm relation with jihadi groups was a strategic error that led to mounting accusations of the group's endorsement of violence, thus hurting the MB more than providing them with any political advantage (El-Houdaiby, 2013). Violent attacks in 2013 against Copts, the military and various state targets amongst others were easily blamed on the MB by association despite the fact that the group suffered from an absence of leaders who would have been able to concert such action after the massive wave of arrests following the military coup.

Equally remarkable was the Brothers' brief, yet intense, honeymoon with the military. Realizing that their grip on power could only be secured by the backing of the military, the effective ruler of the country since the downfall of Mubarak, the MB entered into an unholy alliance with the generals. This alliance manifested itself in several ways, not least of which was the Brothers' tacit support for the military's violent crackdown on protestors including the bloody assaults in Mohamed Mahmood street, outside the Parliament and in the Maspero massacre of unarmed Coptic demonstrators. Not only did the MB refrain from opposing any of this violence, they went so far as to openly attack any critics of the military. In December 2012, an MB member filed a lawsuit against the RS for holding a public talk in which the speakers severely criticized SCAF (Eskandar, 2013). More importantly, the MB cooperated with the military during the post-Mubarak transitional period in producing a constitution that guarantees the military's unparalleled powers and protects its corporate empire.

Despite historical animosity, working with the MB was necessary from the military's perspective for two reasons. Firstly, as the most organized political group with a strong mass base that underpins its electoral power, the MB could not be ignored as a major player. Secondly, after the ousting of Mubarak and dissolution of the NDP, the military's main interest was to find a reliable partner that would be able to secure not only the interests of the military establishment but also help maintain the foundations of the *ancien régime*. Basically, the military wanted to continue its role of ruling the country but behind the scenes without having to do the 'dirty' business of actually running the government. It therefore needed a political partner to provide a civilian face to run the country in its favour in exchange for protecting its privileged position. This civilian partner would also deflect criticism from the military's Western allies who wanted to see a 'democratic', non-military government in post-Mubarak Egypt. Initially, the military regarded the MB as a useful partner. With their conservative approach to economic and political matters, the MB proved their credentials by passing anti-labour laws and keeping the security apparatus untouched – in fact increasing the budget of the ministry of the interior. They also continued negotiations with the IMF and other bilateral donors to further entrench neoliberal policies, ignoring calls to restructure wages. Furthermore, the MB rejected any prospect for national reconciliation programmes or transitional justice to redress the legacy of violence and human rights abuse that took place both during and after the uprising. Moreover, the MB had long accepted and expressed their complete commitment to international agreements, including the Camp David peace treaty with Israel, a red line for the military establishment.

However, the military soon realized that the MB, despite their electoral success, were able neither to provide a stable political environment nor form a political consensus capable of securing the necessary support for their policies in the country as a whole. The MB were fast losing their position. The so-called 'Brotherhoodization' policy which saw the group pack as many of its members as possible into top positions in different state institutions such as government ministries, the diplomatic corps and local government, alienated friends and enraged foes.[11] Morsi's constitutional declaration of 22 November 2012 was, however, the main blow to any hopes of the Brothers' willingness to govern within a genuine democratic and widely-accepted framework. The declaration granted Morsi far-reaching powers and prevented the Islamist-dominated constituent assembly from being dissolved by the judiciary. Pleas from the opposition to correct the biased nature of the assembly were ignored, which led to the withdrawal of Christian, liberal and other non-Islamist representatives.

The Muslim Brothers made grave miscalculations during their brief period in power. The group overestimated its ability to impose its sectarian vision and anchor its power across all state institutions without first establishing a country-wide consensus. It erroneously assumed that its position as the largest party in the lower house of parliament (but without a majority on its own) meant that the country was behind this grab for absolute power. Moreover, the MB ignored the fact that Morsi only garnered about a quarter of the vote in the first round of the presidential election and was narrowly elected largely by default as many non-Islamists wanted to keep out the former regime's candidate. The MB leadership's lack of commitment to or indeed apparent understanding of genuine democratic institutions and practices meant that it felt it had been given a green light to do as it pleased without consultation, let alone cooperation, to achieve a more broadly-based consensus.

Furthermore, the MB overestimated their power over the military and their ability to control state institutions, given that the state bureaucracy has always been hostile to the group. Just as easily as the military had abandoned Mubarak when he proved to be a liability, the generals had no qualms about sacrificing the MB. The failure of the MB to create a broadly-based consensus on the nature of their rule was key to the ease with which the military could depose Morsi and his government in July 2013.

Old men in grey suits and their 'revolutionary' alliances

Mohamed Morsi's constitutional declaration of November 2012 created anger across the political spectrum and led to a wave of popular protest. As a reaction to MB rule in general and the constitutional declaration in particular, a new political coalition was born. The National Salvation Front (NSF) was launched two days after the declaration in an attempt to bring together the fractious opposition forces against the perceived power grab of the MB with Morsi at the helm. The NSF was the most serious attempt by opposition forces to create a political alliance since the parliamentary elections of 2012. The immediate demands of the Front were the retraction of the constitutional declaration, the formation of a new, more representative constituent assembly and the issuing of a law for transitional justice. The NSF included groups from across the political spectrum such as the Wafd, the Egyptian Social Democratic Party, the Nasserist Democratic Party, Tagamou, Free Egyptians and the Egyptian Popular Current among others. The three main leaders of the NSF, who greeted TV cameras on behalf of the opposition and raised hopes for revolutionary change, had come of age during the Nasser and Sadat era: Sabahi, a politician and staunch member of the opposition against Sadat and Mubarak; Amr Moussa, who had occupied top official positions for over a decade as a solid pillar of the Mubarak regime and El-Baradei, who was projected by many as the 'leader' of the pro-democracy movement (see Chapter 4).

Along with other groups, the NSF called for mass protests against the declaration. Tens of thousands took to the street in the following days, which resulted in deadly clashes between pro- and anti-Morsi supporters, especially at the Ittihadiya presidential palace (Hussein and Black, 2012). However, a causal link between the call for protest and the actual pouring of people onto the streets is very doubtful. The protests were much more spontaneous than the NSF leaders would have liked to believe. For a while, the NSF was seen as a welcome effort to unite the divided opposition but it had no links with the Egyptian masses except for the support its individual groups had among certain constituencies. Furthermore, the Front was eyed with suspicion by many supporters of the individual groups constituting the NSF. Many followers of centre-left groups, for example, were critical of the presence of Amr Moussa, who was considered to be a member of the *foloul,* remnants of the Mubarak regime. On the right, there was discontent within the ranks of the Wafd Party

youth, who objected to their party being allied with the Nasserist Popular Current led by Sabahi. They subsequently called on their leader to team up only
with political groups with similar ideological stands (Ahram Online, 2013).

Apart from their opposition to MB rule and Morsi's declaration, the partners within the NSF had nothing in common. They had different ideological
positions and could not agree on even the most basic tactics. They also found
it difficult to establish one clear-cut position on various issues. For example, the
NSF first called upon the electorate to boycott the referendum on the constitution before changing its position by asking people to go out and vote 'no'.
They also declared their intention of running as a coalition in the legislative
elections before subsequently announcing uncertainty about this course of
action. This indecision reflected deep internal disagreements which seemed, if
anything, to weaken and fragment the opposition even further.

More divisions were evident during the NSF leaders' meeting with an IMF
delegation to discuss a government loan request of $4.8 billion. On one hand,
Badawi, head of the right-wing Wafd, adopted the government's position in
declaring that the need for the loan was a matter of urgent necessity. The
Nasserist Sabahi, however, raised serious concerns about the effects of the
loan on the poor and on the issue of subsidies (Mustafa, 2013).

The final blow to NSF unity came with divisions over the military coup
and the heavy-handed clearing of MB supporters from two protest camps in
which almost one thousand people were killed in the summer of 2013. In a
move much criticized by supporters and opponents alike, El-Baradei resigned
from his position as interim vice president for international relations in protest against the violent crackdown against the MB demonstrators. Badawi, on
the other hand, championed the military and announced that the NSF would
back al-Sisi if he decided to run for president. The official statement of the
NSF was staggering:

> The NSF salutes the police and military forces, and bows its head in tri-
> bute and respect for the great people, imposing their will of complete
> victory and continuing to strive for a constitution befitting a civilized
> Egypt, rising to a bright future … . Glory to the people, to the great
> army and to the courageous police.[12]

The pitiful performance of the NFS coupled with the tragic polarization of
the country in the aftermath of the military coup in July 2013 resulted in a
growing process of soul searching among many. In one instance, it led to the
formation of yet another initiative: the Revolutionary Path Front (RPF).[13]
The Front, also known as 'Revolutionaries', was launched by groups of like-
minded individuals, mostly from the left, in order to 'struggle alongside the
people for radical reforms, especially the redistribution of wealth for the benefit
of the Egyptian people, the poor and the downtrodden; for the building of a
popular participatory democracy'. The focus on common principles rather
than the common enemy is what sets this experiment apart from previous

coalitions. The RPF is quite negligible in terms of numbers and any mass influence; it might continue for a bit longer, develop into something more resilient or it might disappear from the political scene altogether. However, the RPF hoped to represent a move towards a realistic conception of coordination among groups with a radical agenda in the hope of combining their efforts.

The example the NFS set with its knee-jerk reactions to fast-changing events, the coming together of disparate opposition groups to face a common enemy and the absence of a clear, shared project has proven the irrelevance of models carried over from the Mubarak era. Coalitions fashioned on these principles have been unable to afford sustainable, effective political forms in the completely different context after the uprising. If anything, the rush of progressive forces to join liberal and right-wing groups to confront the Islamist forces has impeded the development of a revolutionary project. This also helps to explain the ease with which counter-revolutionary forces have undermined the revolutionary process since the 25 January uprising.

Notes

1 Not to be confused with the Freedom and Justice Party formed by the MB after the downfall of Mubarak.
2 The Preparatory Committee for the National Committee of Students, for example, had representation from almost all political groups on campus including the liberal Wafdists, Marxists, Muslim Brothers, Young Egypt, the Nationalist Party and the Student Union of Secondary Schools among others. The National Committee of Workers and Students was the most prominent of all committees created during this period and brought together the liberal Wafdists, nationalists, communists and trade unionists. For more details on coalition-building among students, see Abdallah (1985).
3 Abu al-Fotouh resigned from the MB a few months after the ousting of Mubarak in order to run for president, which the MB had forbidden any of its members to do in an alleged deal with the military at the time.
4 For a history of the bitter struggle between the MB and the left over the definition and direction of the labour movement, see Goldberg (1986).
5 The Popular Unionist Party, Tagamou, has often been dubbed the 'government left' because of its conciliatory approach to the regime.
6 See issues of *Elbosla* at http://elbosla.org.
7 See the webpage of the Communist Maoists at https://www.facebook.com/commaoist.
8 For an English translation of the programme, see the Muslim Brothers' official website at http://www.ikhwanweb.com/article.php?id=811.
9 For more details on this rift between the left and the Brothers, see El-Hamalawy (2002).
10 For a discussion of Salafist groups, their history and position towards political participation, see Meijer (2009) and Al-Anani and Malik (2013).
11 For details of the Muslim Brothers' efforts to appoint their members to a variety of state institutions, see Ezzat (2013) and El-Sheikh (2013).
12 For an English translation of the full statement, see Mikail (2013): http://nilerevolt. wordpress.com/2013/08/14/statement-by-the-national-salvation-front/?utm_content=b uffer56fc9&utm_source=buffer&utm_medium=twitter&utm_campaign=Buffer.
13 For the English translation of the founding statement of the Front, see 'A Revolutionary Front in Egypt' (*Socialist Worker*, 2013).

6   In struggle, divided we stand

Prior to the 25 January uprising, cross-ideological cooperation, joint coordination of activities and cross-fertilization among different groups of activists remained firmly within the boundaries of the middle-class pro-democracy movement. There was no such cooperation within the labour and citizen-based currents of mobilization. Moreover, there was not even meaningful contact between the three streams of mobilization identified in this book, let alone a serious attempt at coordination of activities. The inability to merge the forces engendered by the different struggles under a more broadly-based, cross-sectorial front remains one of the main stumbling blocks to the emergence of a strong revolutionary force. Egypt's different strands of mobilization have remained divided and unable to act as a collective force since the downfall of Mubarak. One of the main lines of fissure is whether the 'economic' or the 'political' sphere constitutes the core of revolutionary struggle. This split has its lineage in the Mubarak era, when workers, farmers and other groups of protesting citizens were portrayed by most of the rest of society, including the pro-democracy movement, as being engaged in narrowly focused struggles for economic demands such as salary increases and access to social provisions. On the other hand, pro-democracy activists were seen, and saw themselves, as striving solely for political liberties and rights. An emphasis on the conceptual unity of the two was missing from most analysis. In the field, very little coordination was taking place between the different struggles beyond symbolic, limited gestures.

In 2008, a small number of activists were already beginning to realize the grave implications of this fragmentation in their fight against the dominant neoliberal order. Nevertheless, the course taken to redress this divide was limited to isolated initiatives and remained ineffective at the time. Since January 2011, no breakthrough has taken place along these lines, to say the least. The Egyptian ruling elite have ensured that none was forthcoming by employing every tactic available to them to drive a wedge and accentuate the supposed differences between 'political' and 'economic' activism. Through their control of legal and media institutions, the military, the Muslim Brothers and capital have set out to deepen this split in the minds of the general public. In particular, protests for 'economic' demands are portrayed not only as peripheral to the course of the revolution but also as a threat to its success. Economic demands and struggles to achieve them are shown as greedy, individualistic and harmful to the economy.

The previous two chapters have explored important challenges facing Egypt's revolutionary forces that can be traced to the experience of activists under Mubarak. The analysis has focused on the nature of social movement strategies and tactics adopted by the activists and how these have severely limited the room for manoeuvre in the post-Mubarak phase. This chapter explores a third challenge that has also undermined the potential of a revolutionary project. Unlike the other two challenges, the questions of organization and coalition-building, the challenge of overcoming the tension between economic and political activism is not simply the outcome of failing strategies and tactics characteristic of new social movements. In the words of Laclau and Mouffe, it is more a 'structural effect of the capitalist state' (1985: 9) and, indeed, one of the mechanisms it employs to maintain its dominance.

Economic struggle *is* political

A compartmentalization of different forms of resistance, by analysts and activists alike, based on the content of their demands, assumes an impossibly neat separation between economic and political struggles. This understanding is born out of a narrow conception of the political sphere and overlooks a theoretical tradition that demonstrates the interconnectedness of the two spheres in which, from Marx to Polanyi, the economic sphere had always been theorized as embedded in the social and political spheres in capitalist societies. Wood (1981: 2) does well to remind us how political Marxism illustrates that the economic sphere rests firmly on the political where the 'disposition of power between the individual capitalist and workers has as its condition the political configuration of society as a whole'. She elaborates how in this analysis the 'base' and 'superstructure' cannot be viewed as compartments or 'regionally' separated spheres 'but rather a continuous structure of social relations and forms' (ibid.: 6).

One of the reasons labour protests are often regarded as separate from larger struggles for political change is rooted in the nature of the capitalist production system. As Wood (ibid.: 14) puts it: 'Class conflict in capitalism is ... encapsulated within the individual unit of production. ... Each individual plant, a highly organised and integrated unity with its own hierarchy and structure of authority, contains within it the main source of class conflict.' This tends to make class struggle in capitalism '*local* and *particularistic*'. In the same vein, Eckstein (1989: 13) elaborates how 'labour's anger typically is directed at their bosses, whom they believe to be oppressing them, not at broad invisible forces like capitalism or distant agents of capitalism, like banks, which may ultimately be responsible for their plight.' Workers expressing anger at the immediate level against their direct superiors does not, however, make their struggles non-political. The so-called 'economism' of working-class attitudes does not so much reflect a lack of political consciousness as an objective shift in the location of 'politics' (Wood, 1981: 14).

Under authoritarian regimes in particular, even the smallest of workers' protests is indeed political. While El-Mahdi (2012) speaks of the effect of a rise in class consciousness within the labour movement under Mubarak, Beinin (2011: 184) argues that 'in an authoritarian state the capacity to organise anything is a political challenge to the regime'. Returning to examine the nature of the demands of previously discussed groups, such as workers, farmers and unorganized groups of citizens, easily shows their overtly political character.

Blocking roads, occupying factories and jamming government offices to demand salary increases, access to potable water, effective rubbish collection and provision of medication for long-suffering patients by disempowered and marginalized groups, rather than by seasoned activists, are political acts that bolster political demands more than anything else. In the absence of any legal channel of political representation through which different groups in society can delegate democratically elected representatives to negotiate their demands, Egypt's disenfranchised have been attempting to represent their own interests directly. They have been putting pressure on the state and demanding that state institutions react, though this pressure is often unsuccessful. More than simply demanding the satisfaction of basic needs, Egyptians have been bringing the state and its agents to account and putting pressure on its institutions to respond in the only way that is left open to them. On a daily basis, these demands have the effect of exposing the government and the nature of its project. The inability of state institutions to provide satisfactory responses to these daily demands has laid bare a crisis of governability and challenged the regime's legitimacy. Similarly, labour protest to demand better pay and secure jobs is necessarily a political act. While most workers' protests since the late 1990s have raised demands for job security, salary increases and improved working conditions, many protests have also broached policy issues. For example, workers have been demanding government re-acquisition of privatized enterprises and the investigation of corrupt management staff as well as even questioning the World Bank privatization programmes in general (Beinin, 2009; El-Merghany, 2013).

The failure to see labour strikes and citizens' protests that are in favour of economic interests as truly political is a major analytical misjudgement. Furthermore, the unwillingness to acknowledge the emergence of 'political' demands by Egyptian labour during the last decade is tantamount to blindness. A few examples from the labour struggle will suffice to demonstrate the nature of these demands. For instance, the elected committee of the momentous strike at Mahalla in 2006 was successful in collecting almost 13,000 signatures of workers for a petition to impeach the head of the official General Union of Textile Workers and to demand free elections for a new union committee. Another major event at Mahalla took place in 2008, when the strike committee called for a national strike to demand raising the national minimum monthly wage to EGP 1200. This demand went beyond an attempt to improve the wage of the Mahalla workers; it was a demand representing the interests of millions of Egyptians and their families across different social groups. The regime's policies of privatization provided the impetus and the focus for the workers' growing collective action. It was not only these policies and their direct effects on living standards that workers were challenging. Labour protests during the first decade of this century took place outside formal labour unions and were clearly opposed to the long-held monopoly of the co-opted ETUF, which workers regard as an extension of the state. By organizing outside, and in spite of, formal unions and by daring to create independent bodies, as the tax collectors did in 2009, Egyptian workers were demanding and effectively enforcing a renegotiation of the relationship between workers and the state. The workers' struggle was in fact against the state–capital nexus and its institutions. The more workers became involved in fights for their rights in the immediate sense, the more their cause became political. Alexander (2011) sums up this reality:

> Egyptian workers took by storm the same rights which other 'political' campaigns for democracy had been forced to abandon under pressure from the state: the right to assemble, the right to protest, to free speech. The strike wave carved out spaces for discussion and organisation in thousands of workplaces across the country, driving the struggle deep into the fabric of Egyptian society.

Conversely, it is also naïve to perceive 'political' struggles as having no roots in economic demands. The pro-democracy movement Kefaya and similar groups relied heavily on the increasing mobilization of associations organized by vocation. Professional groups such as doctors, engineers, lawyers and journalists contested the state's oppressive measures that prevented them from organizing collectively through independent and democratically elected bodies. In many cases these professionals were also placing demands on the regime to reverse their deteriorating living conditions. Like other groups in society, middle-class professionals were suffering the effects of the neoliberal order that markedly affected their living standards and deprived them of their long-held privileges, including job security and social welfare. The 9 March Group, for example, was created to defend academic freedom. The group radicalized large numbers of staff and students and revitalized a culture of political protest. One of its most visible activities was the 2008 march to demand better pay and adequate health care and pension packages (see Chapter 2). Doctors without Rights, a similar group that was established in 2009 to contest the deteriorating working conditions of most doctors in the country, mobilized to demand improvements in doctors' incomes and living conditions. The group's manifesto stated that raising doctors' living standards was a crucial step towards improving the virtually collapsed public health-care system (Mina, 2010). One of the group's efforts was to protest against the government's ban on the doctors' right to strike but the core demands of the group remained focused on issues of overtime, basic pay and support for postgraduate studies (ibid.). The centrality of these demands to the profession was integral to the group's political victory in 2013 when, in tandem with like-minded groups, it took over the doctors' syndicate after decades of domination by the Muslim Brothers.

This is not to say that all struggles are necessarily rooted in the economic sphere but to emphasize that the economic and political spheres are insepar-able without necessarily being fixed in a static, causal relationship. In Rosa Luxemburg's analysis, the economic struggle can at moments be the factor that advances events from one political focal point to another. At the same time, 'the political struggle periodically fertilises the ground for the economic struggle. Cause and effect interchange every second' (Luxemburg, 1906: 201). What is political and what is economic is not fixed; neither is the nature of the link that brings them together. In Egypt, the 'political' and 'economic' struggles, with their ebbs and flows, evolved and organized alongside each other without impeding or overwhelming the other. At moments, the pro-democracy movement seemed to be in the ascendancy, filling the streets and dominating the media with its marches and statements. On other occasions, especially after 2005, the movement seemed to recede while labour action began to dominate, with its peak moment in the Mahalla strikes in 2006.

A fragmented struggle?

Laclau and Mouffe (1985: 10) argue that Luxemburg's work on the mass strike invites us to 'concentrate not only on the plurality of forms of struggle but also on the relations which they establish among themselves and on the unifying effects which follow from them'. The large-scale mobilization, which gained momentum in Egypt over a decade, was characterized by hor-izontal expansion and an intense diffusion of ideas through which groups learned and copied tactics from each other. Despite intersecting paths and cross-fertilization, the different struggles by all these groups were insufficiently connected. The pro-democracy movement and its constituent groups, for example, remained overwhelmingly middle-class in membership and orienta-tion, rendering it unable to reach out to other social groups such as workers, small farmers or slum residents. In the midst of searing popular discontent in every corner of the country, Kefaya failed to join forces or have meaningful coordination with the social groups most adversely affected by neoliberal policies. Kefaya core members and the leadership consistently stressed, in public statements and personal interviews, the need to reach out to these oppressed groups. However, the only actual links the movement had with them were limited to the symbolic issuing of support statements and to organizing under-attended rallies.[1]

The question of the class base of social movements, such as the pro-democracy movement, is a thorny one. According to Gramsci (1971), struggles and movements derive their meaning from their 'hegemonic articulation'. The progressive character of these movements is never assured in advance. Thus, workers' struggles do not always have a unified progressive direction. Similarly, new social movements, which are often middle-class in character, are not necessarily progressive or reactionary. However, the middle-class nature of these movements often determines the way the benefits of their struggles are distributed. While hailed in mainstream literature for their inclusive character, case studies of movements claiming universal representation of non-economic groups, such as peace, environment or feminist movements, show that the benefits they generate often serve members of a particular class – usually the middle class. Rose (1997), for example, shows that members of the middle classes have most often benefited from race and gender quotas, campaigns for resistance to conscription and protective land-use policies.

The rural–urban divide also drew a sharp geographical line between protestors. As far as the urban-based, pro-democracy activists were concerned, Egypt's rural protests could have been taking place on another planet. Such is the total absence of any physical link between the two. Kefaya and its sister organizations were alienated from issues of water, land tenancy and access to markets more by their aversion to entering villages than by class. While the pro-democracy movement had difficulty reaching out to workers, at least workers could be encountered on city streets and syndicates' Cairo headquarters where rallies and meetings are held. However, physically travelling to villages and communicating with their residents was an action totally alien to the urban middle classes. As one activist of the Youth for Justice and Freedom put it:

> Our idea of reaching out to the countryside is to have some presence in the capital *cities* of the Delta like Damanhour or Mansour. We really have no access to villages. They are completely different settings and all of us who grew up in cities have no understanding of their dynamics. We wouldn't even know whom to talk to when we got there even if we managed to summon the will to go.
>
> (Yasser El-Hawary, author interview, Cairo, April 2011)

This deeply-rooted, rural–urban divide is one among several factors explaining the lack of solidarity between the different types of protest. Another major factor was the embryonic nature of the different groups of protestors, whether pro-democracy, labour or citizen-based. None of the three modes of protest developed a solid base or had a sustainable organizational structure from which to reach out and attempt coordination, let alone create a broad coalition. Most of the individual groups were consumed by the task of mobilizing within a certain narrowly defined constituency, be it professional groups such as doctors, academics, judges and engineers or workers within a particular sector such as transport, weaving or food processing. State co-optation of unions and manipulation of syndicates meant that activists were working to circumnavigate the hurdles created by these bodies, to create links within the ranks of their colleagues and plan future activities. Labour protests under Mubarak were a good example. They were localized events and lacked any sectorial or national coordination. Each strike, occupation or sit-in erupted spontaneously and only some developed committees which had the sole purpose of representing striking workers in the negotiating process with the management.

As discussed in Chapter 4, by the end of the first decade of this century, both labour and pro-democracy groups were realizing the importance of creating alternative, yet sustainable, forms of organization. Some groups were grappling with new options while others actually achieved major victories, such as the landmark tax collectors' victory in 2009. The dispersed, citizen-based protests, by definition, had no core and did not possess the potential to develop beyond specific geographic localities. These protests did not develop out of an orderly plan with a grand design. In most cases, they developed spontaneously and as such originated in the manner described by Luxemburg (1906: 48), 'from specific local accidental causes ... and grew with elemental power ... and then they did not begin an "orderly retreat", but turned now into economic struggle, now into street fighting and now collapsed on themselves'. On the eve of the 25 January uprising, the streets of Egypt were teeming with an impressive array of activist networks and protest groups. They were, however, no more than that: nascent groups and loose networks still exploring their potential as a 'movement'.

Another factor that limited a reaching out over the divide and the expression of more concrete forms of solidarity was the level of repression by the state which made it very difficult for protestors to approach other groups. The heavy presence of state security in public spaces, workplaces, universities and other institutional settings, along with the draconian dictates of the emergency law against public meetings and gatherings, contributed hugely to the fragmentation of the struggle against the regime. 'Political' rallies that brought together a few hundred activists would be surrounded by thousands of riot police who prevented more people from joining the kettled demonstrators. The police never hesitated to use violence against protests, thus intimidating others from swelling the ranks of the protestors. The chances of activists being able to enter factories or government offices and associate with striking workers or public-sector employees were even less likely. It was only when workers took their protests onto the streets, for example at the gates of parliament in 2009, that any real chance of joining them was possible. State repression ensured a physical separation between proponents of the 'economic' and 'political' struggles wherever possible.

Moreover, the development of a cross-sectorial coalition, or even a more meaningful coordination of protests, was inhibited by a conceptual impasse. This manifested itself in a prioritization of struggles in which protests for social and economic rights were presented by some activists and political analysts as peripheral to the more serious business of changing the constitution and, at a later date, the regime. Activists within the pro-democracy movement, especially when Kefaya was at the forefront, perceived their own protests as the leading force for change, around which all other groups should and would naturally rally. Labour protests and protests for economic demands were regarded by political activists as important forms of agitation but not as central to the struggle against the regime as their own. Not only the more liberal or Islamist elements of the pro-democracy movement fell for this line. Even factions within the left expressed similar views. In the middle of the intensification of labour protests, Hussein Abdel Razek (2010), a leading member of the Tagamou Party, wrote in *Al-Ahali*, the official newspaper of the party:

> Despite the proliferation of workers' action, there is a lack of consciousness among workers and popular classes of the fact that their conditions will not change without changing the social and economic policies which have come into existence since 1971 ... . Unless they realise that they will not get their rights or achieve any real changes in their living conditions and organisational [union] structures without a fundamental change in the political and constitutional structure based on real democratic foundations, the status quo will persist. At best, their struggles will achieve only isolated, limited gains and their reality will remain the same.

Attempts to bridge the divide

Despite the dominant position among pro-democracy activists who conceptually and practically compartmentalized struggles, there were a few critical voices, especially on the left of the wide-ranging pro-democracy movement, who rejected the conceptualization of workers' activism as 'economic' rather than 'political' and hence as less inclusive and less powerful. The great majority of pro-democracy activists believed that political change could only happen through emphasizing a political message and political demands that had the backing of all social, political and economic groups in the country. A 'trickle-down' logic dominated, in which it was assumed that changes to the apex of the formal political structure would necessarily filter down to positively impact the conditions of different groups at the bottom. As part of this position, many activists not only saw economic demands (*mataleb iqtisadia*) for salary increases and other financial benefits as secondary, but also failed to recognize the struggles to achieve them as the political actions they were. One of the critical members within Kefaya dismissed this attitude, arguing that:

> Political activists do not realize that change is currently taking place at different levels through the efforts of several other actors such as workers, farmers, employees and students who have become capable of organizing and bringing about tangible results by confronting the regime in much

more meaningful ways than simply protests for political demands. These groups are putting the regime under pressure and posing a real threat to its hegemony. This is where *political* change begins.

(Wael Khalil, author interview, Cairo, August 2009)

The majority of the pro-democracy movement chose to believe that political change could only take place by emphasizing a political message and political demands in the narrow sense of constitutional changes. In another account, Yehia Fikry (author interview, Cairo, 2009) voiced concerns about the failure of the pro-democracy groups to become a broad, popular movement that goes beyond the limited base of political activists. The only way out of this impasse, he argued, was to recognize the elitist character of the pro-democracy groups and for their members to develop modalities not just to reach out to but also to follow the masses who are consumed in their own struggles. This mounting criticism had no effect on Kefaya and its sister organizations. However, it resulted in the rise of a young generation of activists disenchanted with the mainstream trend to prioritize political over economic struggle. In the face of the failure to reach out and express solidarity with workers and other groups protesting for social and economic rights, small groups appeared as offshoots of the pro-democracy movement. Initiatives such as *Tadamon* (Solidarity), 6 April, Youth for Justice and Freedom (*Hanghiar*), and the Popular Democratic Movement for Change (*Hashd*) appeared at the end of the decade to articulate a new agenda which aimed to cross the boundaries between economic and political struggles.

The first of these groups to attempt to bridge the divide was Tadamon. Created in September 2007 by a group of core activists of the Kefaya Youth for Change movement, this offshoot developed specifically out of its members' disenchantment with Kefaya's inability or unwillingness to create organic links with other protest movements. Tadamon's declaration of principles, for example, states that its objective is to 'change the state of separation between the movement for democratic change and movements on the street' and to demonstrate that 'democratic struggle can never be separate from economic-ally- and socially-based struggles.' Tadamon's main objective was to provide support for the growing 'economic-based' protests by drawing on the activists' experience in the pro-democracy movement (Gihan Shabaan, author inter-view, Cairo, May 2010). The group organized several activities to this end, such as campaigns for the support of specific protests, providing legal advice and media coverage and helping connect workers with a network of human rights and labour lawyers. Members of Tadamon understood small-scale protests to be the 'stepping stones on a long road towards change'.[2] Instead of assuming to speak on their behalf, Tadamon members went to the places of protest and put themselves at the service of the protestors. One of the group's main objectives was to encourage the creation of links between the different protests by holding meetings to which leaders of protests from different sec-tors were invited to share experiences and discuss potential coordination. The group organized several meetings for this purpose at which activists within the different protest strands came to discuss their experiences or to exchange ideas around specific issues, such as the creation of independent unions.

Tadamon, like most other groups, attracted individuals from diverse political backgrounds including the Revolutionary Socialists, the Al-Aa'mal Party (Labour), the Al-Ghad Party and many independent activists with different leanings. However, the ideological differences between these various members and their disagreements on tactics proved terminal. The massive strike of the Mahalla workers in 2008 was a divisive moment for the group. A split took place when a member originally belonging to the Aa'mal and the (liberal) Ghad parties advocated organizing a general strike in support of the Mahalla protests on 6 April. Other members within the group rejected this proposal on the grounds that the labour movement had not sufficiently matured to galvanize a general strike (Shehata, 2009: 258). The split resulted in the withdrawal of many members to launch a second group working on the same principle of solidarity with workers, the 6 April group.

Taking its name from the planned Mahalla strike of 2008, the 6 April group was created to promote a call for a general, national strike in solidarity with the Mahalla workers. The group launched its Facebook page to this end, attracting tens of thousands of virtual supporters. Offline reality, however, was a different matter. On the day of the strike, it was the Mahalla workers and residents who bore the brunt of the police violence and not Facebook followers. Members of 6 April explained the mission of the group as one to encourage 'people to be active in working-class areas, rather than only staging protests outside the Journalists' Syndicates', in reference to most protests led by pro-democracy groups (Carr, 2012). Despite these good intentions and the huge media attention, the 6 April group attracted, due to its 'youth' and 'social media' brand, the group achieved very little.

Hashd was one of two groups born out of a split within the RS in 2010, the other being the Socialist Renewal Current. An entirely leftist group that was concerned with the same issue of giving struggles for economic and social rights pride of place in any project for change, it attempted to offer a more radical reading of the struggle against capital and Mubarak's neoliberal order. In reference to Kefaya, the launching statement of Hashd questioned the ability of the slogan 'No to succession' and the concomitant demands for constitutional changes and fair elections alone to provide any magical solutions to Egypt's fundamental problems (Hashd, 2010). The group, which had been in existence for only a few months by 25 January 2011, elaborated upon the same message propagated by the other three similar groups, namely that the 'actual force for change is not the tens or hundreds of intellectuals and political activists but the millions of masses in factories, farms, alleys, hamlets ... when they organise and adopt a revolutionary vision for change' (ibid.).

Dissatisfied with the experience of all three previous groups, Youth for Justice and Freedom (Hanghiar) was established to overcome their perceived weaknesses. In a bid to reaffirm the centrality of struggles for social and economic justice, the group went so far as to declare that 'while the struggle for social and economic justice needs to go hand in hand with struggles for democracy, "justice", signifying equal access to social and economic rights, in fact takes priority' (Ola Shohba, author interview, Cairo, 22 June 2011). The group, like its contemporaries except for Hashd, consisted of members of diverse political convictions. However, they were brought together by the belief that 'justice was more important than simple procedural democracy ... hence the group's name giving priority to justice over freedom' (ibid.). From the outset, the group's founding members included activist workers and not just political activists who would represent the workers' interests. To emphasize the role of workers in the group, at the conference announcing its launch in July 2010, the group honoured leaders of prominent labour struggles including Esam Abdallah, Hisham Abu Zeid (who headed the Amonsito and Tanta Flex factory struggles respectively) and Nagui Rashad, who was the first to institute a legal case for increasing the minimum wage (Youth for Justice and Freedom: A New Movement on the Egyptian Street, 2010). In the lead-up to the 25 January uprising, the group launched the campaign 'No to the NDP, No to Mubarak', in which it worked on exposing corruption at the local government level by engaging with different protests against corrupt practices in the provinces (ibid.).

The four groups organized campaigns to support specific acts of protest by workers and other diverse groups by providing them with legal advice and media coverage. They also worked on connecting labour activists and other protestors with a network of human rights and labour lawyers. A small yet highly visible and active number of human rights NGOs and civil society groups were at the forefront of these support and solidarity campaigns. Among them was the Centre for Trade Union and Workers' Services, the Centre for Socialist Studies, the Egyptian Centre for Economic and Social Rights, the Land Centre for Human Rights, the Coordinating Committee for Trade Union and Workers' Rights and Freedom, and the Hisham Mubarak Law Centre.

The sincerity of activists within these initiatives and groups has been undeniable. Their efforts were crucial for challenging the artificial dichotomy of the political and the economic spheres and they struggled with the question of how to develop concrete platforms for broadly-based coalitions. However, these efforts were fraught with challenges. Not least of these was the embryonic nature of the groups, their short history and the small number of activists they relied on for their work. Furthermore, the media attention that these groups attracted often turned their activities into photo opportunities. The Facebook-using, technology-savvy 6 April activists, in particular, became media darlings. Competition over who should take credit for which campaign and who should speak to the media on behalf of workers was a cause of inter-group conflict. Khaled Abdelhamid recounts how Kefaya would attempt to hijack or use the success of some of the workers' victories for its own purposes and to steal the media limelight. 'For example, when the tax employees decided to end their strike after their demands were agreed to, Kefaya members asked them to hold on to their strike for one more day as Kefaya was due to organize a rally in support of their strike' (author interview, Cairo, May 2011). Even among members of these fresh initiatives, there was a rush to claim credit. According to Yasser El-Hawary, a leading member of Hanghiar, 6 April was often credited by the media for activities organized by Hanghiar. Members of 6 April were happy to accept the credit despite the fact that they had very little presence on the ground and were only really involved in social media activism (author interview, Cairo, June 2011).

The inability of these new groups to shed their middle-class background and the attitudes that this engendered in their approach to working with labour was a much more serious factor. Organizing campaigns to support workers' protests was one thing but creating organic links with them was quite a different matter. The almost exclusively middle-class background of their members meant that these groups adopted a paternalistic approach when attempting to mobilize people for political and social action. They came with preconceived ideas about how workers needed to be 'helped' rather than involving the workers in organizing themselves. As a result, many of these campaigns came closer to charity work than joint action. For example, in a major campaign in support of asbestos workers, various activities such as raising funds for workers' medical check-ups and collecting signatures for petitions were done on behalf of the workers, who were never included in planning and organizing the campaign (Mohamed Agati, author interview, Cairo 2011). This should not come as a surprise, however. The creation of a stratum of intellectuals that can organically link with the working classes is a long, slow process. As Gramsci elaborates in *The Modern Prince* (1968: 50–51), 'non-proletarian intellectuals' develop

> much more slowly than any other social group, because of their own nature and historical role … . To think it possible that this type can, as a mass, break with the whole of the past in order to place itself wholeheartedly on the side of a new ideology, is absurd [even] for very many intellectuals taken individually, despite all the honest efforts they make and want to make.

The ruling elite: a strategy for maintaining dominance

The neoliberal order institutionalized under Mubarak has remained untouched in the years that have followed his ousting. Capital has continued to ensure that its interests have remained intact in the face of any demands for radical change of the system. The military complex, for one, has since the early days of SCAF's ascent to power shown single-minded intent in both expanding as well as safeguarding its already substantive economic interests. As shown in the previous chapter, the June 2012 constitutional declaration issued by SCAF, for example, granted the military total control over military matters and a *de facto* veto on the drafting of the new constitution. Both the 2012 and the 2013 constitutions have enshrined the military's autonomy as an economic entity above and beyond the executive. The military's economic projects have also continued to multiply. Between September and November 2013, for example, the military received EGP 7 billion worth of government contracts, including a 2.2 billion contract to implement the government's investment plan in the Sinai region (Soliman, 2013). Most of the other contracts were focused on housing and construction projects. Under a presidential decree passed by the military-appointed interim government, these contracts were accorded to the military without a bidding process.[3] A few weeks later, the cabinet offered the National Service Authority a highly favourable contract to run the Cairo–Alexandria desert toll road, one of the main highways in Egypt.[4]

Similarly, once in power the Muslim Brothers-led government promoted an economic programme not at all dissimilar to that of Mubarak's NDP. While an outlawed group under Mubarak, its leading members, nevertheless, controlled a huge business empire integral to Egyptian capital. The Muslim Brothers have firm roots within the business elite that has benefited from the neoliberal policies of Mubarak and before him Sadat. The group's ideological commitment to a free-market economy goes back to the 1970s. The embourgeoisement of the Muslim Brothers took place during their exile in the oil rich monarchies of the Gulf during the oil boom (Achcar, 2013: 124). This has led some commentators to describe the heavy crackdown on the Muslim Brothers' financial and economic interests in 2007 as simply part of competition between two elements of Egyptian capital (Abu El-Magd, 2012).

In his exposition of the dense network of family–business relations which link members of the Muslim Brothers through marriage and corporate ties, El-Kharabawi, a former member of the group, gives a rare glimpse into the highly secretive business world of the Muslim Brothers. In a 2012 article, he shows the extent of a joint business empire between the business tycoon Hassan Malek, one of the group's major financiers, and Khairat Al-Shater,[5] and their families, including seventy large companies ranging from land reclamation (in Siwa) to real estate (Mostaqbal), construction, clothing and other sectors. While most of these companies were registered in the names of the children and relatives of the Muslim Brothers' members to avoid state harassment, most of their board members were drawn from the top echelons of the Muslim Brothers. The MB business empire was not confined to Egypt but extended to Algeria, Turkey and sub-Saharan Africa (Al-Morshedi, 2013; *Al-Watan*, 2013). One characteristic of this empire is its sole focus on production of consumer goods and services which cater to the Egyptian middle classes.

As the Muslim Brothers constitute a significant segment of Egyptian capital, they have had a keen interest in reproducing existing patterns of capital accumulation developed under Mubarak. In an expression of the vested

interest of the MB in maintaining the same economic order as under
Mubarak, Hasan Malek was quoted in March 2011 as saying that 'Mubarak's
economic policies were on the right track but were marred by corruption and
cronyism' (*Al-Masry Alyoum*, 2011). Malek engineered Morsi's famous business trip to China in August 2012, to which he invited 80 businessmen to
accompany the president in his mission to encourage Chinese FDI in Egypt.
Among them were some of Mubarak's leading business cronies including
Mohamed Farid Khamis (see Chapter 1) and Sherif Al-Gabaly, a close
associate of Gamal Mubarak and member of the NDP. In a goodwill gesture,
Morsi's government also backed SCAF's Decree no. 4 of 2012, which gives
immunity from criminal prosecution to businessmen accused of corruption
under Mubarak and offers them the chance to settle their cases with government commissions (Achcar, 2013: 180). Similarly, the Islamist-dominated
parliament, albeit only briefly in existence, had no problem approving the
2012/2013 budget, which paid only lip-service to issues of redistribution and
social justice. The Muslim Brothers government was also keen to negotiate a
$2.4 billion deal with the IMF, providing continuity with Mubarak's borrowing
habits. Not surprisingly, then, three leading ministers in Morsi's government
were actually drawn from Mubarak's own henchmen. Hanieh (2013: 170)
describes this situation:

> Morsi's cabinet appointments demonstrated the clear continuity of the
> old patterns of rule. His finance minister, Mumtaz al-Said ... [was] an
> ardent proponent of neoliberal policies and strongly pushed for the
> international loans from the IMF and World Bank. Morsi appointed
> Osama Saleh as minister of investment, a man who had been chosen by
> Mubarak as chairman of Egypt's General Authority for Free Zones and
> Investment, an institution that led to the drive to market Egypt as a low-
> wage platform for foreign investors. The minister for trade and industry
> was Hatem Saleh, CEO of Gozour Food Industry Group, a subsidiary of
> the Gulf-linked Citadel Capital.

Confronted with the same impoverishing economic policies and a political
process which shows no regard for the demands of freedom and social justice
in the months and years following the downfall of Mubarak, millions of
Egyptians have continued their struggle. Despite violent repression and overt
attempts at co-optation by the ruling elite, waves of protests have come and
gone only to return driven by new grievances and demands. The repertoire of
action has continued to multiply, including marches against the increasing
powers granted to the military by different constitutions, demonstrations
against Morsi's constitutional declaration, campaigns against the drafting of
a constitution which undermines political liberties and social justice alike and
factory occupations and workers' strikes culminating in an unprecedented
2,400 labour protests in the first three months of 2013. Thousands of workers
across the country from the Nobariah Company that produces fertilizers, the

Suez Iron Company, the Shibin weaving factories, the East Delta Bus Company, Tanta Flax, Pharco Pharmaceuticals and hundreds more have been staging daily action in their worksites and on the streets. As was the case under Mubarak, the post-Mubarak governments are struggling to meet the demands and contain the anger of these workers. Despite the overwhelming coercive power of the old/new ruling elite, the compound and diversified nature of the protests continues to present a challenge to their rule. Due to their disparate nature, these protests are difficult to co-opt or crush entirely. As Eckstein shows in the case of Latin America:

> The more diversified the base of resistance, the more difficult it is for a state to address the varied grievances of groups concomitantly through force or reform. ... The diverse socioeconomic groups that rebelled in Mexico, Bolivia, Cuba and Nicaragua had different reasons for defying the government in power, but the net effect of their combined defection was a breakdown of the existing political and economic order.
>
> (1989: 49)

It is not surprising, therefore, that members of the different elements constituting the ruling elite, who have at times been involved in a contest over power amongst themselves, have all been in agreement on one thing: the need to crush protests and isolate different struggles. Some commentators even argue that the conflict between the Muslim Brothers and the military in the lead-up to Morsi's ousting in July 2013 was partly a competitive struggle between factions of the same class that were nevertheless united in their resolve to undermine any popular uprising (Hanieh, 2013). Finding themselves confronted with an unrelenting revolutionary process, which still involves large sections of the masses, those in power, whether they are the military, the Muslim Brothers, the interim governments, the *foloul* of domestic capital or the well-entrenched state bureaucracy, have all worked, often in unison, to undermine and derail this process. In addition to physical repression, they have drawn on an arsenal of legal and propaganda tools to achieve this end.

The ruling elite has fashioned a legal system to ensure the divided nature of the opposition and the weakening of protests. SCAF's Law 34/2011, which criminalized strikes and protests that curtail production, was one such example. Heavy fines and prison sentences for workers who participate in, call for or publicize strikes was later enshrined in the constitution. The law and others which followed, discussed in Chapter 4, not only criminalized labour strikes, they also strongly curtailed opportunities for workers to organize.

Faced with this constant threat to its interests, Egypt's ruling elite have resorted to isolating different struggles and institutionalizing and strengthening a set of binaries in order to pit different groups against each other. Since 2011, Egyptian politics has become polarized on the basis of a set of binaries, in particular Islamist versus secular, the ballot box versus street protests, and 'political' versus 'economic' struggles. While legal measures have been crucial to attempts to marginalize workers' protests, the use of the media to shape hostile public opinion has been the most powerful weapon. The propaganda campaigns of the official media as well as sections of the private media owned by business magnates have allowed the ruling elite to intensify their vilification of workers and other groups protesting for their 'economic' rights.

Since Mubarak's downfall, the media has promoted a discourse in which protests for economic demands are portrayed as a direct cause of the deteriorating economic conditions in the country. By labelling them as *mataleb fa'awyea* (group or partisan demands), these acts of protest are immediately reduced to the status of narrowly focused, selfish demands that would benefit only members of specific groups regardless of their damaging effect to the economy as a whole. Another term which has become a mantra in the official media is *a'agalet el-intag* ('the wheel of production'), which protests and strikes are allegedly bringing to a halt. In this portrayal, protest by labour and groups of citizens is responsible for reducing national production as well as discouraging foreign investors, whose capital the country desperately needs. In October 2011, the minister of labour was quoted as blaming striking workers for being irresponsible and unreasonable, as they had to 'take into consideration the financial crisis and the huge responsibilities which the government has to shoulder. Making exaggerated demands will not have positive consequences' (Albassel and Khalifa, 2011). Similarly, 'increasing workers' ... strikes, constant protests and unrealistic demands' were blamed by the head of the Investors Association in the industrial zone of Bourg El-Arab for the closures of over one hundred factories in the zone in the months following the ousting of Mubarak (Abdelsalam and Ismail, 2012).

Even the Salafi Nour Party adopted the same line. During a mobilization campaign for a general strike in February 2012, members of Al Nour condemned the campaign as a 'call to destroy the state and to ruin the economy' (*Al Shorouk*, 7 February 2012). At times, the political and business elite argued that any form of protest should be confined to a government-approved location and should only be led by responsible political activists who represent the true demands of the revolution. This draconian, anti-democratic demand was actually made into a highly controversial law in November 2013. An official of the Nour Party was quoted as saying: 'Protest is enough as a form of popular pressure without hampering the economy. ... [in place of strikes] I hope to see 300 or 400 thousand protestors every day in Tahrir to demonstrate the power of the revolution' (ibid.). In the weeks following the election of Morsi, protests by different groups of workers intensified in front of the presidential palace only to be dismissed by Hasan El-Prince, a high-ranking official in the Freedom and Justice Party, as being organized by hired agents working in a state security conspiracy to destabilize the president (*Aswat Masrya*, 2012).

By their use of the media, the military and interim governments have managed to manipulate public opinion not only to refuse to recognize 'economic' forms of struggle as an integral part of a revolutionary process but also to condemn them as impeding a swifter transition to democracy and stability. From the ruling elite's perspective, the fragmentation of protests and demands is an essential strategy to weaken the forces of the revolution. For the business elite, separating the economic from the political sphere and disparaging the struggles articulated within the former has always been one of the most effective defence mechanisms against labour. Fighting for economic demands, however, remains an obvious political statement whose strength is that it not only defies the oppressive tactics of the forces in power but also exposes the liberal forces whose members hope to convince the people to suspend their fight and accept a promise of symbolic representation through elections (Alexander, 2011).

On the part of activists, the surge in new networks formed in the hope of bridging the rift between the activities of different struggles, which rose in the last two years of Mubarak's rule, has receded in the years after his ousting. The marathon of electoral politics, which has come to define the post-Mubarak era, means that most activists who were invested in resolving the rift became completely absorbed in the task of building political parties and contesting elections. However, most political parties that have emerged from this process have been marked by internal splits and other weaknesses. None has been able to devise programmes or seriously engage in the task of creating broadly-based struggles.

Human rights groups and some trade union activists, especially on the left, continue to provide legal and other forms of support to workers and other protesting groups. Providing support, however, is one thing. A genuine commitment to building a project based on the intertwining of different 'economic' and 'political' struggles is another completely. At the beginning of 2014, only some activists and trade unionists on the left genuinely regard these struggles as an integral part of the process of changing the political order. However, these leftist forces are small and fragmented. Furthermore, they have been unable to find a coherent strategy for working with labour. In one harsh analysis, a labour activist argues that the left still has a problematic relationship with labour in which engaging with the labour movement is regarded as optional and not integral to an overall revolutionary strategy (Gabr, 2012). As the left is not organically linked with labour struggles, its reaction to labour fluctuates between soaring elation when workers' strikes peak and total disillusionment when workers go dormant or, even worse, when they fail to rise in response to political activists' calls for a general strike, as was the case in February 2012 (ibid.). It is clear that the left is confronted with a massive task of building organic links with workers. The process, even if successful, will be long and might take many years, if not decades. Leftist activists in the meantime are not always realistic about their ability to play a 'leadership' role for workers or to get them to respond on cue. Arguing against any delusion to that effect, Rosa Luxemburg reminds us that:

> It is clear that the mass strike cannot be called at will, even when the decision to do so may come from the highest committee of the strongest

social democratic party ... even the greatest enthusiasm and impatience of the social democratic troops will not suffice to call into being a real period of mass strike as a living, powerful movement of the people.

(1906: 53)

The logical conclusion to Luxemburg's analysis of the mass strike is the development of a revolutionary situation which engenders unity of the political and the economic struggles – a situation that would necessarily be resolved in a socialist direction. Laclau and Mouffe, on the other hand, wonder if this outlook is not somewhat deterministic. In examining more recent changes in the capitalist system, they ask whether we might experience a situation where the fragmentation of the economic and the political struggles ceases to be an 'artificial product' of the capitalist state and instead becomes a permanent reality (1985: 10). The unfolding events in Egypt reveal that the tension between the two possibilities is still at play although the latter is more in the ascendancy.

Notes

1 For examples of such statements, see Support Asbestos Workers: Enough Hunger ... Enough http://www.ahewar.org/debat/show.art.asp?aid=40609.
2 *Tadamon*'s declaration of principles can be found at 'Who Are We?' http://tadamonmasr.wordpress.com (accessed 16/10/2010).
3 Law 82/2013 was passed on 11 September 2013 to allow direct according of contracts in 'urgent cases'.
4 See Al-Boursa (2013) for details.
5 Deputy leader and a major financier of the MB, Al-Shater was the group's original candidate for the presidency. He had to be replaced at the last minute by Mohamed Morsi after a court ruling prevented him from standing.

Conclusion

The difference between the public mood in Egypt in February 2011 and August 2013 could not have been starker. The euphoria, optimism and sense of grand achievement and boundless potential for the future in which Egyptians had basked after the downfall of Mubarak had all but deserted the streets of the country and the hearts of the people by the time the bloody summer of 2013 arrived. In its place was a country polarized and a people divided. The Muslim Brothers' rapid fall from grace, which astounded even their most ardent critics, ushered in one of the bloodiest and most divisive episodes of Egypt's long revolution. The indifference of the MB under Morsi's presidency to the need to create a consensus in support of their project once in power sealed their fate. The widespread disenchantment with the MB led to the rise of the new adage that 'what the MB built in 80 years, they lost in 8 months'. Tamarod (Arabic for 'revolt'), a campaign which set out in April 2013 to collect signatures for a petition demanding that Morsi step down and call fresh presidential elections, capitalized on this public discontent. A numbers game intensified in the ensuing months between members of Tamarod, who declared at the end of June that they had collected 15 million signatures, and the MB, who insisted that the number was no more than 170,000. On 30 June, the first anniversary of Morsi in office, however, the millions who came out on the streets across the country in support of the Tamarod petition significantly exceeded the number of protestors in the 25 January uprising. The military, already frustrated with Morsi and ready to dispose of him, co-opted the popular campaign and carried out a coup. The coup quickly unfolded in the days that followed the ousting of Morsi with the suspension of the constitution, the appointment of an interim president and a new government and the declaration of a new 'road map'. The mass protests of the pro-Morsi supporters, which culminated in two major demonstration camps in Cairo and Giza, were brutally crushed on 14 August, when the security forces stormed in using bulldozers, tear gas and live ammunition. The military-backed operation, which left at least one thousand dead, many thousands injured and many more under arrest, had the support of a large majority of Egyptians. By the end of the summer, the MB had been completely expunged from the formal political process. After their failure to establish a right-wing or centre-right ruling pact along the lines of Western Christian Democratic parties and to stick to the rules of the liberal democracy game, they were easily deposed by the military. The brutality with which the head of the army, General Sisi, set about crushing the MB during the summer of 2013 saw his popularity soar, with wide popular campaigns demanding his candidacy for the presidency. The overwhelming 'yes' vote in the 2014 constitution, which confirms the independence and power of the military, was in part testimony to this popularity. However, the plan to reproduce and preserve the Mubarak order, of which the military is an integral part, might not prove as simple as the generals and other counter-revolutionary forces would like to believe.

In the midst of rival chants by the millions who took to the streets to give Sisi a mandate to rid the country of MB rule and by the MB supporters demanding the reinstatement of Egypt's 'legitimate' president, a slogan raised by a small group of activists was almost inaudible. In the midst of the bloodshed and the hysteria that reigned supreme, the slogan 'Don't chant Morsi and Sisi: Neither is the first coming back nor is the latter going to be my president' was a cry not only against the polarization that was dividing the country but for a sober assessment of the remaining potential for a revolutionary process. At that moment, a revolutionary way forward seemed stalled by the polarization and an ever-growing atmosphere of distrust, retaliation and vilification.

The popularity of Sisi, as the face of this new/old regime, has come in response to his promise to rid the country of 'terrorism', eliminate the MB and provide security and stability, and presumably also ensure economic recovery and reinstate Egypt as a commanding regional power. A brazen media campaign has been promoting a brand of Sisi drawn from the image of Nasser: a charismatic, fierce general around whom a country in crisis could unite; and a benevolent tyrant who will stop at nothing to crush dangerous dissent in order to grant his people security and prosperity. But Sisi, or anyone in his place for that matter, can never reproduce Nasser's project. For Nasser *did* have history on his side. Nasser was not simply a charismatic leader. He was a charismatic leader whose project of building a modernist, developmentalist state had the backing of a thriving post-war global capitalist order and its institutions. Like other leaders of most newly independent countries, Nasser followed an officially sanctioned route to modernization. Its pillars were huge infrastructure projects, job creation schemes for a rapidly increasing population and the introduction of universal health care and education systems, all of which were enthusiastically supported by global financial institutions and bilateral donors. Nasser's developmentalist state and its public investment strategies drew on resources accrued from the nationalization of private assets and land reform programmes. In the middle of an intense cold war, Nasser could further exploit Egypt's geostrategic position to gain economic and political support for his project from both superpowers.

Alas, for Egypt's current rulers, Nasser's world has all but completely vanished. A Sisi-backed regime could only dream of the material and political resources that were available in the 1950s and 1960s. Even in that period, Nasser's redistribution policies were often limited and symbolic in their achievements. The current global order has no appetite for public investment or redistributive measures. Not only has neoliberalism long done away with such principles, but a protracted crisis of global capitalism is leading to more regimes of austerity across the world. For a country like Egypt, this means more cuts in public expenditure on social services, privatization of public facilities and companies, liberalization of trade and the subjection of labour and environmental concerns to the needs of FDI. Egypt's regional power has also been waning since the 1990s as it has been increasingly eclipsed by actors such as Turkey, Qatar and Iran.

To garner popular support for the current political and economic order, the military-backed regime intends to rely on an inflated nationalist and security discourse to create a consensus. Declaring the MB a terrorist organization has already been a vital first step in constructing an enemy around which to rally nationalist sentiment and foster a sense of fear and insecurity. A national saviour, in the form of the military in general and Sisi in particular, has also been found. Since Mubarak's downfall, the military has been dressing up its secured and growing economic privileges in the garb of a nationalist project. Lucrative public contracts secured by the military, discussed in previous chapters, as well as SCAF's move in 2012 to lend the central bank a sum of $1 billion, have been hailed as part of a nationalist project to build a 'second republic'. Furthermore, in the hope of quelling the continuing protests, especially the most recent wave of labour action, the regime will continue to employ the time-honoured tactics of violence to bolster its rule. The necessary measures have already been enshrined in legislation and a security discourse popularized towards this end. The sowing of discord between elements of the opposition will also be one of the more traditional tactics employed by counter-revolutionary forces in an attempt to underpin the prevailing order. As the book has argued, the coordination of the diverse struggles of the dispossessed is essential for any movement aiming for revolutionary change. However, these struggles are historically both inherently difficult to unify and easy to divide by preying on the fears and insecurities of different social groups and playing them off against each other. Since Mubarak's ousting, Egypt's rulers have attempted to assert an ideological hegemony over the very essence of what constitutes the revolution. Using all the means at their disposal, they are creating in the public mind a pared down notion of revolution to include only the basics of liberal democracy while conducting a comprehensive campaign to demonize 'economic' struggles for justice. This ploy is central to the elite's tactic of reducing Egypt's revolutionary process to an 'orderly transition to democracy'. Thus, the free market will be protected and neoliberal policies can flourish in return for occasional, limited political representation through elections.

The question is: how long will the current rulers be able to survive on the back of a security-centred 'project' which is thinly veiled in nationalist sentiment and backed, for the moment, by millions of Egyptians who saw no alternative to the army for ridding themselves of the MB? To establish and sustain political hegemony will take a lot more than a temporary majority largely sustained by fear. Hegemony requires a position of intellectual and moral leadership that can provide a degree of accommodation of different classes and social groups, and rally sufficient numbers around a strategic vision and programme. Hence, without addressing the glaring injustices and suffering of the majority of the people, this security-driven, nationalist project might find it difficult to suppress continuing public anger and, yes, mobilization. In discussing the crisis of the ruling class in Egypt and Tunisia, Achcar (2013) stresses that the combination of material and political grievances which have driven the revolution in the first place cannot be assuaged, let alone effectively addressed, by the purely cosmetic changes on offer. The slogan of bread, freedom and social justice is, of course, so much more than a slogan and is not going to melt away as long as the material conditions of exploitation and dispossession remain. It hence seems not unlikely, as it becomes increasingly more evident that the army is not the hoped-for saviour – and is in fact 'part of the problem' – that dissatisfaction will grow and consequent mobilization will continue to swell.

One of this book's central premises is that a revolution is a process rather than an event. A revolution is a long process of accumulated struggles with moments of victory, defeat and retreat. A revolution is *not* one grand moment marking a dramatic break and a complete rupture with an old order and its instant replacement with a victorious new one. Egypt's long revolutionary process started well before the 25 January uprising and still continues. The fact that the uprising did not destroy the old regime and immediately create a new order is not a testimony to the 'failure' or the end of a revolutionary process. Neither does the fact that this process is still ongoing mean that the revolution will 'succeed' or reach a satisfactory conclusion for those who initiated it. As Gramsci (1971) saw it, an old society will be destroyed only if a revolutionary movement is capable of constructing and consolidating a new one.

The history of this revolutionary movement in Egypt and an assessment of its potential to establish a common vision and adopt a transformative project to redress social injustice has been the main focus of this book. The book has shown how millions of activists, workers, farmers and unorganized citizens were at the heart of this still inchoate revolutionary movement that battled against the Mubarak regime. The tactics of mobilization and resistance they used were hugely successful in surviving the regime's brutality, challenging its hegemony and eventually removing its head. The book has also shown how the same tactics have proven problematic during a different phase of the revolutionary process. The inability of this movement of disparate elements to coalesce around a coherent project of transformation and to devise strategies for realizing such a project has led to the ease with which counter-revolutionary forces have often been able to dissipate its energies and tame much of its potential. Counter-revolutions are an integral part of the history of any revolutionary process. It is almost always the case that a revolutionary movement of the dispossessed calls into being a reactionary movement of the dominant classes. Gramsci again reminds us that among the main causes of the success of the reactionary forces is the inability of revolutionary groups to give any conscious leadership to spontaneous revolts or to turn them into an effective political force (1971: 119). The main objective of conservative forces in the aftermath of the 25 January uprising has been to control and transform the revolutionary process into the limited, as well as distorted, process of a narrowly defined 'transition to democracy'. The revolutionary forces were faced with a dilemma: to continue their struggle towards a more radical transformation of society and the creation of revolutionary action based on mass mobilization and the rejection of formal traditional institutions or to compete in the electoral process, which was designed and controlled by reactionary forces, with the aim of gaining formal political power. Many believed they could fight on both fronts simultaneously and that the two were not mutually exclusive. Some favoured one path over the other, claiming either revolutionary purity or political pragmatism as grounds for their choice. For those who opted for the latter, joining the formal political process, building political parties and competing in elections has proved a daunting task. Between the two positions, divisions arose within the already fragmented movement, leading to increased polarization along lines not only of economic vs. political and secular vs. Islamist but of autonomous political mobilization vs. electoral 'democracy'.

To understand the root of this dilemma in choosing between autonomous political mobilization and participation in formal politics, we need to remind ourselves of the history of the embryonic revolutionary forces. Over the course of the twentieth century, Egypt's rulers had set up legal constraints, constitutional distortions, regimes of co-optation and measures of repression that very significantly curtailed the freedom of political and civil organizations and their potential to build a mass base. In contrast, the rising popularity of new forms of activism, which were sweeping the world from Seattle to Milan and from Thailand to Moscow, provided activists in Egypt and elsewhere with new analyses and forms of mobilization. These have not only served Egyptian activists to elude the repressive Mubarak regime but even to bring down its chief. Despite their efforts in challenging the regime and its institutions, they had never intended to replace it by themselves. Their focus was to perfect tools and tactics to change the nature of traditional politics, to push its boundaries and to create alternatives to formal, hierarchical structures.

This book has focused on the challenges facing Egyptian activists within their specific national context. However, the case of the Egyptian uprising and its unfolding developments raises theoretical questions on the relationship between protest movements everywhere and the notion of power, questions which have already dominated debates about the future of these protest movements and their potential in creating 'another possible world'. Movements of protest and resistance against a global capitalist order and its nationalist agents have proliferated since the beginning of the twenty-first century. In 2011, in particular, these movements took the world by storm, from Arab 'springs' to Spanish *indignados* to anti-austerity regimes in Greece, Italy, Portugal and Chile to occupy movements starting in the US and spanning the world and anticorruption movements in India, Brazil, Uganda and Thailand. Students, farmers, middle-class professionals, workers, the unemployed, indigenous populations and the rest of those dispossessed by neoliberal global capitalism took to the streets, threw governments off guard and dominated public debate for months. The bravery, ingenuity and single-mindedness of these groups have brought up questions which had remained unanswered for over a decade. Beyond episodic waves of protest and momentary destabilization of authorities, what else do these movements aim to achieve and what transformative projects can they offer? This question becomes paramount during instances when the old order that these movements are challenging is actually going through a period of crisis. However, for most members of these social and protest movements, the very phrasing of this question is itself part of this old order, symptomatic of outdated modes of thinking and praxis.

In 2002, Naomi Klein stressed in a talk at the World Social Forum that 'the challenge to the movement does not lie in finding a vision but in resisting the desire to find one too quickly' (in Pleyers, 2010: 218). In many ways her logic is clear. Expecting activists dreaming of 'another possible world' to choose from a catalogue of existing but usually failed models or expecting them to come up with a blueprint for a new world order using the same failed logic, language and assumptions of the twentieth-century paradigm is self-contradictory. In an extreme reaction to this old world certainty and the mentality of its professional apparatchiks, one author projects the voice of protest movements in celebrating the very absence of a clear vision. Holloway (2002: 251) emphasizes that:

> Our not-knowing is the not-knowing of those who understand that not-knowing is part of the revolutionary process. We have lost all certainty but the openness to certainty is central to revolution. We ask not only because we do not know the way but because not knowing the way *is part of the revolutionary process* itself.

While this position reflects the fluidity of the movement and its openness to a learning process through which an alternative could be born, social movements are not without pre-determined positions. One clear position is the rejection of state power. This is a basic tenet of almost all social movements, whether they are working within the territorial boundaries of the nation-state or transnationally. Members of new social movements cling to the label 'autonomous' not only because they are independent of the state and traditional political institutions but because, first and foremost, they do not want to take over state power. In this vision, a revolution is not about a 'storming of the Bastille' but about everyday transformation of social relations (Sitrin,

2012). As discussed in Chapter 4, activists everywhere have been disillusioned with the potential of state institutions to be a space for radical change. In this regard, Holloway argues:

> For over a hundred years, the revolutionary enthusiasm of young people has been channelled into building the party or into learning to shoot guns, for over a hundred years the dreams of those who have wanted a world fit for humanity have been bureaucratised and militarised, all for the sake of winning state power for a government that could then be accused of 'betraying' the movement that put it there … . Rather than to look for so many betrayals as explanation, perhaps we need to look at the very notion that society can be changed through the winning of state power.
>
> (2002: 29)

This position could not be more different from views which regard the state and the capturing of state power as still the key to any transformative project in the current historical conjuncture. For Harvey, for instance, the choice for these movements is unambiguous: there is no way an alternative social order can be constructed

> without seizing state power, radically transforming it and reworking the constitutional and institutional framework that currently supports private property. Inter-state competition and geo-economic and geo-political struggles over everything from trade and money to questions of hege-mony are also either far too significant to be left to local social movements or cast aside as too big to contemplate.
>
> (2010: 256)

The reticence about identifying a specific vision and the total rejection of state power is the trademark of most social movements of the twenty-first century. One can understand and even sympathize with such a position in light of the disastrous history of anti-systemic movements of the previous century. How-ever, we have to ask ourselves if, at certain moments, this resolutely taken position does not make for self-limiting movements. During moments of intense crisis or moments when a regime or even the entire prevailing order is weakened, the potential perhaps arises to affect the social relations of power. The question then becomes: how can activists ignore a moment pregnant with possibility and continue to struggle in isolated, small-scale ways? Can acti-vists, in their battle to confront the injustices of the current global system and of national governments supporting its hegemony, afford to confine their struggles to critiquing the system and stirring up the streets against its agents without any immediate, practical goal? Or is there now a need for alternative strategies which could take activists beyond networking, protesting and even, unwittingly, bringing down individual heads of the system? Should state power regain its position as the target of activists who have 'elevated' themselves above the constraints of corrupting and ineffective traditional politics? Or should activists, in both the global North and South, redefine their relationship vis-à-vis the concept and reality of power at the current historical conjuncture? Despite the latest global crisis, global financial institutions, the capitalist state and the regimes which bolster their hegemony are likely to survive into the foreseeable future. However, the nature of the crisis, the uncertainty facing the world at so many levels and the continuing waves of mass uprisings and discontent are affording new possibilities for effecting change. For activists challenging this system, history in 2011 seemed to be on their side for one promising moment. No one can predict how long this moment will last and how global capitalism will manage to resolve its latest crisis.

Egypt's long revolution to this point has gone along a tumultuous, yet unsurprising, path dotted with both small and soaring victories, inevitable instances of retreat and moments of dispiriting defeat. The millions who have kept its momentum going, but without being able to guide it towards what they hoped to achieve, will still determine its future, albeit under circumstances not of their own making. However, it would seem that those genuinely intent upon achieving political transformation in this future need to consider transcending the dichotomy of autonomous vs. electoral politics. This will not be an easy task for several reasons, not least of which is the nature and limitations of liberal democracy under current global capitalism. Much theoretical and practical work clearly needs to be done to move sustained challenges to the prevailing order to the next level. Few of the millions struggling for social justice, especially those most disenchanted with the failure of twentieth-century political tactics and strategies, would perhaps be inclined to embrace the advice of Lenin. However, his words affirming that those 'who preserve their strength and flexibility "to begin from the beginning" over and over again in approaching an extremely difficult task, are not doomed (and in all probability will not perish)' are worth remembering by those hoping to keep the banner of 'bread, freedom and social justice' flying.

Bibliography

Abdallah, A. (1985) *The Student Movement and National Politics in Egypt 1923–1973* London: ALSAQI Books.

Abdel Aziz, B. (2011) *Temptation of Absolute Power: Violent Path between the Police and Citizens Across Time* Cairo: Sefsafa Publishing House (in Arabic).

Abdel-Fadil, M. (2011) *Crony Capitalism: A Study in Social Economy* Cairo: Dar Alain (in Arabic).

Abdelrahman, M. (2009) 'With the Islamists? Sometimes … With the State? Never!' *British Journal of Middle East Studies* 36(1): 37–54.

——(2012) 'Ordering the Disorderly: Street Vendors and the Developmentalist State in Egypt' *Jadaliyya* http://www.jadaliyya.com/pages/index/9542/ordering-the-disorder ly-street-vendors-and-the-dev.

Abdel Razek, H. (2010) 'Lelyasar Dor' (To the Left: March!) *Al-Ahali* http://www.ma sress.com/alahaly/2120.

Abdelsalam, F. and Ismail, T. (2012) 'Strikes, Shortage of Natural Resources and Thefts Spread a Shadow over the Closure of 150 Factories' *Al-Ahram*, 15 March.

Abdel Wahab, S. (2011) 'Egypt's Debts: How Did we Reach the Trillion?' *Al-Masry Alyoum*, 11 November.

Abouleinein, S., El-Laithy, H. and Kheir-El-Din, H. (2009) *The Impact of Phasing out Subsidies of Petroleum Energy Products in Egypt* Working Papers Series (145-E) Cairo: The Egyptian Center for Economic Studies.

Aboul Enein, A. (2013) 'Labour Strikes and Protests Double under Morsi' *Daily News*, April 28, http://www.dailynewsegypt.com/2013/04/28/labour-strikes-and-pro tests-double-under-morsi/ (accessed September 2013).

Abu al-Magd, K. (1991) *A Contemporary Islamic Vision* Cairo: Dar Al-Shorouq (in Arabic).

Abu El-Magd, Z. (2012) 'Military Business … the Unknown Economy' *Al-Badeel*, 11 February.

Achcar, G. (2009) 'Egypt's Recent Growth: An Emerging Success Story?' *Development Viewpoint* London: Centre for Development and Policy Research, School of Oriental and African Studies.

——(2013) *The People Want: A Radical Exploration of the Arab Uprising* London: SAQI.

Adib, M. (2011) '3000 Jihadi Return to Egypt from Afghanistan, Chechnya, Bosnia, Somalia and Iran' *Al-Masry Alyoum* http://m.almasryalyoum.com/news/details/ 122653.

Adler, G. and Webster, E. (1999) 'Lessons from South Africa: Unions, Democracy, and Economic Liberalization' *Journal of Labor and Society* 3(3): 9–22.

Adly, A. (2011a) *Mubarak (1990–2011): The State of Corruption* Cairo: Arab Reform Initiative.

——(2011b) 'Will the Revolution Turn Right or Left?' *Al-Masry Alyoum*, 18 February.

Ahram Online (2012) 'Morsi Declaration Hailed by Supporters, Deemed "Coup" by Opposition' http://english.ahram.org.eg/NewsContent/1/64/58950/Egypt/Politics-/Mor si-declaration-hailed-by-supporters,-deemed-cou.aspx.

——(2013) 'Disputes in National Salvation Front Emerge Ahead of Elections' http://english.ahram.org.eg/NewsContent/1/64/76774/Egypt/Politics-/Disputes-in-National-Salvation-Front-emerge-ahead-.aspx (18 July).

Al-Ahram (2003) 'Report on Economic Directions', 28 September.

Al-Ahram Weekly (2002) 'Bringing the Intifada to Egypt', 26 September–2 October.

Al-Agati, M. (2010) 'The Left and Protest Movements in Egypt: AGEG, Popular Committee for the Support of Intifada, March 20 Movement' in D. Shehata (ed.) *The Return of Politics: New Protest Movements in Egypt* (Cairo: Center of Political and Strategic Studies) (in Arabic).

Al-Anani, K. and Malik, M. (2013) 'Pious Way to Politics: The Rise of Political Salafism in Post-Mubarak Egypt' *Digest of Middle East Studies* 22(1): 57–73.

Alavi, Hamza (1972) 'The State in Post-Colonial Societies: Pakistan and Bangladesh' *New Left Review* 74: 59–82.

Al-Bahnasawi, M. and Zalat, A. (2012) 'Officers Rule Egypt Ministries' *Al-Watan*, 5 January (in Arabic).

Al-Balad (2012) 'Head of the Central Auditing Authority Wonders What the Link Is between Armed Forces-run Wedding Halls and National Security?' http://www.el-balad.com/303191#sthash.4MZQbxLx.dpuf.

Albassel, A. and Khalifa, R. (2011) 'Labour Strikes: A Landmine in the Way of the Government'. *Digital Ahram*, 21 October.

Al-Boursa (2013) 'Armed Forces Receives Rights to Complete and Manage the Cairo–Alexandria Desert Road for 50 Years' http://www.alborsanews.com/2013/10/31.

Alexander, A. (2008) 'Inside Egypt's Mass Strike' *International Socialism* http://www.isj.org.uk/?id=428.

——(2011) 'The Growing Social Soul of Egypt's Democratic Revolution' *International Socialism* 131 (June) www.isj.org.uk/index.php4?id=741&issue=131 (accessed 2 July).

Al-Haddad, A. (2013) 'Effects of the Global Crisis on the Egyptian Textiles and Clothing Sector: A Blessing in Disguise?' *ISRN Economics*, ID 941695, doi:10.5402/2012/941695.

Ali, K. *et al.* (eds) (2009) *Workers and Social Resistance* Cairo: Coordinating Committee for Workers' and Union Rights, Land Centre for Human Rights, Hisham Mubarak Legal Centre (in Arabic).

Al-Khalsan, M. (2011) 'What Are the Secrets of the Military's Budget?' *Elw3y Alarabi* http://elw3yalarabi.org/modules.php?name=News&file=article&sid=11166 (in Arabic).

Al-Masry Alyoum (2011) 'MB Businessman Hasan Malek: Mubarak's Policies Correct but Marred with Corruption', 28 November.

Almeida, P. (2005) 'Multi-Sectoral Coalitions and Popular Movement Participation' in Patrick Coy (ed.) *Research in Social Movements, Conflicts and Change* Emerald Group Publishing Limited: Bingley UK.

Al-Morshedi, R. (2013) 'Freezing the Muslim Brothers' Assets is a Mission Impossible' *Al-Watan* http://www.elwatannews.com/news/details/329500.

Al-Naggar, A. (2013) 'What Does the West Want from the Military Economy?' *Al-Ahram* 8 October.

Al-Shab Al-Gadid (2012) 'Names and Positions: Egypt's Map of Generals' http://elshaab.org/thread.php?ID=31222.

Al-Watan (2013) 'Al-Watan Continues to Expose the MB Spider Web' http://almogaz.com/news/politics/2013/09/16/1097119.

Ashour, O. (2013) 'Egypt: Return to General's Republic' *BBC News Middle East*, 21 August, http://www.bbc.co.uk/news/world-middle-east-23780839.

Aswat Masrya (2012) 'Prince: Partisan Demands in front of Presidential Palace ... Conspiracy against the President', 4 July.

Ayeb, H. (2012) 'The Marginalization of the Small Peasantry: Egypt and Tunisia' in Ray Bush and Habib Ayeb (eds) *Marginality and Exclusion in Egypt* London: Zed Books.

Ayubi, N. (1988) 'Arab Bureaucracies: Expanding Size, Changing Roles' in A. Dawisha and W. Zartman (eds) *Beyond Coercion: The Durability of the Arab State* London: Croom Helm.

Azambuja, C. (2003) 'The New Face of the Antiglobalization Movements' WWW. cubdest. Org/0312/cazambuje.html.

Baker, R. (2003) *Islam Without Fear: Egypt and the New Islamists* Cambridge: Harvard University Press.

Bandy, J. and Smith, K. (2005) *Coalitions Across Borders: Transnational Protest and the Neoliberal Order* Maryland: Rowman & Littlefield Publishers, Inc.

Bargawi, H. and McKinley, T. (2011) *The Poverty Impact of Growth and Employment in Egypt (1990–2009)* UNDP: Arab Development Challenges Background Paper 2011/01.

Bassiouny, M. and Said, M. (2008) *Rayat Al-Idrab* (Protest Flags) Cairo: Socialist Studies Centre.

Bayat, A. (2009) *Life as Politics: How Ordinary People Change the Middle East* Cairo: The American University in Cairo Press.

——(2011) 'Paradoxes of Arab Re-folutions' *Jadaliyya* http://www.jadaliyya.com/pages/index/786/paradoxes-of-arab-refo-lutions.

Beck, U. (1992) *Risk Society: Towards a New Modernity* London: Sage.

Beinin, J. (2009) 'Workers' Struggles under "Socialism" and Neoliberalism' in R. El-Mahdi and P. Marfleet (eds) *Egypt: A Moment of Change.* London: Zed Books, 68–86.

——(2010) *Justice for All: The Struggle for Workers' Rights in Egypt* Washington, DC: Solidarity Center.

——(2011) 'A Workers' Social Movement on the Margin of the Global Neoliberal Order, Egypt 2004–9' in J. Beinin and F. Vairel (eds) *Social Movements, Mobilization, and Contestation in the Middle East and North Africa* Stanford: Stanford University Press.

——(2012) 'The Rise of Egypt's Workers' Carnegie Papers June 28, Carnegie Endowment for International Peace http://carnegieendowment.org/2012/06/28/rise-of-egypt-s-workers/coq6.

——(2013) 'Workers, Trade Unions and Egypt's Political Future' *Middle East Research and Information Project* (*MERIP*), January.

Beinin, J. and Lockman, Z. (1998) *Workers on the Nile: Nationalism, Communism, Islam and the Egyptian Working Class, 1882–1954* Cairo: The American University in Cairo Press.

Bianchi, R. (1989) *Unruly Corporatism: Associational Life in Twentieth-Century Egypt* Oxford: Oxford University Press.

Bonefeld, W. (1993) *The Recomposition of the British State during the 1980s* Dartmouth: Dartmouth Pub. Co.

Brayez, A. (2013) 'On the Military and its Economic Empire in Egypt: Questions in Methodology' *Jadaliyya* (in Arabic).

Browers, M. (2009) *Political Ideology in the Arab World: Accommodation and Transformation* Cambridge: Cambridge University Press.

Brown, N. and Nasr, H. (2005) *Democracy and Rule of Law: Egypt's Judges Step Forward: The Judicial Election Boycott and Egyptian Reform* Washington, DC: Carnegie Endowment for International Peace.

Bush, R. (2009) 'The Land and the People' in R. El-Mahdi and P. Marfleet (eds) *Egypt: The Moment of Change* London: Zed Books.

——(2012) 'Marginality or Abjection? The Political Economy of Poverty Production in Egypt' in Ray Bush and Habib Ayeb (eds) *Marginality and Exclusion in Egypt* London: Zed Books.

Bush, R. and Ayeb, H. (eds) (2012) *Marginality and Exclusion in Egypt* London: Zed Books.

Carnegie Endowment (2012) *Guide to Egypt's Transition: Parties and Alliances* http://egyptelections.carnegieendowment.org/category/political-parties (accessed 25/8/2012).

Carr, S. (2012) 'April 6: Genealogy of a Youth Movement' *Jadaliyya* http://www.jadaliyya.com/pages/index/4950/april-6_genealogy-of-a-youth-movement.

Castells, M. (1996) *The Rise of the Network Society* Oxford: Blackwell.

Centre of Socialist Studies (2007) *The Working Class Is the Alternative* Cairo: Centre of Socialist Studies.

Charbel, J. (2012) 'Labor Activists: New Decree Eyes "Brotherhoodization" of Unions' *Egypt Independent*, 26 November.

Choueiri, Y. (2000) *Arab Nationalism: A History* Oxford: Blackwell Publishers.

Clement, F. (2009) 'Worker Protests under Economic Liberalisation in Egypt' in Nicholas Hopkins (ed.) *Political and Social Protest in Egypt* Cairo Papers in Social Science 29(2/3) Cairo: The American University in Cairo Press.

Cohen, R. and Rai, S. M. (eds) (2000) 'Global Social Movements: Towards a Cosmopolitan Politics' in R. Cohen and S. M. Rai (eds) *Global Social Movements* London: The Athlone Press.

Coleman, R. (2003) 'Images from a Neoliberal City: the State, Surveillance and Social Control' *Critical Criminology* 12(1): 21–42.

Crozat, M. (1998) 'Are the Times a Changin'? Assessing the Acceptance of Protest in Western Democracies' in *The Social Movement Society: Contentious Politics for a New Century* ed. David S. Meyer and Sidney Tarrow. Lanham, MD: Rowman and Littlefield, 59–82.

Davies, J. C. (1962) 'Toward a Theory of Revolution' *American Sociological Review* 27: 5–19.

della Porta, D. (2005) 'Multiple Belongings, Tolerant Identities, and the "Construction" of "Another Politics": Between the European Social Forum and the Local Social Fora' in D. della Porta and S. Tarrow (eds) *Transnational Protest and Global Activism: People, Passions, and Power* Oxford: Rowman & Littlefield.

De Smet, B. (2012) 'The Prince and the Pharaoh: The Collaborative Project of Egyptian Workers and their Intellectuals in the Face of the Revolution' Unpublished PhD dissertation, Ghent University.

Dessouki, A. (1994) 'Ideology and Legitimacy in Egypt: The Search of a "Hybrid Formula"' in Oncu, A., Keyder, C. and Ibrahim, S. E. (eds) *Developmentalism and Beyond: Society and Politics in Egypt and Turkey* Cairo: The American University in Cairo Press.

Dwivedi, O. P. (1999) *Bureaucracy and the Alternatives in World Perspective* London: Macmillan Press.

Eckstein, S. (ed.) (1989) *Power and Popular Protest: Latin American Social Movements* Berkeley CA: University of California Press.

Edelman, M. (1984) 'New Political Movements and Changes in Processes of Information' *Social Science Information* 23(6): 1–48.

Egyptian Initiative for Personal Rights (2011) 'The National Initiative to Rebuild the Police: A Police for the Egyptian People' Cairo: Egyptian Initiative for Personal Rights http://eipr.org/sites/default/files/pressreleases/pdf/national_initiative_for_poli ce_reform_en.pdf.

El Amrani, I. (2010) 'The Murder of Khaled Said' *The Arabist* http://arabist.net/blog/ 2010/6/14/the-murder-of-khaled-said.html.

El-Ghobashy, M. (2005) 'The Metamorphosis of the Egyptian Muslim Brothers' *International Journal of Middle East Studies* 37: 373–95.

——(2011) 'The Praxis of the Egyptian Revolution' *MERIP* 258.

El-Ghonemy, M. R. (1998) *Recent Changes in Agrarian Reform and Rural Development Strategies in the Near East* FAO Corporate Document Repository http://www. fao.org/docrep/w4760e/w4760e0i.htm.

El-Guindy, Z. (2012) 'Updated: Revolution Youth Coalition Disband with End of Egypt's Transitional Phase' *Al-Ahram English*, 25 August.

El-Hamalawy, H. (2002) 'Same Side, Different Teams' *Cairo Times* 6(11).

——(2007) 'Comrades and Brothers' *Middle East Research and Information Project* 242 (Spring) Retrieved 27/10/2008, http://www.merip.org/mer/mer242/comrades. brothers.

El-Hennawy, N. (2010) 'We Are All Khaled Saeed: Redefining Political Demonstration in Egypt' *Egypt Independent*, 4 August.

El-Houdaiby, I. (2013) 'A Nonviolent Muslim Brotherhood?' Washington: Middle East Institute, 4 October, http://www.mei.edu/content/nonviolent-muslim-brotherhood.

El-Kharabawi, T. (2012) 'The Muslim Brothers Business Families Rule Egypt' *Tahrir*, 30 October, http://tahrirnews.com.

El-Mahdi, R. (2009) 'Enough! Egypt's Quest for Democracy' *Comparative Political Studies* 42(8): 1011–39.

——(2010) 'Does Political Islam Impede Gender-Based Mobilization? The Case of Egypt' *Totalitarian Movements and Political Religions* 11(3–4): 379–96.

——(2012) 'Labour Protests in Egypt: Causes and Meanings' *Review of African Political Economy* 38(129): 387–402.

El-Merghany, E. (ed.) (2013) *Social Protests in 2012* Cairo: The Egyptian Centre for Economic and Social Rights.

El-Sheikh, M. (2013) 'Brotherhood Struggles to Translate Power into Policy in Egypt' *New York Times*, January 19.

El-Wassal, K. (2013) *Public Employment Dilemma in Egypt: Who Pays the Bill?* Dubai: Proceedings of 20th International Business Research Conference.

Eskandar, W. (2013) 'Brothers and Officers: A History of Pacts' *Jadaliyya*, January 25.

Ezzat, Dina (2013) 'Muslim Brotherhood Figures Seek Egypt Diplomatic Posts' *Al-Ahram English*, 19 January.

Fathi, Y. (2011) 'Workers Protest in Front of Egypt's Cabinet' *Ahram Online*, April 4, http://english.ahram.org.eg/NewsContent/1/64/9295/Egypt/Politics-/Workers-protest-in-front-of-Egypts-Cabinet.aspx.

Frisch, H. (2001) 'Guns and Butter in the Egyptian Army' *Middle East Review of International Affairs* 5(2): 1–14.

Gabr, M. (2007) 'Evicting Basatin Residents' *Al-Masry Alyoum*, 10 September.

Gabr, H. (2012) 'Labour "Option"' *Al-hewar Al-Mutamaden* 3602, www.ahewar.org/debate/show.art.asp?aid+290904 (accessed 10 June).

Galal, A. (2004) 'The Winners and Losers from the Emerging Informal Economy in Egypt' *Working Papers Series* 14, Cairo: Center for International Private Enterprise (CIPE).

Gamal, W. (2010) 'Founding Myths of Economic Policy during Nazif's Reign: The Rich Pay Less Tax for the Good of Society' *Shorouk* http://www.shorouknews.com/columns/view.aspx?cdate=27102010&id=09adce25-0b34-4550-b471-75b09edd520a0 (in Arabic).

——(2012) 'SCAF: Our Projects are the "Sweat" of the Defence Ministry' *Shorouk* http://www.shorouknews.com/news/view.aspx?cdate=27032012&id=0de8ea0c-136a-4270-9a7c-79b576b91b51 (in Arabic).

Gamson, W. 1990 *The Strategy of Social Protest* Belmont: Wadsworth Publishing.

Giddens, A. (1990) *The Consequences of Modernity* Stanford, CA: Stanford University Press.

Goldberg, E. (1986) *Tinker, Tailor, and Textile Worker: Class and Politics in Egypt, 1930–1952* Berkeley: University of California Press.

——(1992) 'The Foundations of State–Labor Relations in Contemporary Egypt' *Comparative Politics* 24(2): 147–61.

——(2012) 'Morsi and his Adversaries' *Jadaliyya* http://www.jadaliyya.com/pages/index/8676/morsi-and-his-adversaries.

Goodwin, J. (2001) *No Other Way Out: States and Revolutionary Movements, 1945–1991* Cambridge: Cambridge University Press.

Gordon, T. (2005) 'The Political Economy of Law-and-Order Policies: Policing, Class Struggle, and Neoliberal Restructuring' *Studies in Political Economy* 75: 53–77.

Gotowicki, S. (1997) *The Role of the Egyptian Military in Domestic Society* Fort Leavenworth, KA: Foreign Military Studies Office Publications.

Gramsci, A. (1968) The Modern Prince and Other Writings, transl. Louis Marks, New York: International Publishers.

——(1971) *Selections from Prison Notebooks of A. Gramsci*, ed. Q. Hoare and G. N. Smith, New York: International Publishers.

Grodsky, B. (2012) *Social Movements and the New State: The Fate of the Pro-Democracy Organizations when Democracy Is Won* Stanford, CA: Stanford University Press.

Hamdy, I. (2010) 'Academics in Opposition Politics: Agents for Change?' Paper presented at the conference of the World Congress for Middle Eastern Studies (WOCMES), Barcelona, July 19–24.

Hanieh, A. (2013) *Lineages of Revolt: Issues of Contemporary Capitalism in the Middle East* Chicago, IL: Haymarket Books.

Hansen, B. and Radwan, S. (1982) *Employment Opportunities and Equity in Egypt* Geneva: International Labor Office.

Harman, C. (1994) 'The Prophet and the Proletariat' *International Socialism* 64: 3–64.

Harvey, D. (2003) *The New Imperialism* Oxford: Oxford University Press.

——(2005) *A Brief History of Neoliberalism* Oxford: Oxford University Press.

——(2010) *The Enigma of Capital and the Crisis of Capitalism* Oxford: Oxford University Press.

Hashd (2010) 'Towards a Popular Democratic Movement for Change' http://www.e-socialists.net/node/5826 (Hashd founding statement: http://7ashd.blogspot.com/).

Hassan, M. and Sassanpour, C. (2008) *Labor Market Pressures in Egypt: Why Is the Unemployment Rate Stubbornly High?* Cairo: Arab Planning Institute.

Helmy, O. (2005) *The Efficiency and Equity of Subsidy Policy in Egypt* Cairo: The Egyptian Centre for Economic Studies Working Paper Series, 105-E.

Heydemann, S. (2004) (ed.) *Networks of Privilege in the Middle East* New York: Palgrave Macmillan.

Holloway, J. (2002) *Change the World without Taking Power: The Meaning of Revolution Today* London: Pluto Press.

Howeidy, A. (2006) 'What's Left of the Left?' *Al-Ahram Weekly* 778 (January) Retrieved on 20/7/2009, http://weekly.ahram.org.eg/print/2006/778/eg8.htm.

Human Rights Watch (HRW) (2004) 'Egypt's Torture Epidemic' www.hrw.org/English/docs/2004/02/25/egypt7658.htm.

——(2005) 'Reading between the "Red Lines": The Repression of Academic Freedom in Egyptian Universities' 17(6), http://www.hrw.org/sites/default/files/reports/egypt0605.pdf.

——(2012) ' Egypt: Revoke Ban on Strikes, Demonstrations' www.hrw.org/news/2011/03/25/egypt-revoke-ban-strikes-dem accessed 12/5/2012.

Hussein, A. and Black, I. (2012) 'Cairo Presidential Palace Restored to Uneasy Calm after Deadly Clashes' *Guardian*, 12 June, http://www.theguardian.com/world/2012/dec/06/cario-presidential-palace-calm-deadly-clashes.

International Crisis Group (2003) *The Challenge of Political Reform: Egypt after the Iraq War*, Cairo/Brussels, September.

Joya, A. (2011) 'The Egyptian Revolution: Crisis of Neoliberalism and the Potential for Democratic Politics' *Review of African Political Economy* 38(129): 367–86.

Kalleberg, A. (2011) *Good Jobs, Bad Jobs: The Rise of Polarized and Precarious Employment Systems in the United States, 1970s to 2000s* New York: Russell Sage Foundation.

Kandil, H. (2012) *Soldiers, Spies and Statesmen: Egypt's Road to Revolt* London, New York: Verso.

Kazan-Allen, L. (2005) 'Victory for Egyptian Asbestos Workers' International Ban Asbestos Secretariat http://ibasecretariat.org/lka_vict_egypt_asb_wrks_0905.php.

Kohstall, F. (2012) 'Free Transfer, Limited Mobility: A Decade of Higher Education Reform in Egypt and Morocco' *Revue de Mondes Musulman et de la Méditerranée* 131: 91–109.

Koopmans, R. (1993) 'The Dynamics of Protest Waves: West Germany, 1965 to 1989' *American Sociological Review* 58: 637–58.

Laclau, E. and Mouffe, C. (1985) *Hegemony and Socialist Strategy: Towards a Radical Democratic Politics* London: Verso.

Land Centre for Human Rights (LCHR) (2002) *Farmers Struggle Against Law 96 of 1992*. Cairo (in Arabic).

——(2006) *Documenting the Events of Sarando* http://www.lchr-eg.org/archive/88/88-16.htm.

——(2007) *Land Centre for Human Rights Newsletter*, January.

——(2008) *Land Centre for Human Rights Newsletter*, August.

——(2011) *The Harvest of the Labour Movement in the First Half of 2011* Cairo (in Arabic).

Lee, K. and Kofman, Y. (2012) 'The Politics of Precarity: Views Beyond the United States' *Work and Occupation* 39(4): 388–408.

Lim, M. (2012) 'Clicks, Cabs, and Coffee Houses: Social Media and Oppositional Movements in Egypt, 2004–2011' *Journal of Communication* 6: 231–48.

Lipset, S. M. (1981) *Political Man* Baltimore MD: Johns Hopkins University Press.

Luxemburg, R. (1906) *The Mass Strike Document* London: Bookmarks.

Marshall, S. and Stacher, J. (2012) 'Egypt's Generals and Transnational Capital' *MERIP* 42, http://www.merip.org/mer/mer262/egypts-generals-transnational-capital.

Mayer, J. (2005) 'The Secret History of America's "Extraordinary Rendition" Program' *New Yorker*, 8 February.

Mayo, M. (2005) *Global Citizens* London: Zed Press.

Meijer, R. (ed.) (2009) *Global Salafism: Islam's New Religious Movement* London/New York: Hurst & Co./Columbia University Press.

Melucci, A. (1989) *Nomads of the Present* Hutchinson, Philadelphia: Temple University Press.

Meyer, D. and Tarrow, S. (eds) (1998) *The Social Movement Society: Contentious Politics for a New Century* Lanham, MD: Rowman and Littlefield.

Mikail, A. (2013) 'Update: Official Statement by the National Salvation Front' http://nilerevolt.wordpress.com/2013/08/14/statement-by-the-national-salvation-front/?utm_content=buffer56fc9&utm_source=buffer&utm_medium=twitter&utm_campaign=Buffer.

Mina, M. (2010) *Doctors without Rights: Doctors' Right for a Decent Life, Citizens' Rights for a Real, Good Quality Health Service* Cairo: Egyptian Centre for Economic and Social Rights.

Mitchell, R. (1969) *The Society of Moslem Brothers* Oxford: Oxford University Press.

Moody, K. (2005) 'Toward an International Social-Movement Unionism' in L. Amoore (ed.) *The Global Resistance Reader* Abingdon: Routledge.

Moseley, M. (2010) 'The Normalization of Protest in Latin America' *Americas Barometer Insights* 42, www.AmericasBarometer.org.

Moustafa, T. (2007) *The Struggle for Constitutional Power: Law, Politics, and Economic Development in Egypt* Cambridge: Cambridge University Press.

Munson, Z. (2001) 'Islamic Mobilization: Social Movement Theory and the Egyptian Muslim Brotherhood' *Sociological Quarterly* 42(4): 487–510.

Mustafa, A. (2013) 'Questions Surround Unity of Egypt's National Salvation Front' *Al-Monitor* http://www.al-monitor.com/pulse/politics/2013/04/unity-egypt-opposition-national-salvation-front.html.

Nader, M. (2008) 'Hepatitis C Patients Rally to Protest the Absence of Interferon Injections' *Al-Masry Alyoum*, 20 February.

Naguib, S. (2006) *The Muslim Brothers: A Socialist Perspective* Cairo: Centre for Socialist Studies (in Arabic).

——(2009) 'Islamism(s) Old and New' in R. El-Mahdi and P. Marfleet (eds) *Egypt: The Moment of Change* London: Zed Books.

——(2011) 'Egypt's Unfinished Revolution' *International Socialist Review* 79 (September-October) http://www.isreview.org/issues/79/features-egyptianrevolution.shtml.

Nahdet Masr (2009) 'Governor to Borolus Residents: If you Block the Road, we Will Cut your Throat' http://www.masress.com/nahda/2983660.

Neocleous, M. (2000) *The Fabrication of Social Order: A Critical Theory of Police Power* London: Pluto Press.

Norris, P. (2002) *Democratic Phoenix: Reinventing Political Activism* Cambridge: Cambridge University Press.

Offe, C. (1981) 'The Attribution of Public Status to Interest Groups: Observations on the West German Case' in S. Berger (ed.) *Organizing Interests in Western Europe* Cambridge: Cambridge University Press.

O'Neill, K. (2004) 'Transnational Protest: States, Circuses, and Conflict at the Front-line of Global Politics' *International Studies Review* 6: 233–51.

Owen, R. (1992) *State Power and Politics in the Making of the Modern Middle East* London: Routledge.

Petras, J. (1978) 'Socialist Revolutions and their Class Components' *New Left Review* 1(111) September–October.

Picard, E. (1988) 'Arab Military in Politics: From Revolutionary Plot to Authoritarian State' in A. Dawisha and W. Zartman (eds) *Beyond Coercion: The Durability of the Arab State* London: Croom Helm.

Pleyers, G. (2010) *Alter-Globalization: Becoming Actors in the Global Age* Cambridge: Polity Press.

Pousney, M. (1993) 'Irrational Workers: The Moral Economy of Labour Protests in Egypt' *World Politics* 46(1): 83–120.

Pratt, R. (1978) 'Toward a Critical Theory of Revolution' *Polity* 11(2): 172–99.

Pratt, N. (2012) 'Bringing the Revolution to Campus: An Interview with March 9 Activist Laila Soueif' *Jadaliyya* http://www.jadaliyya.com/pages/index/5457/bringing-the-revolution-to-campus_an-interview-wit.

Ragab, A. (2005) *Deregulation of the Airline Industry: Opportunities and Challenges* Cairo: Egyptian Centre for Economic Research Working Paper Series 109-E.

Reed, T. V. (2005) *The Art of Protest: Culture and Activism from the Civil Rights Movement to the Streets of Seattle* Minneapolis, MN: University of Minnesota Press.

Refaat, A. (2003) *Trade-Induced Protectionism in Egypt's Manufacturing Sector* Working Paper Series (WP85-E) Cairo: Egyptian Center for Economic Research.

——(2006) *Assessing the Impact of the QIZ Protocol on Egypt's Textile and Clothing Industry* Working Paper Series (WP113-E) Cairo: Egyptian Center for Economic Research.

Reid, D. (1990) *Cairo University and the Making of Modern Egypt* Cambridge: Cambridge University Press.

Richards, A. (1993) 'Economic Imperatives and Political Systems' *Middle East Journal* 47(2): 217–27.

Rimlinger, G. (1977) 'Labor and Government: A Comparative Historical Perspective' *Journal of Economic History* 37(1): 210–25.

Riyad, A. (2011) 'The Cement Industry in Egypt: Between Monopoly and the Need for Development' *Zawya* http://www.zawya.com/story/The_Cement_industry_in _Egypt_between_monopoly_and_the_need_for_development-ZAWYA20111025054229/.

Rose, F. (1997) 'Toward a Class-Cultural Theory of Social Movements: Reinterpreting New Social Movements' *Sociological Forum* 12(3): 461–94.

Rutherford, B. (2008) *Egypt after Mubarak: Liberalism, Islam, and Democracy in the Arab World* Princeton: Princeton University Press.

Saad, R. (2008) 'Middle Class and the Changing Face of Rural Resistance' Unpublished paper presented at the Middle East Studies Association (MESA) conference, Washington, 22–25 November.

Saber, K. (2006) 'Agrarian Policy, Legislation and Violations of Human Rights in Egypt: Land Privatization and Farmers' Evictions in Egyptian Countryside' Dialogues, Proposals, Stories for Global Citizenship website http://base.d-p-h.info/en/fiches/dph/fiche-dph-6922.html.

Said, A. (2006) *Judges and the Battle against the Dictator* Centre for Socialist Studies http://www.e-socialists.net/node4430, accessed 12/8/2011.

Sasson, A. (1982) *Approaches to Gramsci* New York: Writers and Readers Publishing & INC.

Sayigh, Y. (2012) 'Above the State: The Officers' Republic in Egypt' *The Carnegie Papers* Washington, DC: Carnegie Middle East Centre.

Schmitter, P. and Lehmbruch, G. (1979) *Trends towards Corporate Intermediation* London: Sage Publications.

Schock, K. (2005) *Unarmed Insurrections: People Power Movements in Nondemocracies* University of Minnesota Press.

Seif El-Dawla, A. (2009) 'Torture: A State Policy' in R. El-Mahdi and P. Marfleet (eds) *Egypt: The Moment of Change* London: Zed Books.

Sewell, W. (1980) *Work and Revolution in France: The Language of Labor from the Old Regime to 1848*. Cambridge: Cambridge University Press.

Sfakianakis, J. (2004) 'The Whales of the Nile: Networks, Businessmen and Bureaucrats During the Era of Privatization in Egypt' in Heydemann, S. *Networks of Privilege in the Middle East* New York: Palgrave Macmillan.

Shahine, G. (2005) 'University Staff Joins Protests' *Al-Ahram Weekly*, May 26–June 1.

Shehata, D. (2009) *Islamists and Secularists in Egypt: Opposition, Conflict, and Cooperation* London: Routledge.

Sitrin, M. (2012) *Everyday Revolutions: Horizontalism and Autonomy in Argentina* London: Zed Books.

Socialist Worker (2012) 'Egyptian Strikers Face Torture', 15 March.

——(2013) 'A Revolutionary Front in Egypt' http://socialistworker.org/2013/10/10/a-revolutionary-front-in-egypt.

Soliman, S. (1999) 'State and Industrial Capitalism in Egypt' *Cairo Papers in Social Science* 21(2) Cairo: The American University in Cairo.

——(2011) *The Autumn of Dictatorship: Fiscal Crisis and Political Change in Egypt under Mubarak* Stanford: Stanford University Press.

Soliman, M. (2013) 'The Military Receive Government Contracts Worth 7 Billion' http://www.masrawy.com/news/Egypt/Economy/2013/November/24/5766489.aspx.

Springborg, R. (1989) *Mubarak's Egypt: Fragmentation of the Political Order* Boulder, CO and London: Westview Press.

——(2011) 'The Political Economy of the Arab Spring' *Mediterranean Politics* 16(3): 427–33.

Tammam, H. (2006) 'The Muslim Brothers ... Organisation Fetish' *Al-Bosla* http://bosla.blogspot.co.uk/2006/06/blog-post_115628608882082440.html.

Tilly, C. (1978) *From Mobilization to Revolution* Reading, MA: Addison-Wesley Publishing Company.

Totonchi, E. (2011) 'Laboring Democratic Spring: The Past, Present and Future of Free Trade Unions in Egypt' *Journal of Labour and Society* 14: 259–83.

Tucker, R. (ed.) (1978) *The Marx and Engels Reader* New York: WW Norton Company.

UNDP (2008) *Egypt Human Development Report* Cairo: UNDP.

Upchurch, M. and Mathers, A. (2011) 'Neoliberal Globalization and Trade Unionism: Toward Radical Political Unionism?' *Critical Sociology* 38(2): 265–80.

USAID/IBM Business Consulting Services (2004) *Privatization in Egypt, 2004 Report* Cairo: USAID Privatization Implementation Project.

Utvik, B. (2006) *The Pious Road to Development: Islamist Economics in Egypt* London: Hurst.

Verhulst, J. and Walgrave, S. (2009) 'The First Time Is the Hardest? A Cross-National and Cross-Issue Comparison of the First-Time Protest Participants' *Political Behaviour* 31: 455–84.

Wade, N. (2013) 'Egypt: What the Poll Results Reveal about Brotherhood's Popularity' *BBC News*, 30 August.

Wallerstein, I. (2002) 'New Revolts against the System' *New Left Review* 18, November–December: 29–39.

Walzer, M. (1998) 'Intellectuals, Social Classes, and Revolutions' in Theda Skocpol (ed.) *Democracy, Revolution, and History* Ithaca and London: Cornell University Press.

Wickham, C. R. (2004) *Mobilizing Islam: Religion, Activism and Political Change in Egypt* New York: Columbia University Press.

Wood, E. M. (1981) 'The Separation of the Economic and the Political in Capitalism' *New Left Review* I(127) (May–June) http://newleftreview.org/I/127/ellen-meiksins-wood-theseparation-of-the-economic-and-the-political-in-capitalism (accessed 10 July 2011).

World Bank (2004) *Unlocking the Employment Potential in the Middle East and North Africa: Toward a New Social Contract* Washington, DC: World Bank.

——(2010) *Most Improved Business Reformers in Doing Business* Washington, DC: World Bank.

World Bank and Ministry of Economic Development, Arab Republic of Egypt (2010) *Egypt's Food Subsidies: Benefit Incidence and Leakages* Cairo: World Bank.

Youth for Justice and Freedom: A New Movement on the Egyptian Street (2010) http://www/nmisr.com/vb/showthread.php?t=154522.

Index

Please note that page numbers relating to Notes will have the letter 'n' following the page number. References to names beginning with Al will be filed under the first significant name, e.g. Al-Maghraby will be sorted under 'Maghraby'.

Party, 109–10; and the left, 96–7; and
Nasserists, 96; networks, 79;
organization skills, 76–9; and
post-Mubarak alliances, 111–14;
pragmatism, 104–5; professionalism,
77; *see also* MB Youth
*The Muslim Brothers: A Socialist
Perspective* (Naguib), 100
Mustafa, Abdel Galil, 51n

NAC (National Association for
Change), 45–6, 94
Nadeem Centre for Psychological
Management and the Rehabilitation
of Victims of Torture and Violence,
31, 34, 95
Al-Naggar, A., 28n
Naguib, Sameh, 90, 100, 107
Al-Nahhas, Safwat, 25
Nasr, General Mahmoud, 24
Nasser, Gamal Abdel, 7, 12, 13, 14, 18,
20, 24, 40, 42, 53, 76, 94, 137;
Democratic Nasserist Party, 95; 'de-
Nasserization' project (Sadat), 97
Nasserists, 32, 34, 35, 41, 62, 68, 77;
acrimonious relationships with other
groups, 96, 98; and coalitions, 93, 94,
95, 96–7, 98, 100, 101, 104, 105, 106,
107, 108, 109, 110, 115; Karama
Party, 39, 95, 105, 109–10; and
liberals, 49, 93, 98, 105
National Association for Change
(NAC), 45–6, 94
'National Conference on Justice'
(1986), 43
National Defence Council, 76, 91n
National Democratic Party (NDP), 7, 8,
41, 59, 89–90, 102, 112, 129
National Investment Bank, 15
National Salvation Front (NSF), 114
National Service Projects
Administration, 22, 23
Nawar family, Sarando village, 67–8
Nazif, Ahmed (Prime Minister), 8, 15,
55, 56
NDP (National Democratic Party), 7, 8,
41, 59, 89–90, 102, 112, 129
neoliberalism, 4, 7, 8–9, 16, 20, 26;
crony capitalism, 10, 11; features, 10;
new order, 12; policing, 16–20
New Islamist Trend, 103
New Social Movements (NSMs),
80–6, 140
newspapers, independent, 70

'New Thinking,' 7
New Urban Communities Authority, 25
9 March Group for Academic Freedom,
37, 39–42, 98, 120
Nobariah Company, 130–1
non-discrimination rule, 10
'non-movement movements,' 66
non-proletarian intellectuals, 128
'normalization' of protests,
68–71
Nour, Ayman, 45
Nour, Mounir Abdel, 9
Nour Party, 86, 111, 112
NSF (National Salvation Front), 114
NSMs (New Social Movements),
80–6, 140

occupational groups, 52–72; farmers,
66–8
Offe, C., 54
old social movements, 80, 81
oligopolies, 10
opposition movements, 97–8
organization, 73–91; brothers and
generals, 75–80; new forms, 60–4;
New Social Movements, 80–6;
pro-democracy activists, 80–6;
workers, 5, 86–91
Oriental Weavers, 9
Osman, Mohamed, 104, 109
Osman, Osman Ahmad, 10

Pakistan, 21
Palestinian Intifada, second (2000), 2,
30, 45, 59, 93, 104
'Palm Hills,' 11
peasants, 14
Pensioners' Federation, 87
People's Assembly, 78
Petras, J., 75
Petrojet (Egyptian oil company), 89
police, 16–20, 68; riot, 30, 71; torture,
17, 18–19; see *baltagya*
political, economic struggle as, 118–21
political parties, Egypt, 32, 53, 81, 83,
111, 133, 139; banning, 53, 94, 98,
109; law governing, 90; leftist, 68, 85,
94, 95, 97, 98, 100, 101, 102, 110, 114,
126; liberal, 85, 101; liberals, 38, 45,
49, 93, 94, 95, 98; new, 85, 86, 90;
Wasateya (middle ground), 103; *see
also* Revolutionary Socialists (RS)
organization; *specific parties, such as
Al-Ghad Party*

CPSIA information can be obtained at www.ICGtesting.com
Printed in the USA
BVOW02*0321220515

401421BV00004B/36/P

9 780415 633048